ROUTE SUMMARY TABLE

Stage number	Start/finish					Page
1	Lausanne to Vevey					39
2	Vevey to Aigle	24.8km	253m	200m	6½hr	47
3	Aigle to Saint-Maurice	17.2km	417m	414m	5hr	53
4	Saint-Maurice to Martigny	16.7km	261m	205m	4½hr	58
5	Martigny to Orsières	18.3km	987m	572m	6hr	63
6	Orsières to Bourg-Saint-Pierre	14.0km	989m	239m	5hr	67
7	Bourg-Saint-Pierre to Col du Grand-Saint-Bernard	12.5km	1062m	224m	5hr	71
8	Col du Grand-Saint-Bernard to Aosta (intermediate stop possible at Echevennoz 15.1km)	28.7km	455m	2347m	7hr	77
9	Aosta to Châtillon	27.8km	1088m	1149m	8¼hr	86
10	Châtillon to Verrès	18.3km	803m	955m	5¾hr	92
11	Verrès to Pont-Saint-Martin	16.0km	289m	338m	4½hr	97
12	Pont-Saint-Martin to Ivrea	23.1km	570m	655m	6½hr	105
13	Ivrea to Viverone	20.3km	401m	355m	5½hr	112
14	Viverone to Santhià	16.4km	150m	268m	4½hr	116
15	Santhià to Vercelli	27.5km	85m	137m	7hr	120
16	Vercelli to Robbio	18.6km	195m	208m	5hr	132
17	Robbio to Mortara	14.5km	49m	59m	3¾hr	136
18	Mortara to Garlasco	20.1km	46m	63m	5hr	140

Stage number	Start/finish	Distance	Total ascent	Total descent	Duration	Page
19	Garlasco to Pavia	24.3km	234m	242m	6½hr	144
20	Pavia to Santa Cristina e Bissone	28.1km	305m	317m	7½hr	150
21	Santa Cristina e Bissone to Orio Litta (4.1km to Corte S. Andrea boat)	16.3km	155m	168m	4¼hr	155
22	Orio Litta to Piacenza	25.9km (19.0km boat option)	235m (174m boat option)	233m (172m boat option	6½hr (5½hr boat option)	159
23	Piacenza to Fiorenzuola d'Arda	32.1km	347m	325m	8½hr	169
24	Fiorenzuola d'Arda to Fidenza	21.9km	268m	271m	5¾hr	175
25	Fidenza to Fornovo di Taro	33.8km	789m	720m	9½hr	180
26	Fornovo di Taro to Berceto (intermediate overnight option at Cassio 21.0km)	31.5km	1658m	1000m	10hr	187
27	Berceto to Pontremoli (intermediate overnight option at Ostello della Cisa 7.0km)	28.2km	1270m	1833m	8½hr	194
28	Pontremoli to Aulla	32.1km	725m	912m	9hr	203
29	Aulla to Sarzana	17.1km	892m	923m	5½hr	210
30	Sarzana to Massa	29.0km	635m	600m	8hr	215
31	Massa to Camaiore	25.7km	651m	681m	7¼hr	222
32	Camaiore to Lucca	24.6km	673m	684m	7hr	228
Total		**726.4**	**17,300m**	**17,663m**	**205hr**	

Staging in this book varies slightly from that of the European Association of Via Francigena ways. Please consult www.viefrancigene.org for additional staging information and Appendix A for a useful stage planning table.

WALKING THE VIA FRANCIGENA

PART 2

LAUSANNE AND THE GREAT ST BERNARD PASS TO LUCCA

by Sandy Brown

JUNIPER HOUSE, MURLEY MOSS,
OXENHOLME ROAD, KENDAL, CUMBRIA LA9 7RL
www.cicerone.co.uk

© Sandy Brown 2021
First edition 2021; reprinted 2024 (with updates)
ISBN: 978 1 78631 086 6

Printed in China on responsibly sourced paper on behalf of Latitude Press Ltd

A catalogue record for this book is available from the British Library.
Route mapping by Lovell Johns www.lovelljohns.com
All photographs are by the author unless otherwise stated.
Contains OpenStreetMap.org data © OpenStreetMap contributors, CC-BY-SA. NASA relief data courtesy of ESRI

Updates to this guide

While every effort is made by our authors to ensure the accuracy of guidebooks as they go to print, changes can occur during the lifetime of an edition. Any updates that we know of for this guide will be on the Cicerone website (www. cicerone.co.uk/1086/updates), so please check before planning your trip. We also advise that you check information about such things as transport, accommodation and shops locally. Even rights of way can be altered over time. We are always grateful for information about any discrepancies between a guidebook and the facts on the ground, sent by email to updates@cicerone.co.uk or by post to Cicerone, Juniper House, Murley Moss, Oxenholme Road, Kendal LA9 7RL

Register your book: To sign up to receive free updates, special offers and GPX files where available, create a Cicerone account and register your purchase via the 'My Account' tab at www.cicerone.co.uk.

Note on mapping

The route maps in this guide are derived from publicly available data, databases and crowd-sourced data. As such they have not been through the detailed checking procedures that would generally be applied to a published map from an official mapping agency. However, we have reviewed them closely in the light of local knowledge as part of the preparation of this guide.

Front cover: The path descends to the valley below the Col du Grand-Saint-Bernard (Stage 8)

Symbols used on maps

〰	main route	▬ ∙ ▬ international boundary	🏰 castle
✎	alternative route	regional boundary	🌿 viewpoint
〰	main route (alternative stage)	**11.1** distance marker	☆ ➊ point of interest
Ⓢ	start point	3.2 alt distance marker	▮ obelisk/monument
Ⓕ	finish point	= footbridge	park area
■◉	bus stop/bus station	≍ bridge	)====(tunnel
■◉	railway station	■ building	⊕🏛 church/cathedral /monastery
		▲ summit	

Facilities

🏠 Accommodation
  🏠 ostello (hostel)
  🏠 hotel
  🏠 camere (rooms)
  🏠 B&B
  🏠 agriturismo
▲ ▲ camping

🍴 Catering
  🍷 bar
  🍽 restaurant
  ☕ café

  🛒 groceries
  🚻 public toilets
  🏧 ATM
  💧 drinking water tap
  🌳 rest/picnic area
  ⊕ pharmacy
  Ⓗ hospital
  ⊕ medical clinic
  ⓘ tourist/pilgrim information
  🧺 launderette

Relief
in meters

800–1000	
600–800	
400–600	
200–400	
0–200	

MAP SCALES
Route maps at 1:100,000
Town maps at 1:25,000 unless
otherwise stated (see scale bar)

SCALE: 1:100,000

0 kilometres	1	2
0 miles		1

SCALE: 1:25,000

0 kilometres	0.25	0.5
0 miles		0.25

Dedication

When I welcomed him into the world some thirty-four years ago, I had no idea Luke Brown would turn into the soulful, creative, beautiful friend that he is. With admiration, respect, and deep love, this book is dedicated to him.

Acknowledgments

A village of supporters helped move this volume toward publication. Erinn Zavaglia followed up with dozens of pilgrim accommodations to get their details just right. Luca Bruschi and Sami Tawfik cheered the project on and offered key support, and European Association of Via Francigena ways (EAVF) Vice-president Gaëtan Tornay reached out at a key moment with much-needed input. Even while COVID-19 had brought the travel world to a halt Jonathan and Joe Williams of Cicerone Press invested in the project, and then Andrea Grimshaw applied her keen eye for detail as editor, while the talented John Bingley oversaw design and layout. The late Alison Raju's preceding guidebooks helped open the door to the Francigena, and her historical research set a high bar that this volume can only hope to meet. No matter the scenery, friendships are always the best part of pilgrim trekking, and dear friends made along the way include Charles Collin of Canada, Greg Stewart and Julia Black of England, Corrado Morelli, Damiano Menegolo, Franco Martinetti, Fabio Graziani, Paolo Ciumino, and Beatrice Moricci of Italy, and many, many others. A group walk on this route in 2023 introduced important insights from Italian hiking guides Giovanni Ramaccioni and Mauro Cappelletti. Swiss-American friends Bob and Cindy Aiello provided fabulous and detailed input as well. The accommodation listings of the Fédération Française Via Francigena and Gronze.com were invaluable for keeping up to date with accommodation listings. Fresh eyes bring a lot to a text, and when Hank and Joyce Landau reviewed the initial layout proof they made very helpful suggestions. I treasure memories of walking the paths of the Via Francigena with my best friend and beloved, Theresa Elliott, who is without doubt the most carefree and fun pilgrim who ever walked a trail.

CONTENTS

St Christophe's Romanesque church tower (Stage 9)

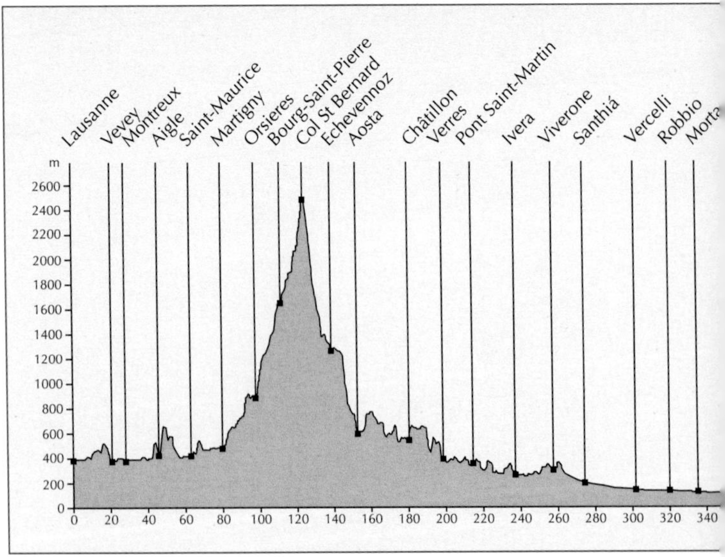

Lausanne
Vevey
Montreux
Aigle
Saint-Maurice
Martigny
Orsieres
Bourg-Saint-Pierre
Col St Bernard
Echevennoz
Aosta
Châtillon
Verres
Pont Saint-Martin
Ivera
Viverone
Santhiá
Vercelli
Robbio
Morta
m
2600
2400
2200
2000
1800
1600
1400
1200
1000
800
600
400
200
0
0
20
40
60
80
100
120
140
160
180
200
220
240
260
280
300
320
340

Alpine peaks fill the horizon over fields of rice and a decaying farmhouse near Vercelli
(Stage 16)

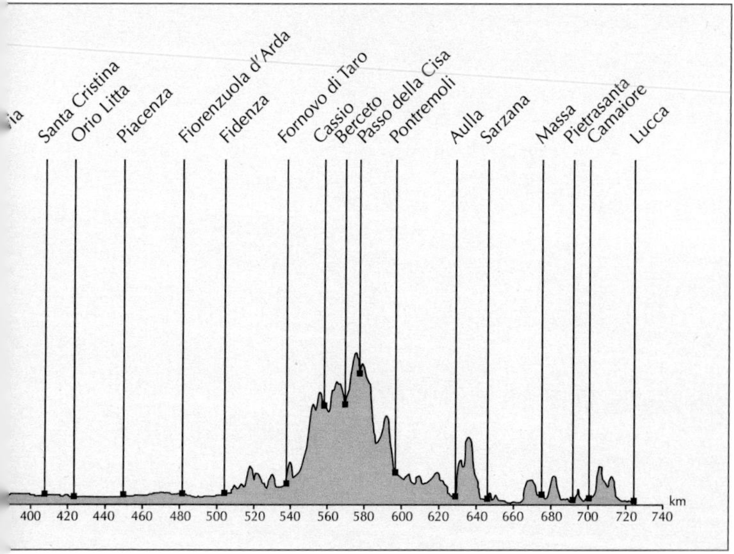

Santa Cristina · Orio Litta · Piacenza · Fiorenzuola d'Arda · Fidenza · Fornovo di Taro · Cassio · Berceto · Passo della Cisa · Pontremoli · Aulla · Sarzana · Massa · Pietrasanta · Camaiore · Lucca

km
400 420 440 460 480 500 520 540 560 580 600 620 640 660 680 700 720 740

A statue of Saint Bernard stands atop Great Saint Bernard Pass at the Swiss-Italian border (Stage 7)

FOREWORD

The Via Francigena – Road to Rome – was designated a Cultural Route by the Council of Europe in 1994. The European Association of Via Francigena ways (EAVF) is a voluntary association of regions and local authorities in England, France, Switzerland and Italy, which currently has more than 190 members. It was established on 7 April 2001 in Fidenza (Italy) to promote the Via Francigena – 3200km (2000 miles) from Canterbury to Rome and, in the Via Francigena del Sud (certified since 2019), to Santa Maria di Leuca.

The route travels from Canterbury in the UK through France and Switzerland to Rome, and continues to the south of Italy, heading toward Jerusalem. It passes through 16 European regions (Kent; Hauts-de-France; Grand Est; Bourgogne-Franche-Comté; Vaud; Valais; Valle d'Aosta; Piedmont; Lombardy; Emilia-Romagna; Liguria; Tuscany; Lazio; Campania, Basilicata, Apulia) in four countries (UK; France; Switzerland; Italy). The association carries out activities to enhance and promote the route at all institutional levels: local, regional, national and European. In 2007 the Council of Europe declared the EAVF the Lead Agency of the Via Francigena, assigning it the role of official reference point for safeguarding, protecting, promoting and developing the Via Francigena in Europe.

This guide to the Via Francigena from Lausanne and the Great Saint Bernard Pass to Lucca is the result of collaboration between the EAVF, Cicerone Press and local associations. It is aimed at walkers and pilgrims who want to discover the beauty of the Swiss and Italian sections of this historic European route. The itinerary includes superb Swiss landscapes, the iconic passage of the Great St Bernard Pass (highest point on the Via Francigena), wonderful passages through Northern Italy, a transit over the forested Apennines, and finally the entrance to Lucca, one of Tuscany's most beloved cities. This is a journey to the heart of Europe, a fascinating way to encounter its traditions, cultural heritage, art treasures, and people.

The Via Francigena was defined as a 'bridge of cultures between Anglo-Saxon Europe and Latin Europe' by the famous medievalist Jacques Le Goff. The Via Francigena of the third millennium is a path of peace, tolerance and dialogue between cultures, religions and countries.

We wish you all a good journey! *Buon viaggio!*

European Association of Via Francigena ways (EAVF)
For information, visit www.viefrancigene.org, or follow us on social media:
Facebook: @ViaFrancigenaCulturalRoute
Instagram: viafrancigena_aevf

The Roman bridge at Pont-Saint-Martin gracefully spans the Lys River with the Castello Vecchio high on the hill above (Stage 11)

INTRODUCTION: THE VIA FRANCIGENA FROM LAUSANNE TO LUCCA

A trail marker points toward Lunigiana near Pontremoli (Stage 27)

It may be true that all roads lead to Rome – but few roads lead to Rome with as many marvels as the Lausanne to Lucca stretch of the Via Francigena. This glorious route begins along the shaded promenades of Lake Geneva (Lac Léman), turns upward on breathtaking mountain trails to cross the Alps, descends to flat farmland roads in the Po Valley, climbs into mountains again at Cisa Pass, and hugs the hillsides near its end in Lunigiana to enjoy sweeping vistas of the sea. Sprinkled along the way are the stone cloisters of ancient convents, the crumbling towers of tall castles, the cobblestone streets of quaint villages, and the contrasting cultures of two Swiss cantons and six Italian regions.

The literal high point of the walk is the tall wall of the mighty Alps in Switzerland and Italy, the two countries connected at the Great Saint Bernard Pass. In summer this mountain crossing is a wonderland of narrow trails among moss-covered boulders set to the music of burbling streams before the backdrop of jagged granite peaks. At its summit stands the pilgrim hospice that has steadfastly safeguarded pilgrims and travelers for nearly 1000 years. A full third of the distance from Lausanne to Lucca is spent climbing up, through, and down these mighty Alpine peaks, with each day offering another unforgettable view.

This beauty is echoed later in the route while crossing the Apennines at Cisa Pass. Though lower than the Alps and covered in an emerald carpet of oak and pine, the Cisa Pass offers some of the most thrilling scenery in all of Italy. From the summit of windswept Monte Valoria or nearby Il Cucchero peak you stand not on a mountain pass, but a mountain-top, with spectacular 360° views of the surrounding peaks in clear weather.

With mountains like bookends to the flat stretches of the Po Valley it would be easy to think of the walk's middle third as less dramatic, except here the villages and people themselves become the focus. As Piedmont's rolling hills flatten first into Lombardy and then Emilia-Romagna the agrarian roots of these great Italian regions become clear – the vast fields of rice are transformed into risotto, while the fields of corn become polenta. The corn, hay and alfalfa feed dairy cows that produce the renowned Parmigiano-Reggiano (Parmesan) cheese of Emilia-Romagna. And as a break from the endless fields, you can pay the boatman to ferry you across the Po and experience this mighty waterway up close, with wind blowing through your hair and a smile on your face.

After a few sumptuous days along the coast you arrive at the cobblestone streets of lovely Lucca, where this tan and terracotta town introduces you to the charms of Tuscany. It is a treasure chest of Italian wonders and another unforgettable moment on the road to Rome.

Impressive sights dot the landscape. Enjoy the views of Lake Geneva from the Cathedral of **Lausanne**, the town that also hosts the International Olympic Museum. Feed your sweet tooth in **Vevey**, home of milk chocolate and the Nestlé company. Stop at fairy-tale Chillon Castle just after **Montreux**, and plan a visit to the Abbey of **Saint-Maurice** where prayers have been raised continuously for 1500 years. The Hospice at **Great Saint Bernard Pass** is a must-sleep-there overnight, after which the charming pedestrian streets of **Aosta** will satisfy all your shopping and

Warm colors of the painted apse greet visitors to the interior of the Parish Church of San Pietro above Châtillon (Stage 9)

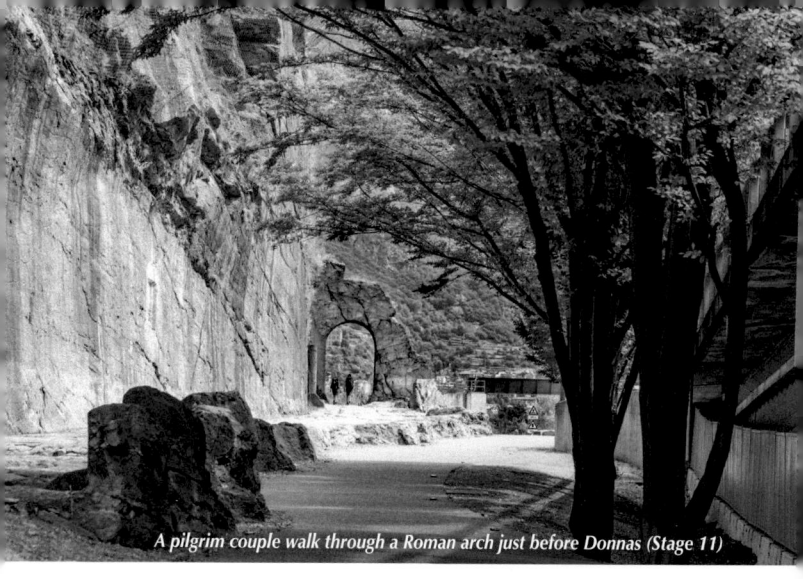

A pilgrim couple walk through a Roman arch just before Donnas (Stage 11)

strolling needs. Stay at the Canoa Club hostel in **Ivrea** and watch kayakers navigate the turbulent waters outside your window. Hospitality at the pilgrim hostel in **Vercelli** is unmatched. Wander inside the holiest brick pile in **Pavia** to see the startling white interior of the cathedral. Pull up a chair in Piazza San Francesco in **Piacenza** and enjoy the town's café culture. In **Fidenza**, use your imagination to fill in details of the stories depicted in the Romanesque carvings on the outer walls of the Cathedral of San Donnino. Make it your plan in good weather to stand atop windy **Monte Valoria** after Berceto, and when you arrive in **Pontremoli**, why not stay in the hostel housed inside the castle? Along the coast, each town between Sarzana and Massa offers its own charms, and more intrepid pilgrims will depart from the itinerary and walk down to the coast for a dip in the waters of the Ligurian Sea. And finally, in charming **Lucca** hear the story of the Volto Santo

and pause in Piazza Anfiteatro to celebrate your accomplishment over a glass of your favorite drink, with memories of land and sea and sky in your journey of many days and miles and wonders.

A BRIEF HISTORY OF THE VIA FRANCIGENA

Two-way traffic between Rome and the British Isles is documented as early as the 1st c. BC, and the Roman Empire strengthened the overland connection between the two by subduing the Alpine Celtic Veragri and Salassi tribes in AD 43 to build its own road over what we now call the Great Saint Bernard Pass (French: Col du Grand-Saint-Bernard, Italian: Colle del Gran San Bernardo). Due to its relatively low elevation, this became the preferred crossing over the western Alps and for over 1000 years soldiers, travelers and pilgrims from throughout Western Europe and the British Isles funneled through

Montreux to make their way up the Rhône, Dranse and Dranse d'Entremont valleys to cross into northern Italy.

After the fall of Imperial Rome and the city's emergence into ecclesiastical importance, the route became a two-way thoroughfare for English pilgrims and Irish missionaries who sought to sow traditional Christianity among the conquering pagan or Arian tribes that had settled north of Rome. Most famous among the Irish evangelists was Saint Fridianus of Ulster, whom the Pope appointed Bishop of Lucca in 556.

One of the most famous English pilgrims would be Sigeric the Serious, in the year 990 the newly appointed Archbishop of Canterbury. Sigeric followed the overland route from Canterbury to Rome, visited several churches while he was there, then returned. History would have forgotten this unremarkable archbishop except that someone in his retinue made a list of the churches he visited in Rome and of his overnight stops on the return journey. When scholars rediscovered these notes in the late 19th c. they knew they had stumbled onto a prize – a documented itinerary, something not unlike Santiago's *Codex Calixtinus* – that outlines a route lost in time. (See Appendix D for a translation of the route and how it relates to modern locations.)

It was never a single road – more a route within a network of roads. According to historian Giovanni Caselli the name 'Via Francigena' (way of the Frankish people) in the late Middle Ages referred to the stretch of the road below Vercelli, where French soldiers traveled south to defend the Papacy. North of Vercelli the route would have been called the Via Romea or Voie des Anglais, but as the route gained prominence in modern times the Italian name would feel most apt.

The rooftops of Lucca (photo: Rod Hoekstra, Stage 32)

THE MODERN VIA FRANCIGENA FROM CANTERBURY TO ROME

While scholars studied Sigeric's route as early as the late-19th century, it was in 1985 that Caselli surveyed the entire itinerary from Canterbury to Rome. He brought technicians of the Italian Military Geographical Institute to map the route and at the 1000-year anniversary in 1990 published his guidebook *Via Romea: Cammino di Dio.*

Aiming to make a viable, modern pilgrim route to Rome in anticipation of the 2000 Year of Jubilee, the Italian Ministry of Tourism pulled together regions and local governments along the way to collaborate in building a suitable pilgrim infrastructure, and in 1994 the Via Francigena was recognized as an official 'Cultural Route of the Council of Europe.' Now this epic walk was ready to be rediscovered by pilgrims looking for history, adventure and inspiration.

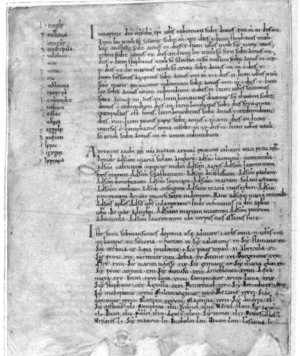 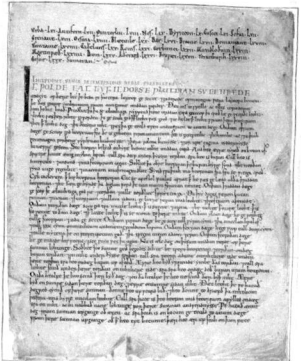

The 11th c. manuscript containing Sigeric's itinerary in Rome and from Rome to the English Channel (courtesy of the British Library)

PLANNING YOUR WALK

Careful planning is key to a smooth pilgrim walk. Here are some tips to consider as you make your preparations. Appendix A includes a helpful stage planning guide that lists intermediate distances between pilgrim accommodations.

WHERE TO BEGIN AND HOW TO GET THERE

It's not necessary to begin in Canterbury to enjoy the Via Francigena – many places along the way offer excellent starting points. Between Lausanne and Lucca the most common starting points are as follows.

Lausanne: A good international airport at Geneva and a quick train connection to Lausanne make it an excellent starting place as the first 1½ days' walking are either spent on quiet lakeside paths or on a picturesque passenger ferry as far as Villeneuve. It's also possible to take the efficient and clean Swiss trains as far as Orsières, then climb for two short but steep and spectacular days to the top of the Great Saint Bernard Pass. The last, Alpine stage before the pass is unforgettable and makes a start in Switzerland well worth the extra days.

To get to Lausanne fly into Geneva and take the convenient Swiss train directly from the airport to the Lausanne station (www.sbb.ch, 5 departures per hour, CHF10, approx 1hr). Trains also connect from Lausanne to many stops along the Swiss portion of the route, including Vevey, Montreux, Villeneuve,

Aigle, Saint-Maurice, Vernayaz, Martigny, Sembrancher and Orsières, each of which also makes a suitable starting point. French trains from Chamonix and Saint-Gervais-Les-Bains intersect the route at Vernayaz, giving another option if you are coming from the south of France (www.sncf.com).

Great Saint Bernard Pass: The literal highpoint of the Via Francigena presents some of its most difficult travel connections and has the disadvantage of being closed to all but the hardiest travelers for much of the year.

To get to the Great Saint Bernard Pass from the Swiss side, take the train to Martigny or the end of the tracks at Orsières, where in late spring through early fall you can catch a bus to the Pass (www.tmrsa.ch). Otherwise the Pass is closed to vehicles and can be accessed only on foot with suitable Alpine gear in favorable conditions. From the Italian side it is easiest to take the train to Aosta and then a bus partway to the pass (www.arriva.it), which is also accessible by vehicles from this side only late spring through early fall.

Aosta, Ivrea, Vercelli, or Pavia: A start in Aosta avoids most of the winter weather complications of the Great Saint Bernard Pass and still allows several days of walking in the lovely Aosta Valley. A start at Ivrea leaves the mountains behind, but still offers touring of the charming villages in the rolling Piedmont region. Those who look forward to walking through the flat expanses of the Po Valley can begin at

A farmer turns corn stalks to mulch after harvest on a field before Orio Litta (Stage 21)

Vercelli or later at Pavia. Each of these cities is easily accessed by train (www.trenitalia.com) from international airports at Milan, Turin or Bologna.

Piacenza or Fidenza: Some prefer to skip the flat, agricultural Po Valley, so a start makes sense at Piacenza, with its many services, or Fidenza, the last stop in the Po Valley before Apennine foothills. Both locations are easily accessible by train from any of Northern Italy's international airports (www.trenitalia.com).

Sarzana: If you want to skip the challenging yet beautiful days in Cisa Pass, a start at Sarzana brings you right to the coastal flatlands, though the official route does include some low climbs on hillsides offering Mediterranean views. Fly into Pisa or Florence to make your train connections to Sarzana.

WHEN TO WALK

Two main scheduling considerations apply: getting over the Great Saint Bernard Pass (GSB) and avoiding hot summer weather in Italy. Given its elevation and the high annual snowpack, the footpath to the pass is reliably open to walkers only in July, August and September (though the auto road is plowed and open for cars and walkers in June and July). The snow-covered walking path is sometimes passable in May and June with snowshoes and other winter hiking gear. In these months make sure to call the Hospice at the pass the day before to confirm that weather and avalanche forecasts allow a safe walk (tel 027 787 12 36).

The disadvantage of waiting for passable conditions on the Great Saint Bernard Pass is that a summer crossing puts you into Italy just in time for high summer temperatures. If you want to avoid walking in the heat, or if a spring or fall crossing is critical for your personal schedule, you'll need to cross the pass in the spring by bus from Martigny, Orsières or Bourg Saint Pierre on the Swiss side (www.savda.it). The bus crosses under the pass in a tunnel and can drop you at Saint-Rhémy,

The Château d'Aigle stands among the vineyards (Stage 3)

Echevennoz or Aosta on the Italian side (see Stage 7 for more details).

(see Stage 7 for more details).

CYCLING ALL OR PART OF THE ROUTE

A complete, well-marked bicycle route in Italy has been set by the European Association of Via Francigena ways (EAVF) with more information available at www.viefrancigene.org. Much of the walking route is on hardpack dirt roads, and the route steers the cyclist onto asphalt roads when trails are inaccessible for bikes. A new bike route for Switzerland is available on the www.viefrancigene.org website. Between Martigny Croix and Sembrancher there is no safe option for bicycles, and cyclists should instead take the train through this narrow mountain gorge.

Given the flat and fairly uniform terrain some people choose to bike Piemonte and the Po Valley, combining stages on bicycle to save as many as 265km on foot. With the exception of one narrow stretch along the dykes after Palestro (Stage 17) this entire Ivrea to Fidenza segment is feasible by mountain bike on the walking as well as the biking route.

WHERE TO STAY

Switzerland

In Switzerland, Via Francigena infrastructure is sparse between Lausanne and the Great Saint Bernard Pass, and pilgrims find themselves choosing among lower-cost tourist options to offset Switzerland's high prices. Campgrounds often have bungalows or mobile homes available as well as tent pitches. Lausanne and Montreux offer youth hostels, while Orsières and Martigny churches make space available. Bourg-Saint-Pierre has hostel beds, and the Great Saint Bernard Pass has its famous and picturesque (but not inexpensive) hospice dormitories and posh hotel. Otherwise pilgrims rely on low-cost hotels and B&Bs, with average costs for a double room between CHF60 and CHF100 per night.

Italy
In Italy, by contrast, pilgrims benefit from a strong infrastructure of low-cost parochial or municipal hostels (Italian: *ostello* or plural, *ostelli*) on almost every stage between the Great Saint Bernard Pass and Rome. Many *ostelli* are *donativo*, which actually means €10 or more is expected. A blanket and pillow are usually provided for use on bunk beds in dormitory rooms with shared bathrooms. Some pilgrims will pay more for the assurance of a reservation and the comfort of bed linens, and hotels and B&Bs are more likely to have an online reservation system available. The extra services or a hotel or B&B will cost around €50–70 per night.

Italian locals also rent out rooms – *camere* – which may be in a separate house or in the host's own apartment and may include access to a kitchen for self-catering. An *agriturismo* is a farm authorized by the Italian government to provide overnight stays. Costs can vary greatly, but accommodations are hotel-like, with comfortable beds, linens and private bathrooms. Camping is allowed in Italy in designated campgrounds in public parks or with permission of a private landowner. Pilgrims who brought along camping gear for early stages of the Via Francigena often send their gear back home by the time they arrive in Tuscany due to the ample supply of low-cost hostel beds. In addition to this guidebook, two excellent resources for finding accommodation are the handbook of the Fédération Française Via Francigena (€12, www.ffvf.fr) and the Gronze website (free, www.gronze.com/via-francigena).

A dormitory at l'Hospice du Grand-Saint-Bernard (Stage 7)

Storefront of the Liddes supermarket (Stage 6)

WHAT AND WHERE TO EAT

Hostel kitchens are seldom available in Switzerland, so pilgrims find themselves at cafés and restaurants for breakfast and dinner. Food for lunch and snacks is readily available in local stores. In Italy, the occasional hostel kitchen allows for self-catering, but otherwise it is best to plan for café and restaurant breakfasts and dinners, with lunches and snacks purchased at grocery stores and eaten along the way. A good strategy is to ask at your breakfast café for a *panino da portare via*, a sandwich for takeaway or 'to go'. Non-Italians find themselves adjusting to the Italian *riposo*, the siesta-like pause in the afternoon when shops and restaurants close. Bars remain open and will usually make a *panino* sandwich for a hungry pilgrim. Italian restaurants open for dinner around 7:30pm, which calls for a mid-afternoon snack at a local bar until dinner is served.

SHOULD I MAKE RESERVATIONS AHEAD?

In Switzerland and Italy it is always best to make hostel reservations 1–2 days in advance of your stay. Call the hostel, tell them your date and approximate arrival time, and your name and nationality. Some hostels will ask you to call back on the morning of your arrival to remind them you're coming so they'll remember to be nearby to share the key. Some will post their phone number on the door so you can call when you arrive. If your French or Italian language skills are not strong, ask your host the night before to make your next-day's reservation for you. Be aware that local Italian pilgrims fill hostels on weekends, so reservations are more important on Friday and Saturday nights. Hotels, B&Bs and *agriturismi* usually have an online portal where you can book your room.

HOW MUCH MONEY SHOULD I BUDGET?

Switzerland
The strong Swiss Franc (CHF) and the high cost of living in Switzerland make it the most expensive of the Via Francigena's host countries.
- Hostel lodging CHF45 (average for youth hostel bed and half board)
- Breakfast CHF7 (sometimes included with lodging)
- Sack lunch CHF7
- Afternoon snack CHF5
- Dinner CHF25 (if not included with lodging)
- Incidentals CHF5
- Total CHF70–95 per day

Italy
The strong network of pilgrim hostels in this stretch of the Via Francigena offers many options for an economical trip.
- Hostel lodging donation €10 (€20 with dinner)
- Breakfast (included)
- Sack lunch €5
- Afternoon snack €5
- Dinner €15 (if not included with lodging)
- Incidentals €5
- Total €35–40 per day

Add more for the occasional glass of wine or beer, for hotel overnights, for more elaborate dinners, for museum admission fees, etc.

Cheesemongers set up shop early on market day in Pontremoli (Stage 28)

HOW DO I SECURE MY CREDENTIAL?

The pilgrim credential (*credenziale*) is a document that certifies the bearer is a pilgrim who is walking, biking or riding horseback. It allows pilgrims to stay in overnight pilgrim lodging and, if stamped for at least the last 100km before Rome (200km for cyclists), qualifies the bearer to receive a Testimonium completion certificate at the Vatican in Rome. To be certain you have it at the start of your walk, it's best to order your credential in advance. The EAVF offers credentials with space enough for the Italian portion of the Via Francigena through its partner, SloWays at www.viefrancigene.org/en (€5 plus shipping, allow 1–2 months for delivery).

Appendix B contains a list of locations on the Via Francigena where you can collect a credential in person. Plan to hunt down one stamp (*timbro*) corresponding to each overnight along the way. This is usually done at lodgings, but can also be secured at many bars, churches, museums, tourist offices and city halls. When you arrive in Rome, present your credential at the Vatican's Opera Romana Pellegrinaggi just off Saint Peter's Square to receive your Testimonium (Piazza Pio XII, 9, open 09:00–17:00 Mon–Sat, 09:00–13:00 Sun).

A Via Francigena pilgrim credential

TIPS FOR MAKING THE MOST OF YOUR WALK

TOPOGRAPHY OF THE VIA FRANCIGENA FROM LAUSANNE TO LUCCA

The portion of the Via Francigena covered in this book can be divided into four regions:

The Vaud and Valais: From Lausanne to Martigny the route follows bike and pedestrian paths – with the occasional jaunt up a mountainside for views – to climb almost imperceptibly through then above the Rhône Valley through these two Swiss cantons.

Crossing the Alps: After Martigny the climb over the Alps begins in earnest, with genuine Alpine hiking on a stretch between Martigny Croix and Sembrancher (Stage 5) that less-agile pilgrims may find difficult. The route gradually steepens between Sembrancher and Bourg-Saint-Pierre, until it becomes a treeless and steep Alpine footpath between Bourg-Saint-Pierre and the top of the Great Saint Bernard Pass (Stage 7). After the pass the footpath quickly descends, crossing the tree line and continuing downhill to Aosta, mostly following undulating mountainside paths until just after Pont-Saint-Martin.

Piemonte, Lombardia and Emilia-Romagna: The low, rolling hills of Piemonte flatten out to the fertile farmlands of the Po River Valley beginning at Santhià (Stage 15) which continue on through Lombardia and into Emilia-Romagna for the next 230km to Fidenza (Stage 26). The route here follows flat, two-track farmroads and dyke-top gravel roads.

The Apennines and Lunigiana: Following a day of foothills after Fidenza (Stage 26) the climb over the Apennines leads on sometimes-steep paths to the 1041m Cisa Pass. Here you enter Tuscany and walk the long downhill stages to the coastal plain of Lunigiana, which straddles the regions of Liguria and Tuscany. Via Francigena stewards have chosen mountainside vistas over the flat and urban coastal plain, providing some climbs and descents until the route turns inland at a low pass through the Apuan Alps on its way to Camaiore and ultimately, Lucca.

UNDERSTANDING LOCAL CULTURES

After centuries of domination by the French, the Swiss regions of the Vaud and Valais – as well as the Aosta Valley in Italy – speak French. In this part of Switzerland, hello is *grüezi* and goodbye is *adieu*. Besides French, Swiss children in this region also learn either German or Italian in school, since all three are official languages in Switzerland. Statistics suggest that about two-thirds of Swiss people speak at least some English as well.

Italian culture is diverse, with many regional differences. Still, there are some aspects of Italian culture that are widely shared throughout the country. Pilgrims are often surprised to find Italian streets

The village of Rivaz is nestled among the hillside vineyards with views to Vevey and the Alps (Stage 1)

empty in the afternoon. This is the Italian *riposo*, or 'rest,' in which everything grinds to a halt. Bakeries, restaurants, offices and businesses are generally closed between about 12:30 and 4:30 for a long lunch break, rest and family time. No matter how much pilgrims may want to leave at the crack of dawn, it's general practice that breakfast comes at about 7:30 or 8:00 each morning. If you want an earlier departure, make sure to notify your hosts. Restaurants open for dinner at 7:30pm, which means that a pilgrim who wants to be in bed by 9:00 will have to sleep on a full stomach. In Italy it's traditional for residents to head out in the evening, particularly on Sundays and holidays, for a relaxing stroll – a *passegiata* – on one of the main shopping streets or a large park. In urban areas about a third of Italians speak some English, but in rural areas not as much. It's wise to become familiar with your Italian-English dictionary or phrasebook,

otherwise a good smartphone translation app will be a big help. Spanish and French speakers will find a quicker entry into Italian and both languages are sometimes understood in Italy.

TRAINING FOR YOUR WALK

While anyone who is of average or better fitness can complete a walk of this kind, the experience is much more pleasant with some advance training. Training prepares the muscles and tendons of your legs and feet for the daily regime of long walks and gives you time to fix any shoe or sock problems that might lead to painful blisters.

For a person of average fitness, a training program should include walks of increasing distance over varied terrain for 2–3 months in advance of your trip, building toward at least two successive walks of 20–25km in the week prior to your departure.

If blisters develop in training walks, adjust the socks and shoes, sandals or boots you are using. Try to duplicate the conditions of your pilgrimage by walking with a loaded pack on varied terrain during training, which benefits cardio conditioning and duplicates the stresses your feet will undergo as you walk in Italy.

WHAT TO PACK

Many Via Francigena pilgrims have already walked at least one Camino de Santiago, so will understand the benefits of packing light. As a rule of thumb a fully loaded pack should weigh less than 10% of a pilgrim's body weight.

A good packing list includes:
- Backpack: 35–40 liters
- Clothes: layers, max 2–3 pants (trousers) and shirts
- Rain gear: poncho, rain jacket or trekking umbrella
- Sun gear: sun hat; sunscreen, sunglasses
- Bedding: hostels are generally equipped with wool blankets, so take a sleeping bag liner in summer, and a lightweight sleeping bag otherwise
- Walking shoes and camp shoes (for around town)
- Hydration system – reusable bottles or bladder
- Basic first-aid kit and blister kit
- Toiletries
- Hiking towel
- Smartphone/camera and charger
- Travel and identity documents
- Debit and credit cards
- Toilet paper and a few plastic bags
- Trekking poles as needed

A two-level arcaded passageway connects two buildings in Filetto (Stage 28)

• Miscellaneous: zippered mesh bags are helpful for keeping your items organized inside your pack. Some like to bring along a small clothes-line and clothespins for drying just-washed items as well as earplugs for a restful sleep.

BAGGAGE TRANSPORT AND STORAGE

Baggage transport in Switzerland is limited and is often arranged through booking companies like www.eurotrek.ch. Some hotels will arrange taxi or train transfers for your baggage. At present, organized baggage transport service is only available for groups in the stages between Aosta and Lucca (€15/each, info@sloways.eu, min 5 bags from Aosta to Pontremoli, min 4 bags from Pontremoli to Lucca). After Lucca single bag service is available from SloWays and other providers (for

details, see Appendix B). Otherwise, your overnight accommodation may be able to suggest how to transport your bags to your next lodging.

TELEPHONES

SIM cards and international plans
Pilgrims from outside the EU may find it expensive to use their cellphone pro-vider's international calling plan. If you anticipate heavy usage you may want to purchase a European SIM card for your unlocked smartphone. Although this SIM card will work throughout the EU, calls and data are more expen-sive when you roam outside the host country, so the least expensive option is to purchase a prepaid SIM card at a local phone shop when you cross a border. Switzerland's largest providers are Swisscom (www.swisscom.ch) and Sunrise (www.sunrise.ch), with several

A pilgrim finds shade on the outskirts of Belgioioso (Stage 20)

The hamlet of Piazzano between Valpromaro and Lucca (Stage 32)

shops located between Lausanne and Martigny. Italy's largest providers are Vodafone (www.vodafone.it), TIM (www.tim.it) and Wind Tre (www.wind tre.it), each with shops in Aosta and larger cities on the route.

Country prefixes

If you are dialing from an international phone, always use the country code – for Switzerland +41 and Italy +39. Because the need for country codes depends on the nationality of your SIM card, in this guidebook country codes are not included before local phone numbers. On Swiss calls from outside Switzerland – or from inside with a non-Swiss SIM card – it is necessary to add the prefix '0' after the country code. In Italy it is common for phone numbers to begin with '0' (and to have 8–11 digits).

HEALTH AND WELL-BEING

Switzerland and Italy have state-of-the-art national telephone systems to contact ambulance and police, with English-speaking operators available 24/7 to answer emergency calls.

Emergency phone numbers:

Switzerland

117 Police
118 Fire
144 Ambulance
1414 or 1415 Helicopter rescue

Italy

112 Carabinieri – Nationwide number for emergencies
113 Local police
115 Fire department
117 Finance police (if you've been cheated in a retail transaction)
118 Medical emergencies – this is the best number to call if you have a health-related emergency and need an ambulance or emergency room
1515 Forest fires

If you become sick or injured and don't feel it's an emergency, a good starting place for information is the local pharmacy, which is marked throughout Europe with the sign of a green cross above the storefront. If the pharmacist can't help you, he or she will recommend a nearby clinic or hospital. Your overnight host is a valuable source of information about local transportation, clinics, hospitals and doctors.

HOW TO USE THIS GUIDE

As part of Cicerone's pilgrimage series, this guide is loaded with helpful information for your walk. Since the main body of research for the guide was completed, the world has been struck by the COVID-19 virus. It is likely that facilities and accommodation will be affected by this pandemic for some time after publication. We have checked information as close to publication date as practicable, but please do let us know of any serious problems (see Updates to this guide section). There may be regulations on social distancing, group mixing, masks and other matters for some time so check the latest requirements in Switzerland and Italy before setting off. Communal accommodation in particular may be impacted – please take the required precautions to protect yourself and your fellow pilgrims.

ROUTE DESCRIPTIONS

Each stage is laid out in the following format:

Route summary information

Information is included at the start of each stage that provides the specific starting and ending point as well as information summarizing the walk.

Total distance: Unless otherwise specified, the distance given is based on the official route with extraneous waypoints carefully edited out and the tracks smoothed to one waypoint for each 30m in distance. Expect the unedited tracks

from your recreational GPS, smart-phone app or step counter to add about 10–15% to the stage total.

Total ascent and descent: These figures record the up-and-down bumps as you gain and lose elevation through the day. Elevation figures for GPS tracks in this book are provided through www.gpsvisualizer.com using the best of either ODP1, ASTER or NASA altitude data.

Difficulty: Using a formula that balances total distance, steepness and ascent/descent amounts, all stages are awarded one of four designations: 'Easy,' 'Moderate,' 'Moderately hard,' and 'Hard.'

Duration: No two pilgrims walk at exactly the same speed, so this book uses a formula that calculates duration based on 4km/hr with an additional 5min added for every 100m of ascent, rounding the result to the nearest ¼ hour. Rest stops are not included in the duration total, so you'll need to add those to your shedule.

Percentage paved: This shows how much of the walk is on hard surfaces like concrete, tarmac, asphalt and cobblestones rather than softer surfaces like gravel, dirt roads and dirt paths.

Hostels: Distances from the start of the stage to all hostels are included in order to help you plan your stages.

Overview: This paragraph summarizes the stage and shares any special tips, recommendations or warnings walkers should know before beginning the walk.

*Waymarkers for the Via Francigena (anticlockwise from top left):
trail 70 and black bordered arrows or diamonds in Switzerland;
trail 103 on the GSB; and red/white tape blazes in Italy*

Walking directions, distances and municipality information headings

Since the Via Francigena between Lausanne and Lucca is quite well marked, only moderately detailed walking descriptions are given for most stages. Bold type is used when a landmark is also labelled on the route map, and useful intermediate distances are provided in the text between municipalities. Because underlying distance calculations are based on 100ths of a kilometer while intermediate distances are shown at 10ths of a kilometer, some minor decimal rounding discrepancies result when intermediate distances are added together.

Municipalities with pilgrim lodgings have their own headings with 10 codes that indicate available services. The municipality headings also show the distance from the previous municipality and the distance remaining to the end of the Via Francigena at Rome. Figure 1 gives an example and shows the meaning of the various symbols and codes.

Accommodation listings

The EAVF has done an excellent job of creating a network of pilgrim-specific hostels located in churches, monasteries, convents, municipal facilities and church retreat houses that are not included in typical tourist resources like Booking.com. Accommodation listings in this guide focus on simple and inexpensive pilgrim hostels, since these low-budget lodgings are least likely to have an online presence. Other resources like Booking.com usually offer mid-range and more expensive properties and are easy to find and

book online. There are 11 important infrastructure elements to help you make your choice. See Figure 2 for an example and an explanation of symbols used.

Elevation profiles

Helpful elevation profiles are included for each stage so you see a graphical representation of distances and topography. Where possible, optional routes are included, but the distances of the options may be shown out of scale in the interest of simplicity and clarity.

Maps

The maps in this guidebook are 'north up' and show the entire stage route at a scale of 1:100,000. Six cities – Lausanne, Aosta, Ivrea, Pavia, Piacenza, Lucca – are shown at around 1:25,000. The route is depicted by a solid red line, with optional route lines in dashed red and longer variants in solid blue. See the map key at the start of the book for more details about map symbols.

GPX TRACKS AND ACCOMMODATION DOWNLOADS

GPX tracks for the route in this guidebook are available to download free at www.cicerone.co.uk/1086/GPX. GPX files are provided in good faith, but neither the author nor the publisher accepts responsibility for their accuracy.

A printout of the accommodation listings can be downloaded from www.cicerone.co.uk/1086. Always remember to visit the book's page on the Cicerone website to find the latest updates.

Figure 1: Example of stage description and municipal information

total distance from
previous municipality   elevation population   distance remaining to Rome

infrastructure

5.0KM FUCECCHIO (ELEV 46M, POP 23,082)

▥ ⊕ ▢ ▣ ⊛ ◉ ⊕ ⊕ ⊕ ❶ (372.9KM)

Called 'Arne Blanca' by Sigeric and listed as his Stage XXIII, its current name
derives from the Latin Ficeclum (tr: 'fig plantations'), which gives a hint at the
town's one-time main crop. The 14th c. brought a decimating plague and near
desertion of the town until in the 16th c. it caught the attention of Florence's Medici
family, who began its redevelopment. The medieval town was centered around the
castle, abbey and churches atop Monte Salamartano, most notable of which is the
12th c. **Abbey of San Salvatore**, rebuilt in the 16th–17th c. The church houses an
important painting on the Immaculate Conception by High-Renaissance master
Jacopo Chimenti, a notable 1626 organ, as well as a remarkable 15th c. wooden
crucifix said to have miraculous healing qualities. Adjacent is the neo-classical
Church of San Giovanni Battisti, austere in its bare brick façade, though richly
decorated inside. Fucecchio is the setting for the Puccini opera, *Gianni Schicchi*.
(Train: Fucecchio shares a train station with San Miniato Basso, www.trenitalia.it.
Bus: www.capautolinee.it, www.copitspa.it, www.pisa.cttnord.it.)

place
description

🏠 Monastero Santissimo Salvatore ▣ ▣ ▣ ▣ ▨ , 3/6, €15 Donation,
Piazza Poggio Salamartano 4, tel 057 120 325.

facilities

As the Via Roma leads out of town under tall boulevard trees a pedestrian
path appears to the right, which you follow to the Arno River (1.1km). Tuscany's
most important river, the Arno flows 241km from the Apennines through Florence
before emptying into the Tyrrhenian Sea near Pisa. After crossing the river on the
sidewalk of the road bridge, turn left and pass behind a paper factory, joining a
road along the south bank of the river that leads to another dyke that crosses the
valley floor. After you walk under the **SR436** highway bridge (1.1km) you can see
on the distant hill the towers of San Miniato. To the right, inaccessible because
of the highway; however, the VF veers left to miss the
busy highway and aims instead for the village of **Otraino** (1.7km, bar). Continue
zigzagging on dykes toward San Miniato, walking first under a **railway bridge** and
then under the Pisa–Florence highway bridge (**2.0km**). Scramble up a low, grassy
bank to come to the red-painted bike path leading into central **San Miniato Basso**.

distance
between
intermediate
points

total
distance
from
previous
municipality

6.7KM SAN MINIATO BASSO (ELEV 29M, POP 6050)

▥ ⊕ ▢ ▣ ⊛ ◉ ⊕ ⊕ (366.2KM)

The original village was clustered along the Pisa–Florence road, near the...

distance
remaining
to Rome

Infrastructure symbols

catering: restaurants,
bars or cafés   supermarket/groceries   accommodation   ATM   bus   train   hospital   clinic   pharmacy   tourist info

🍴 ⊕ 🏠 € ■ ■ Ⓗ ✚ ✚ *i*

Figure 2: Example of accommodation listing

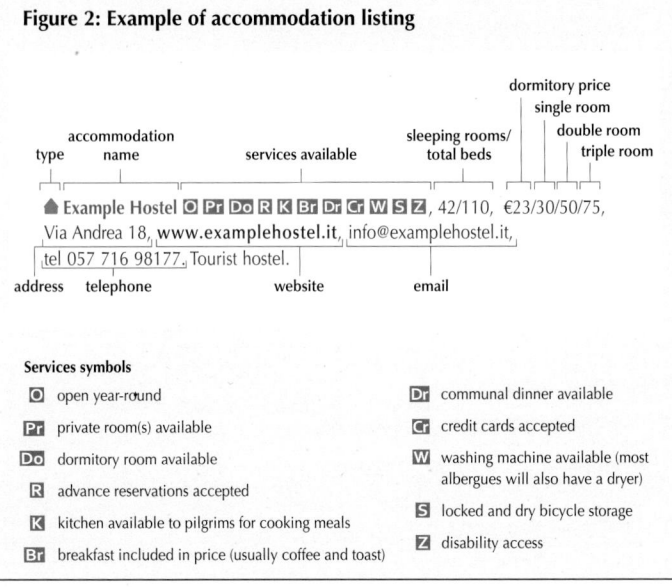

Services symbols

O	open year-round	**Dr**	communal dinner available
Pr	private room(s) available	**Cr**	credit cards accepted
Do	dormitory room available	**W**	washing machine available (most albergues will also have a dryer)
R	advance reservations accepted		
K	kitchen available to pilgrims for cooking meals	**S**	locked and dry bicycle storage
Br	breakfast included in price (usually coffee and toast)	**Z**	disability access

SECTION 1: THE VAUD AND VALAIS

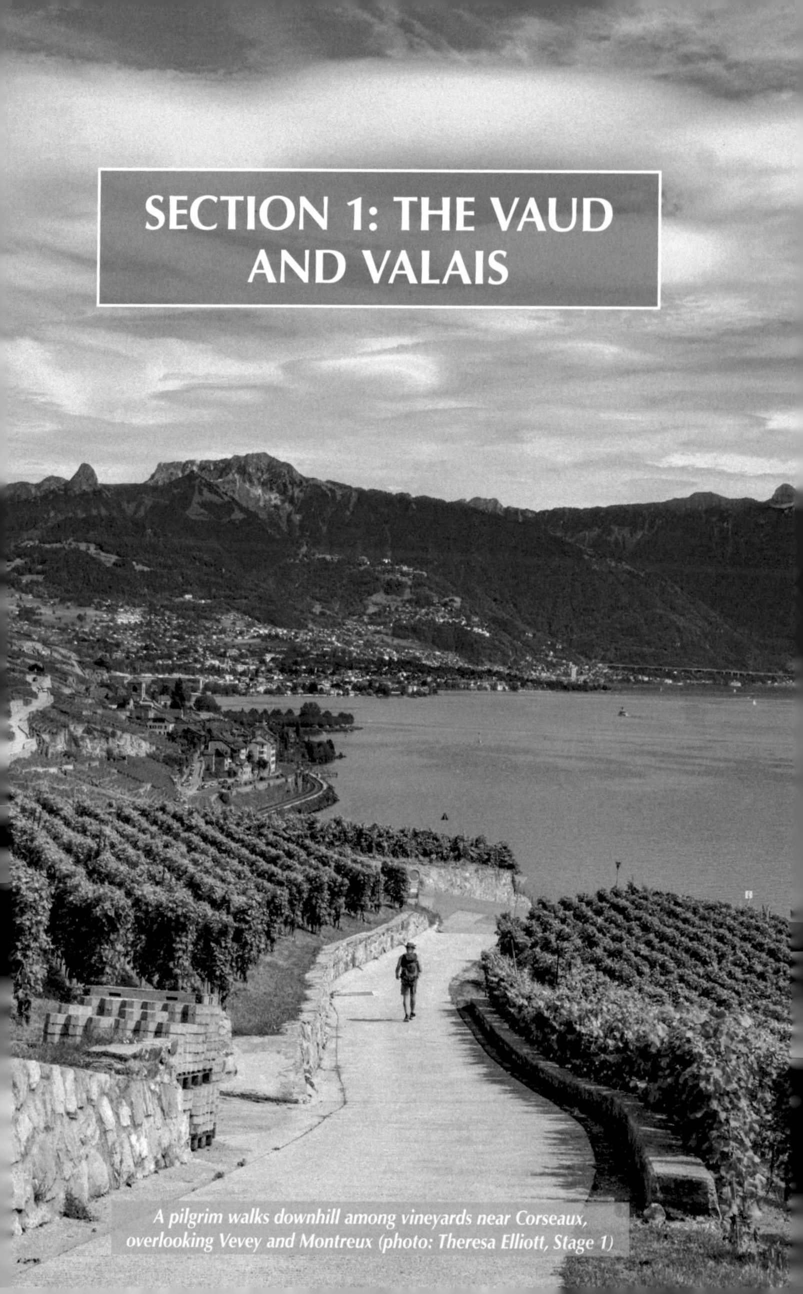

A pilgrim walks downhill among vineyards near Corseaux, overlooking Vevey and Montreux (photo: Theresa Elliott, Stage 1)

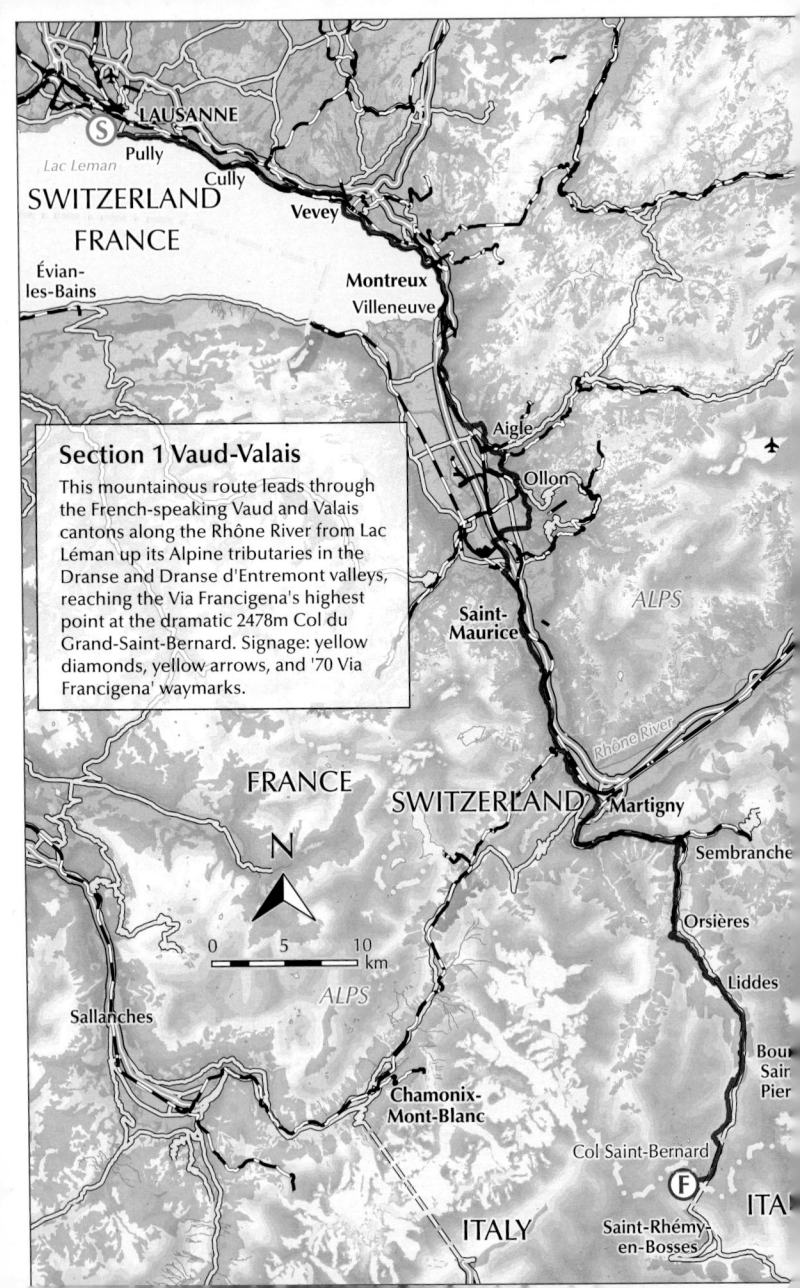

Section 1 Vaud-Valais

This mountainous route leads through the French-speaking Vaud and Valais cantons along the Rhône River from Lac Léman up its Alpine tributaries in the Dranse and Dranse d'Entremont valleys, reaching the Via Francigena's highest point at the dramatic 2478m Col du Grand-Saint-Bernard. Signage: yellow diamonds, yellow arrows, and '70 Via Francigena' waymarks.

STAGE 1

Lausanne to Vevey

Start	Lausanne, Place de Jeux, Ouchy
Finish	Vevey, ferry landing
Distance	21.2km
Total ascent	363m
Total descent	366m
Difficulty	Moderate
Duration	6hr
Percentage paved	99%
Hostels	Cully 9.0km (camping only), Vevey 21.2km

The walk has two distinct highlights – the scenic lakeside pathway and the undulating vineyard terraces on the mountainsides above. On a sunny day the steep and shadeless climb among terraces can make this feel like a very hot and dry stage, but frequent stations at the many towns along the path offer respite and the opportunity to skip ahead by train (www.sbb.ch). Another enjoyable alternative to walking the stage is to take the scenic passenger ferry, which has stops at Lausanne, Pully, Lutry, Cully and Vevey and on the next stage at La Tour, Clarens, Montreux, Territet, Château de Chillon and Villeneuve (www.cgn.ch).

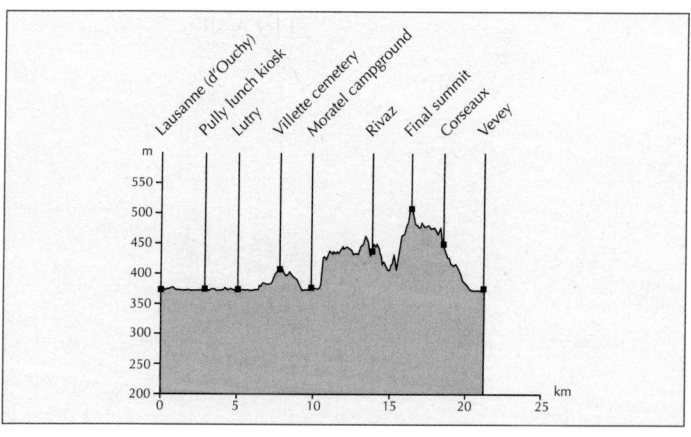

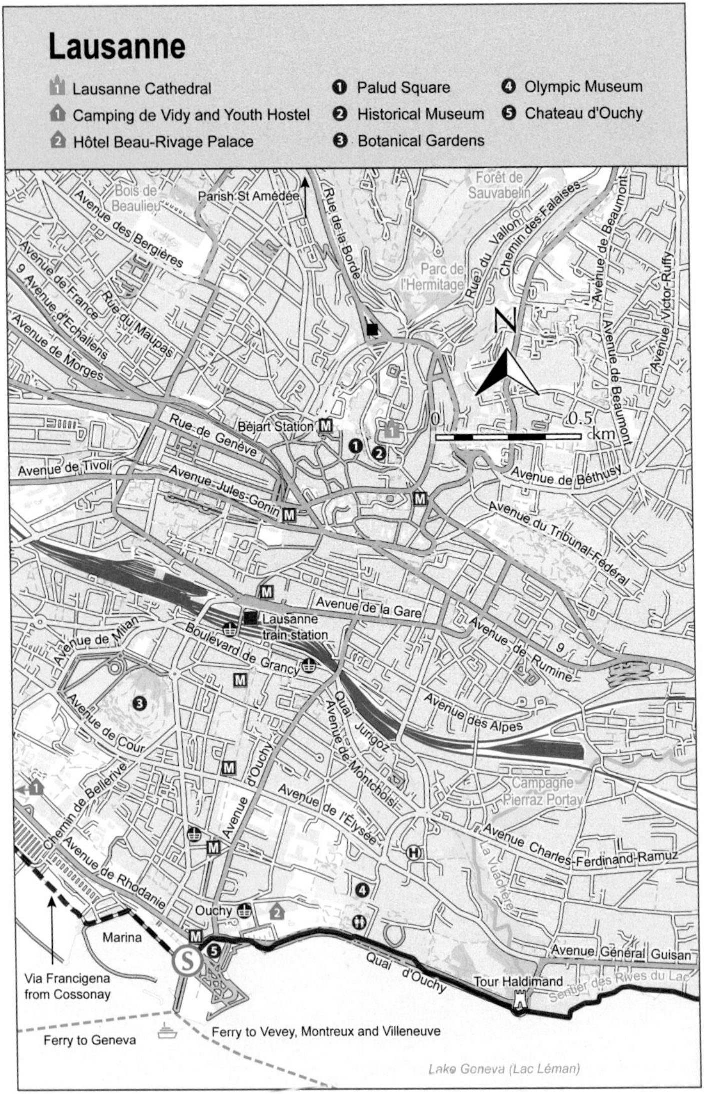
Lausanne
Lausanne Cathedral
Camping de Vidy and Youth Hostel
Hôtel Beau-Rivage Palace
1 Palud Square
2 Historical Museum
3 Botanical Gardens
4 Olympic Museum
5 Chateau d'Ouchy
Bois de Beaulieu
Parish St Amédée
Rue de la Borde
Forêt de Sauvabelin
Chemin des Falaises
Rue du Vallon
Avenue de Beaumont
Avenue Victor-Ruffy
Parc de l'Hermitage
Avenue des Bergières
Avenue de France
9 Avenue d'Echallens
Rue du Maupas
Avenue de Morges
N
0
0.5
km
Rue de Genève
Béjart Station
Avenue de Tivoli
Avenue Jules-Gonin
Avenue de Béthusy
Avenue du Tribunal-Fédéral
Avenue de la Gare
Lausanne train station
Avenue de Rumine
9
Avenue de Milan
Boulevard de Grancy
Avenue des Alpes
Quai Jurigoz
Avenue de Montchoisi
Avenue de Cour
Avenue d'Ouchy
Avenue de l'Elysée
Campagne Pierraz Portay
Chemin de Bellerive
Avenue Charles-Ferdinand-Ramuz
La Vuachère
Avenue de Rhodanie
Ouchy
Marina
Quai d'Ouchy
Avenue Général Guisan
Tour Haldimand
Sentier des Rives du Lac
Via Francigena from Cossonay
Ferry to Geneva
Ferry to Vevey, Montreux and Villeneuve
Lake Geneva (Lac Léman)

0.0KM LAUSANNE (ELEV 526M, POP 139,056) 🍴 ⊕ 🛏 🏧 ⊚ ⊚ ⊕ ⊕ Ⓗ *ℹ*
(1136.9KM)
This prosperous and scenic city is capital of the canton of Vaud in the French-speaking region of Romandy and is the fourth-largest city in Switzerland. Home to the International Olympic Committee and other international sports organizations, it is also center of the Swiss wine-growing region. In the 1st C. AD the Romans built a military camp and then a city called Lousanna along the lakeside where ruins can be viewed today. After the fall of Rome the town was moved to a more defensible location on the hill high above, where central Lausanne now sits, and this is likely where Archbishop Sigeric stayed at the end of his Stage LIV. Colleagues of Geneva's John Calvin brought the Protestant Reformation to the Vaud, and the beautiful 13th c. **Cathedral of Notre Dame of Lausanne** (CHF5, open 09:00–19:00 Apr–Sep) atop the city belongs to the Evangelical Reformed Church. The cathedral tower's seven bells chime the hour until 22:00 – after that a town crier shouts the hours 365 nights a year, as he has done since 1405. A trip to the cathedral provides a view of the church interior (pilgrim stamp in gift shop) and a majestic viewpoint toward Lac Léman (Lake Geneva) and the French Alps across the lake.

Below the cathedral is **Palud Square**, medieval center of town, home to many quaint eateries and shops and on Wednesday and Saturday mornings a farmers' market. Also here is the 17th c. Town Hall adjacent to the 16th c. Fountain of Justice crowned by the colorful Statue of Justice. Lausanne's belle époque **Ouchy neighborhood** is stretched along the lakeshore and sprinkled with cafés and shops among its parks and pathways. The VF route passes the **Olympic Museum** which showcases torches and medals from all modern Olympic games (Quai d'Ouchy 1, www.olympic.org/museum). The monuments, restaurants and shopping of Lausanne are set high above the lakeshore, but can be accessed through a convenient tram system with stops between the lakeshore and the Cathedral of Lausanne (CHF8.80 for an all-day pass). (Train to Vevey, Aigle, Saint-Maurice, Martigny and Orsières: www.sbb.ch.)

🛏 Auberge de Jeunesse de Lausanne 🄾 🄿r 🄳o 🄡 🄱r 🄳r 🄲r 🅆 🅂 🅉 117/320, CHF57/105/140/-/228, Chemin du Bois-de-Vaux 36, www.youthhostel.ch/en/hostels/Lausanne-jeunotel, lausanne@youthhostel.ch, tel (0)21 626 02 22. Located 100m from Lac Léman.

🛏 ▲Camping de Vidy 🄾 🄳o 🄡 🄚 🄲r 🅆 🅂 9/30, CHF-/-/60/90, Chemin du Camping 3, www.clv.ch, info@clv.ch, tel (0)21 622 50 00. Bungalows with bunk beds plus camping. Lakeside with restaurant onsite.

The view just after dawn from Lausanne Cathedral overlooking the city, Lac Léman, and the French Alps beyond

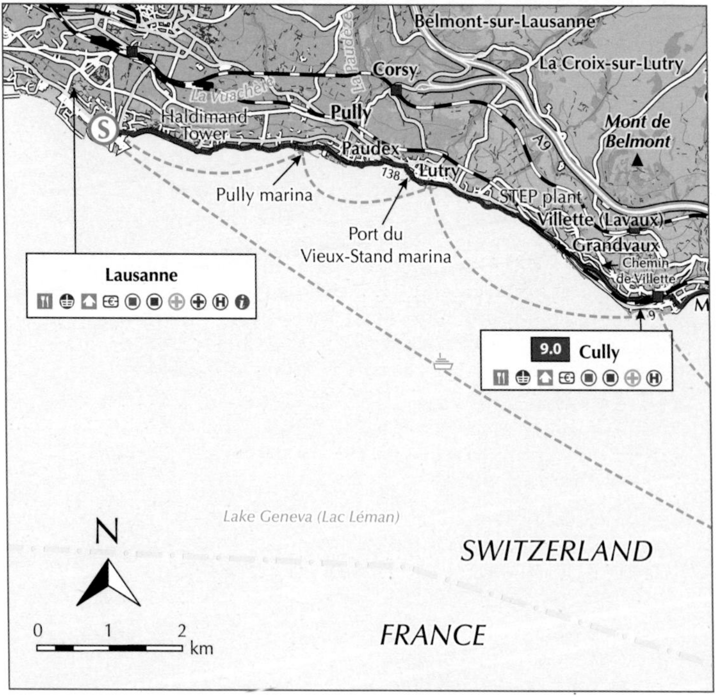

The Sentier des Rives du Lac is the lakeside trail that will lead you much of the way around lovely **Lac Léman**. With the lake at your right hand, follow this pedestrian walkway past the Château d'Ouchy, amid the upscale cafés and crêperies that line the main roadway, the Quai d'Ouchy, of this Lausanne suburb. Pass the faux-ruin **Haldimand Tower** (**1.2km**) and walk along a sandy beach to **Pully marina** (**1.6km**, restaurants), after which you walk along the road with a large park and swimming pool complex on the lakefront to the right. Just afterward comes the town of **Paudex** whose commercial center is a few blocks above this now-familiar maze of marinas and beachfront parks. Continue along the lakeshore to return to the roadside at the Port du Vieux-Stand marina (**1.6km**, restaurants). After the concrete walks of the Vieux-Port marina of **Lutry**, the lakeshore path varies between narrow concrete walkways, flagstones and sometimes the small stones of the beach itself.

After the large concrete **STEP waste water treatment plant** appears on the left, follow the signs leading to a stairway that takes you to the Route de Lavaux highway (**2.0km**) above. Turn right to walk alongside the highway, pass the **Villette** train station

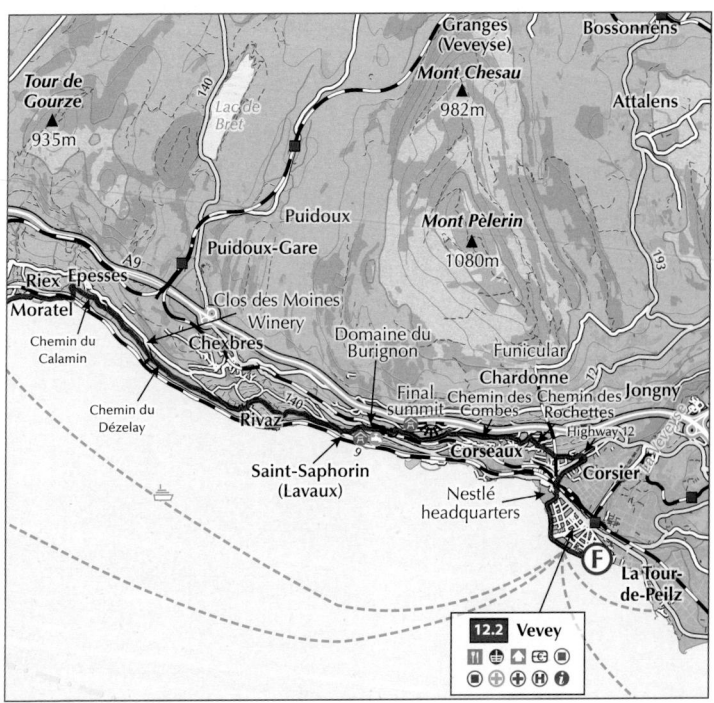

above and cross the road through the pedestrian tunnel (**0.7km**) that leads to Villette church on the opposite side of the tracks. Turn right just before the church wall and follow it to the cemetery beyond. Go through the metal gate of the cemetery and arrive at the narrow **Chemin de Villette** among terraced vineyards. This is a just a taste of the mountainside vineyard walk, as just after **Cully train station** you cross under the tracks and head back down to the lakeside, with a lovely collection of restaurants and shops and a carousel in the summer (**2.0km**).

9.0KM CULLY (ELEV 374, POP 1752) 🍴 ⊕ 🏠 🎒 🅿 🔁 ⊕ 🏥 (1127.9KM)
The closely clustered homes on narrow streets betray Cully's medieval past, though recent archaeology shows the village has roots in Neolithic times. Its first documentary mention is from 967 under the name 'Cusliacum.' The town served as capital of the Lavaux district until it was subsumed into the district of Lavaux-Oron. Many buildings in the village, particularly on its main road, the Route de Vevey, hail from the 16th–19th c. The graceful park along the lake is shaded by trees and has many cafés and wine shops nearby. (Train: www.sbb.ch.)

▲ **Camping de Moratel** 🆁 🅶 🆆 🆂 1/3, CHF15 tent site, Route de Moratel 2, camping.moratel@bluewin.ch, tel (0)76 499 93 31. Open Mar–Oct. Tent sites only. On lakeshore.

The beachside promenade continues through the village of **Moratel** (**0.5km**, WC), where it is interrupted by a campground then a small marina. At **Epesses** (**0.8km**) come again to a concrete stairway, aiming up through a tunnel under the train tracks and then under the highway, continuing up on the other side as it climbs the mountain with a rivulet burbling alongside. Turn right at the top onto the paved Chemin du Calamin among the terraces, heading higher and higher on the mountainside with sweeping views of Montreux, the lake, and the Alps themselves. Pass **Clos des Moines Winery** (**1.8km**) where the road becomes the Chemin du Dézaley. Come to a summit, and not long afterward to the tiny settlement of **Rivaz** (**1.7km**, WC).

The Temple de Cully stands amid the narrow streets of this ancient lakeside village

Small boats gently bob in the water at one of the many marinas along the lakeside walk

While the Romans first grew wine here, it was in the 12th c. that Cistercian monks brought **Chasselas vines** to the Dézelay hillsides to take advantage of what are called the 'three suns' – the sun itself, the heat emitted by the walled terraces, and the light reflected from the lake. The area produces some of the finest Swiss wines and is protected as a UNESCO World Heritage Site (www.dezaley.ch/en).

For centuries this terraced hillside of Dézelay has been home to vineyards of Chasselas grapes

Though it is tempting to head down toward the lake here, instead head back uphill once more among the terraces. After another summit come to **Saint-Saphorin** (**1.6km**, restaurants). Keep the lovely church on your right, passing in a colonnade to a steep stairway just after the church where you begin the longest climb of the day, up to another series of vineyard-covered terraces along the mountainside. Pass a drinking fountain and rest area and the red-roofed ♠ **Domaine du Burignon B&B** (**0.5km**, www.burignon.ch) then a tunnel beneath the railroad tracks. Continue along the mountainside terraces to a **final summit** and rest area (**0.5km**) with sweeping views. Continue on the **Chemin des Combes** and, as houses gather to the right, turn right onto the **Chemin des Rochettes** (**1.9km**) and descend very steeply to the Vevey suburb of **Corseaux**. Pass over the funicular tracks (**0.5km**). An optional ride downhill takes you into Vevey (CHF2.4, www.sbb.ch).

Cross **Highway 12** toward a gas station with a small market, keeping the station on your right. After crossing a small creek into the town of **Corsier** (**0.5km**), turn right on a narrow and quiet road leading steeply to the bottom of the hill. Pass the lower funicular station, cross under the rail tracks, pass the Volkswagen car dealership and then cross Avenue Nestlé. Keep the **Nestlé corporate headquarters** on your right as you head downhill to the lake on Avenue de Savoie. Turn left onto the lakeside pedestrian path which you follow to the Vevey ferry landing, finding the center of **Vevey** just two blocks to your left (**2.0km**).

12.2KM VEVEY (ELEV 374M, POP 17,676) 🏨 🏤 🏧 🏪 Ⓒ Ⓢ ⊕ ⊕ Ⓗ 𝒊 (1115.8KM)
Here in 1867 Henri Nestlé began his milk-based baby food factory and today it is the largest food company in the world. Its modern steel and glass headquarters stands in stark contrast to the historic homes and civic buildings of central Vevey, known as Vivaec when Sigeric visited here as his Stage LIII. In medieval times the town was a crossroads for pilgrims from France to the west or Germany to the east, a fact remembered in the name of Mont Pélerin (tr: 'Mount Pilgrim'), a peak northwest of town. The many-turreted, neo-Gothic 19th c. **Château de l'Aile** replaces a 16th c. castle on the same site and is just a block from the prosperous charming and historic center. Vevey was the home in exile for British-American actor Charlie Chaplin, who lived here from 1952 until his death in 1977. Sets of his films are recreated at **Chaplin's World museum** (from CHF19, www.chaplinsworld.com). Look for a sculpture of Chaplin at the lakefront, along with the 'World's Largest Fork' that has stood in the lake opposite the **Alimentarium Food Museum** (CHF13, www.alimentarium.org) since 2009. Every 20 years a temporary 20,000-seat amphitheater is built in the center city to house the live shows of the Fête des Vignerons that showcases regional wines. The next festival is set for 2039. (Trains to Villeneuve, Aigle and beyond: www.sbb.ch.)

▲ Camping de la Pichette Ⓡ Ⓚ Ⓦ Ⓢ Ⓩ 1/3, CHF8 per person, CHF6 per tent, Chemin de la Paix 37, camping.pichette@vevey.ch, tel (0)21 925 35 07. Tent camping only, no indoor beds. Lake swimming. Small pizzeria.

♦ Vevey House Ⓞ Ⓟⓕ Ⓡ Ⓒⓕ 22/44, CHF-/63/72/90, Grande Place 5, www.veveyhouse.com, reservation@veveyhouse.com, tel (0)21 922 35 32.

STAGE 2
Vevey to Aigle

Start	Vevey, ferry dock
Finish	Aigle, Tourist information office
Distance	24.8km
Total ascent	253m
Total descent	200m
Difficulty	Easy
Duration	6½hr
Percentage paved	96%
Hostels	Montreux 6.9km, Villaneuve (tourist lodgings) 12.3km, Aigle 24.9km

A delightful stroll along the cultivated and elegant lakeside path with cosmopolitan Montreux and medieval Chillon as highlights. Afterward lies a somewhat tedious slog along canals and tracks, and then a punishing though skippable climb to Vers Moray before arriving in Aigle. On sunny days take sunscreen and extra water. The promenade between Vevey and Villeneuve is gorgeous, but it's possible to opt instead for the charming passenger ferry, which lands at Vevey, La Tour, Clarens, Montreux, Territet, Château de Chillon and Villeneuve (www.cgn.ch).

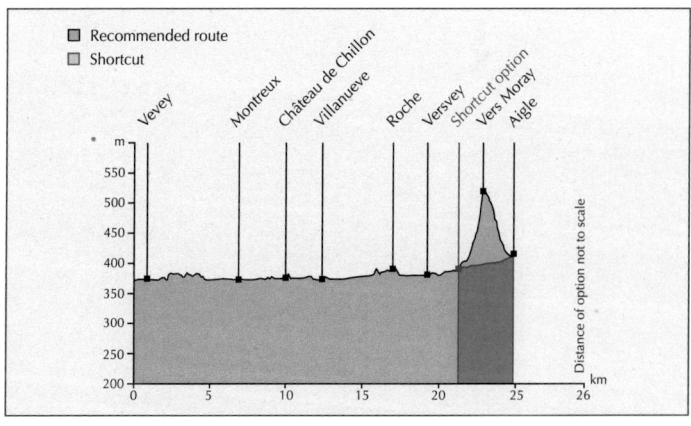

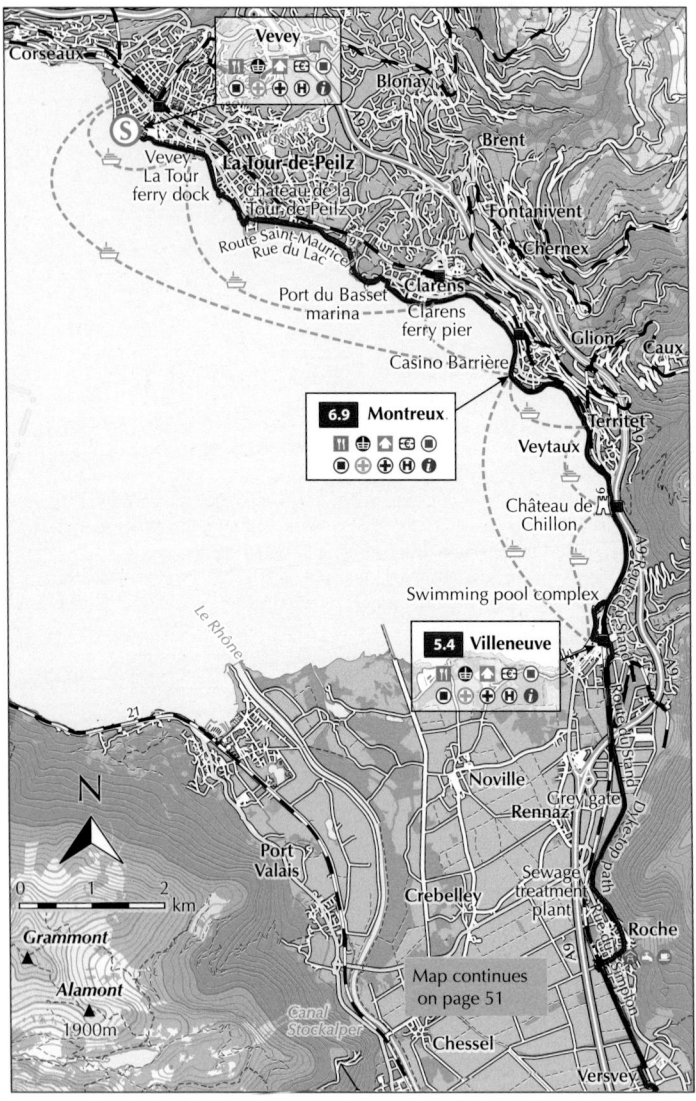

The passenger ferry service offers a picturesque voyage along the Lake

The charms of Vevey are on display as you continue east along the lakeside path –
restaurants and bars on the left and lawns and beaches on the right. Continue along
the walkway, passing the **Vevey/La Tour ferry dock** (**0.6km**), then follow signs after
the **Château de la Tour de Peilz** (**1.5km**) directing you up to the Route Saint-Maurice/
Rue du Lac roadway. Here you must bid adieu to the lake and content yourself with
the sidewalks of this wide and noisy arterial road among smart homes. After the **Port
du Basset marina** (**2.4km**, WC) on the right and Shell gas station on the left, return to
the waterfront promenade, whose wide lakeside parks include volleyball courts and
sandy beaches. After the **Clarens ferry pier** (**1.0km**) enter the outskirts of Montreux,
with carefully tended flowerboxes separating the path from the lake itself and earning it the name 'Quai des Fleurs.' On the left are belle époque estates behind hedges
and carved stone banisters, and to the right is a series of sculptures, many highlight-
ing international luminaries, like Igor Stravinsky, who made Montreux their home. As
central **Montreux** approaches, the restaurants of the lakeside hotels multiply to serve
the international collection of well-dressed tourists strolling the lakeside path (**1.3km**).

6.9KM MONTREUX (ELEV 374M, POP 25,980) 🍴 ⊕ ⬆ 🅒 ⊙ ⊚ ⊕ ⊕ ⒣ 𝒊
(1108.9KM)

Though Montreux is best known for its annual July **Montreux Jazz Festival**, attract-
ing international attention here since its inception in 1967, it has been important
since ancient times as the place where the road from the Alps forks either toward
Germany or France. In the 19th c. the favorable climate and Alpine scenery
attracted tourists, leading to a profusion of belle époque hotels, homes and commercial buildings that give today's city its charm. Famous ex-patriot residents
include David Bowie, Noël Coward, Vladimir Nabokov, Stravinsky, Tchaikovsky
and Freddie Mercury, whose statue adorns the lakeside and in whose honor an
annual festival is held here the first weekend of September. (Trains: www.sbb.ch.)

🏠 **Youth Hostel Vaud Montreux** Pr Do R Br Gf W S Z 23/106, CHF45/96/-
/-, Passage de l'Auberge 8, www.youthhostel.ch/en/hostels/montreux,
montreux@youthhostel.ch, tel (0)21 963 49 34. Near the lakeshore before
Chillon. Closed Nov–Mar. Dinner available CHF18.50.

Lake waters lap at the base of the towers and turrets of Château de Chillon, with Montreux in the background

After the **Casino Barrière** the flower planters become more sparse and the walkers fewer as Montreux begins to fade into the background. Ahead now is Château de Chillon and to the left a high viaduct above the suburb of Veytaux. The mountain walls push more narrowly toward the lake now and as the path rises toward the tracks come to the entry to **Château de Chillon (3.4km)**, a favorite among bus and train tourists and a site well worth an hour's visit.

The tiny, limestone island of **Chillon** has for centuries offered a highly defensible outpost at the place where the German and French roads over the Alps join together. The first written record of the castle is from 1005, and its current structure derives from an expansion project by the Count of Savoy in the 13th c. From the 16th to 18th c. it served as a prison and later as a munitions depot until its restoration in the late 18th c. when it became a popular tourist destination. The castle is setting of Lord Byron's poem 'The Prisoner of Chillon' (1816) and figures in the Henry James novel, *Daisy Miller* (CHF26, www.chillon.ch).

The path continues past a **swimming pool complex (1.2km)** and lakeside park into **Villaneuve**, which sits astride the Rhône River delta at the head of the lake. Coming to the ferry dock **(0.8km)**, turn left into Villaneuve and bid a final goodbye to Lake Geneva as you start your way up the valley toward the Great Saint Bernard Pass and Italy.

5.4KM VILLANEUVE (ELEV 372M, POP 5767) 🍴⊕🛏⊕🄬⊚◉⊕⊕🄷ⓘ
(1103.5KM)
Listed in the Inventory of Swiss Heritage Sites, Villaneuve features a charming main street, the Grand Rue, with cafés and shops set among historic buildings. (Train: www.sbb.ch. Commercial lodgings available.)

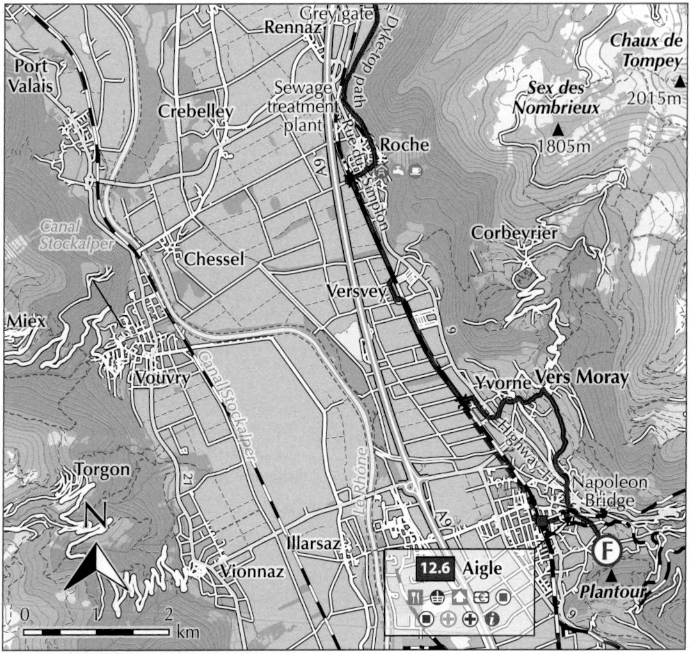

The main street of Villeneuve, last town on the lake

Follow signs to the **train station**, leading to a tunnel under the tracks. Turn right at the first street and follow signs to a path alongside the tracks. Just before the A9 highway overpass (**1.5km**), the path veers onto the shoulder of the **Route du Stand** roadway and, immediately after the bridge and a retail outlet, obscure signs direct you across the road and under a **grey gate** (**0.3km**) at the start of a **dyke-top path**, which you follow for several kilometers, first on the left and then, after a bridge, on the right side. After a series of small factories and a **sewage treatment plant** (**2.0km**), veer right and pick up a road that follows the trajectory of the canal, landing soon in **Roche** (**1.0km**, café).

At a small park with benches and a water fountain turn right, crossing the **Route du Simplon** highway in a few blocks and to come to the train station beyond. A tunnel under the tracks leads to a road going left alongside the tracks. Follow this for several flat and shade-deprived kilometers, diverging only briefly to walk the back streets of tiny **Versvey** (**2.2km**, no services). Some scholars believe this is the location of Sigeric's Stage LII Burbulei. Continue along the track-side road until signs point you toward a bridge (**1.9km**) on the left where the route crosses the tracks and heads up the hillside rather than directly into Aigle, which otherwise lies a few flat kilometers ahead (see map for shortcut option). If you've remained on the official track, climb uphill through **Yvorne** (**1.1km**) to **Vers Moray** (**0.5km**, water) and back downhill into **Aigle**, veering left just before the busy **Highway 11** to cross the **Napoleon Bridge** and the center of Aigle just ahead (**2.0km**).

12.6KM AIGLE (ELEV 414M, POP 10,134) 🏨 ⊕ 🏧 🄲 ⊙ ⊚ ⊕ ⊕ 🅸 (1090.9KM)

With its position on the road to the Alps, the market town of Aigle (French for 'eagle') grew up around trans-Alpine trade. Archeologists have found proof of Bronze Age settlement here, as well as settlement by the Romans, who called it Aquilas (Latin for 'eagle'). The 12th c. **Église du Cloître** is thought to have been the site of a priory and is listed as a Swiss Heritage Site. Aigle's 1725 **Pont Napoléon** over the Grande-Eau River was likely used by Napoleon and his troops who overnighted here on 16 March 1800. The grand **Château d'Aigle** was built in the 12th–15th c. and served as headquarters for the Lords of Compey, vassals of the powerful House of Savoy. Today it houses the **Museum of the Vine** (CHF40, www.chateauaigle.ch). (Trains to Saint-Maurice, Martigny and Orsières: www.sbb.ch.)

🛏 **Le Relais du Château** ⓞ 🄿 🅁 🄱 🄶 2/4, CHF-/70/125/-, Chemin de Rochebord 20, www.bnb-aigle.ch, info@bnb-aigle.ch, tel (0)24 466 63 31.

🛏 **Parisod B&B** ⓞ 🄿 🅁 🄶 2/4, CHF-/60/120/-, Chamin Roc de l'Aigle 11, tel (0)24 466 57 70.

STAGE 3

Aigle to Saint-Maurice

Start	Aigle, Tourist information office
Finish	Saint-Maurice, Place du Parvis
Distance	17.1km
Total ascent	417m
Total descent	414m
Difficulty	Moderate
Duration	5hr
Percentage paved	82%
Hostels	Ollon 4.5km, Saint-Maurice 17.1km

Aigle sits at the edge of the last wide place in the Rhône Valley, while Saint-Maurice lies upstream beyond a very narrow gap in the mountains around 10km away. While the two towns are not separated much in distance or elevation, the official track adds two Alpine trails to make the day both more photogenic and more challenging. Two shortcuts offer flatter options. Lovely Saint-Maurice has been a pilgrim destination in its own right for over 15 centuries, and its abbey museum is well worth an afternoon's visit.

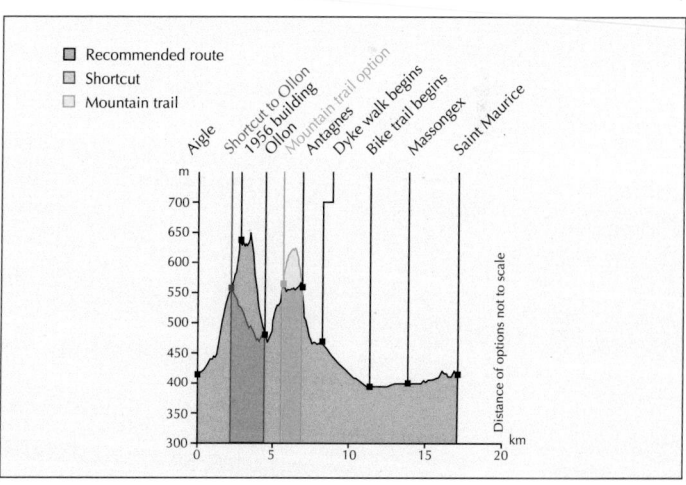

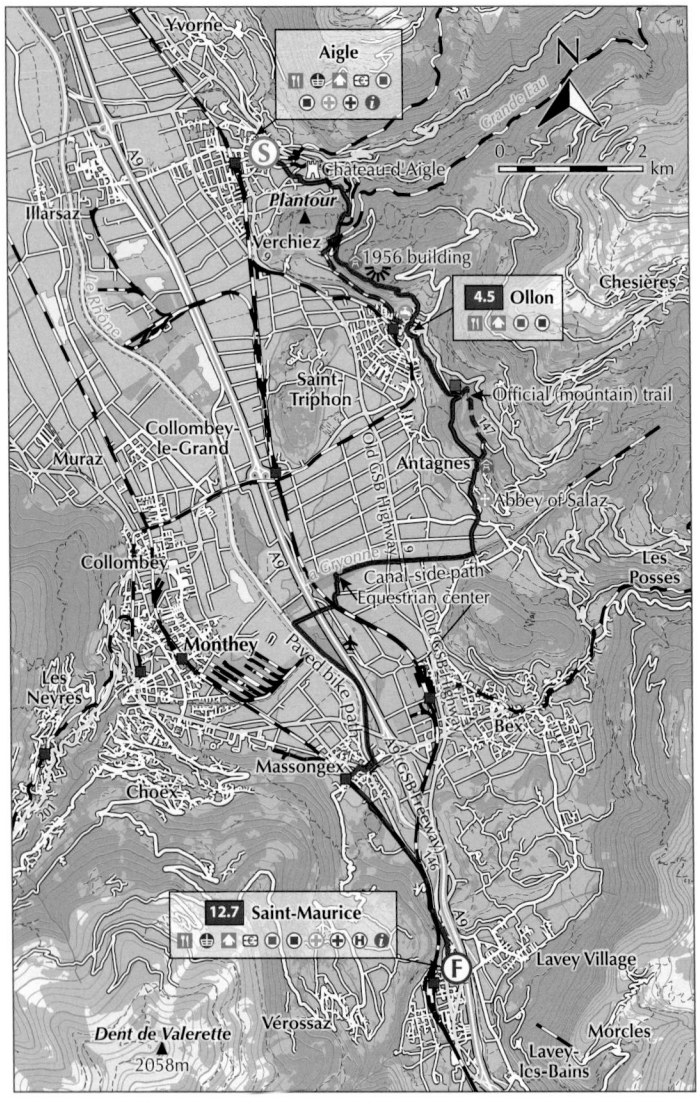

The tower of the Temple d'Ollon stands at the heart of the village

Cross the main road from central Aigle and head up Rue du Cloître toward the **Château d'Aigle** (**0.6km**), finding the best views of this grand edifice among the vineyards on its opposite side. Watch carefully for the right-hand turn that takes you into the woods for your first climb of the day. The asphalt road leads steeply uphill through a dark forest and then through the vineyards of the small settlement of **Verchiez** (**1.5km**), twice crossing the tracks of a narrow-gauge railway. Just after passing under the arched train bridge a right fork offers a shortcut to Ollon down the quiet Route de Verschiez. The main track forks left and, after a final crossing of the tracks, pick up a dirt path heading even more steeply uphill. The summit comes at a picnic table and small **building** marked '1956' (**0.7km**). Head steeply downhill with dramatic views opening to the valley a few hundred meters below. The back streets of **Ollon** are punctuated by boisterous water fountains at most every barn on the way to the center of town with its church and two cafés (**1.7km**).

4.5KM OLLON (ELEV 476M, POP 7461) 🏨 🛖 ⊚ ⊚ (1086.4KM)
The village of Ollon was originally part of the estates of the abbey at Saint-Maurice. Its Temple d'Ollon church and diminutive Château de la Roche date from the 13th c. (Train: www.sbb.ch.)

⌂ La Fontaine **Pr R Br** 1/2, CHF-/30/40/-, Place de l'Hôtel de Ville 5, tel (0)24 499 25 26.

⌂ The Traditional à Ollon **O Pr R Br W S Z** 1/double, CHF-/-/90/-, Chemin du Collège 25, pweber273@gmail.com, tel (0)79 848 83 16. English-speaking.

Cross the road, veering left, and wind your way through the stucco homes and board-and-batten barns toward the hillside beyond. The road becomes a two-track gravel lane, slowly rising as it traverses the mountain ahead with sweeping views to the right, soon leaving the vineyards and heading into the forest. Before long come to a quiet asphalt road at a **bus stop** (**1.2km**) on the Aigle/Monthey line. Turn right and follow the road about 75m to come to an option. At a curve, the official path climbs very steeply on the left, adding a 75m climb. For a shortcut, stay on this quiet, fairly flat, paved road which rejoins the steeper route at the hamlet of **Antagnes** (**1.1km**) with its lumberyard.

In 100m comes a small rest area where a poorly marked right turn leads you diagonally downhill on a virtually invisible path through a vineyard below. After 100m of wondering whether you've made the wrong turn, the surface of the path turns to concrete, taking you very steeply downhill. At an unmarked intersection, this time at a small parking lot with a large garbage receptacle, turn right and continue downhill. Come finally to the valley floor at the **Abbey of Salaz** (**0.8km**, www.abbaye-de-salaz. ch), now a restaurant and winery. The abbey was originally an outpost of the Abbey of Saint-Maurice and the current buildings date from the 12th c. A right turn just afterward leads you through cornfields – a nice variation from endless vineyards – and then to the woods beyond.

Once in the woods, immediately cross a deep canal and turn right on a **canal-side path** (**0.7km**), which you will follow across the **old GSB highway** (**1.0km**). Pass an iron bridge and continue on the path until the gravel ends in grass. Here a left turn off the canal (**1.0km**) puts you on a path through the woods and onto the long driveway of an **equestrian center**. The driveway veers right, meets a road, and passes under railroad tracks. Continuing on, the route passes over the new GSB highway (A9) and then ends at a **paved bike path** (**1.0km**) just before the **Rhône River**, which we see now for the first time. Turn left on the riverside bike path, following it until a pedestrian bridge (**2.4km**) on the right brings you to the town of **Massongex** (**0.2km**)

Archeological digs have uncovered foundations of earlier buildings at the Saint-Maurice Abbey site

Evidence exists for **Roman-era baths** and a Roman bridge here spanning the river. Since this was one of the last navigable ports on the Rhône it was important as the change-point between river and overland transit over the Alps. The sparse offerings of the modern town include a couple of cafés and a Japanese restaurant, all closed on Mondays. (Train: www.sbb.ch.)

Cross the main road in Massongex, and head to the **train station**. After crossing the tracks (**0.3km**), turn left on a narrow, asphalt **track-side road** and follow it to join the highway a few hundred meters shy of **Saint-Maurice**, which is just around the bend (**2.9km**).

12.7KM SAINT-MAURICE (ELEV 416M, POP 4571) ⑪ ⊛ ⬜ Ⓒ ⊙ ◉ ⊕ ⊕ Ⓗ ⓘ (1073.8KM)

Saint-Maurice was Archbishop Sigeric's Stage LI Sancta Maurici, and by the time he arrived there its monastery, named in honor of Saint Maurice, was already centuries old. According to ancient stories, when the Theban Legion sent in the 3rd c. by Rome to subdue the Great Saint Bernard Pass was given instructions to conduct pagan sacrifices and harass local Christians at Agaunum, its Christian soldiers and commander, Maurice, refused to cooperate. The Emperor Maximian punished the disobedient legion by ordering every tenth soldier be executed. This 'decimation' was repeated until the entire legion had been exterminated. Agaunum was renamed in honor of Saint Maurice and the **Abbey of St Maurice d'Agaunum** was built here against a cliff on the site of a 1st c. Roman shrine. Monks have offered prayers uninterrupted here since the year 515. While the current church dates from the 17th c., remains of its predecessors can be viewed, along with the abbey's fascinating museum (CHF15, www.abbaye-stmaurice. ch). Saint-Maurice offers a variety of scenic trails, including a seven-chapel 'Chapelles' route and a 6.6km walk up to the **Chapel of Nôtre-Dame du Scex** perched on a cliff above town (www.saint-maurice.ch). (Trains to Martigny and Orsières: www.sbb.ch.)

⌂ Saint-Maurice Abbey ⓅⓉ Ⓡ Ⓚ Ⓢ 7/8, CHF35/person, Avenue Agaune 15, www.abbaye-stmaurice.ch, abbaye@stmaurice.ch, tel (0)24 486 04 04. Shared bathrooms. Open 1 Jun–1 Nov, otherwise inquire at Gatehouse. Arrival after 17:00 preferred. Book through website.

⌂ Saint-Maurice Hôtellerie Franciscaine Ⓞ ⓅⓉ Ⓡ Ⓖ Ⓢ Ⓩ 40/70, CHF-/-/98/-, Antoine de Quartery 1, www.hotellerie-franciscaine.ch, tel (0)24 486 11 11. Reservation required. Capuchin mass daily. Laundry CHF10.

STAGE 4
Saint-Maurice to Martigny

Start	Saint-Maurice, Place du Parvis
Finish	Martigny, Parish of Notre Dame de la Visitation
Distance	16.7km
Total ascent	261m
Total descent	205m
Difficulty	Easy
Duration	4½hr
Percentage paved	61%
Hostels	Evionnaz 5.8km, Martigny 16.7km

A short and easy stage spent walking along mountain paths, interspersed sometimes with sidewalks of the old GSB highway and never too far from a bar or store with provisions. An option through the commercial district of Vernayaz offers additional refreshment possibilities before Martigny, the last full-service city until Aosta, Italy.

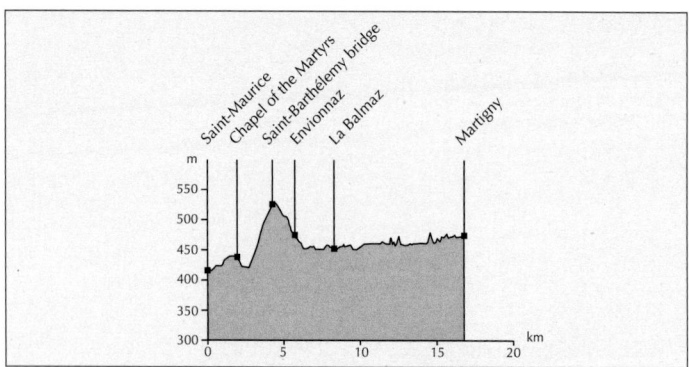

Follow signs to the **train station** and once there turn left to walk through the parking lot. Cross a bridge to follow the tracks on the opposite side where the tracks veer left and you find yourself walking among homes of suburban **Verolliez**. Above and to the right, on a clear day you can see the tall spire of the Cime de l'Est peak of the Dents du Midi. The route turns left and you pass the tall, orange **Christus Regnant**

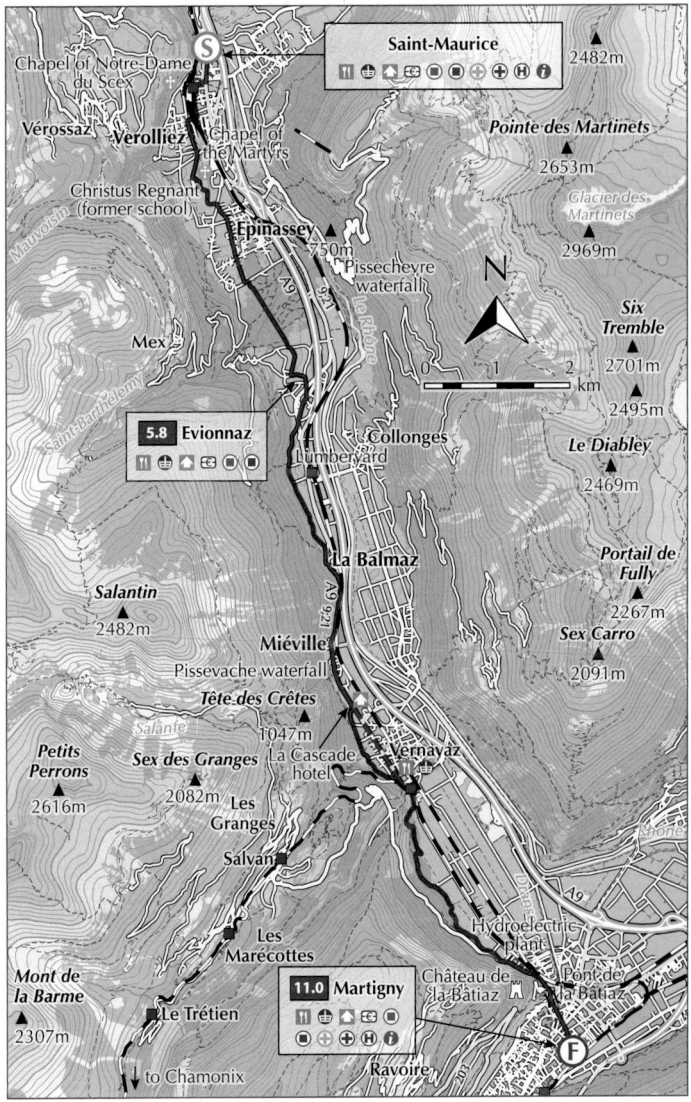

Saint-Maurice

Chapel of Notre-Dame du Scex

Vérossaz   Verolliez   Chapel of the Martyrs

Christus Regnant (former school)

Épinassey   750m
Pissecheyre waterfall

Mex

5.8 Evionnaz

Collonges
Lumberyard

La Balmaz

Salantin
2482m

Miéville
Pissevache waterfall

Tête des Crêtes
1047m

Sex des Granges
2082m
Les Granges

La Cascade hotel   Vernayaz

Petits Perrons
2616m

Salvan

Les Marécottes

Mont de la Barme
2307m

Le Trétien

to Chamonix

11.0 Martigny

Château de la Bâtiaz   Pont de la Bâtiaz

Hydroelectric plant

Ravoire

Pointe des Martinets
2653m

Glacier des Martinets
2969m

Six Tremble
2701m
2495m

Le Diabley
2469m

Portail de Fully
2267m

Sex Carro
2091m

2482m

N   0   1   2
km

The grand 1900 Christus Regnant building of Verolliez

(**2.0km**) building. Don't miss the small, stucco building on the left called **Chapel of the Martyrs**. Tradition says this is the true place (Verolliez from *vrai lieu* meaning 'true place') of the martyrdom of the Theban Legion. The route zigzags through a grassy field and crosses a road to enter **Epinassey**. Head up the hill more steeply into a sparse forest under power lines, crossing the **Saint-Barthélemy stream** (**1.0km**), eventually emerging onto an asphalt road that leads into the town of **Evionnaz**. Aim to the left of the tall spire (**1.8km**) to reach the heart of the town.

5.8KM EVIONNAZ (ELEV 471M, POP 1265) 🍴 ⊕ ⌂ € ⊚ ◉ (1068.0KM)
Originally a Celtic settlement (Celtic *eve* = 'water'), in 563 the town was buried in the collapse of nearby Mount Taurus. In the Middle Ages it was subject to the Abbey of Saint-Maurice, whose rule was ended with the French Revolution in 1798. The most notable landmark today is the **Evionnaz Adventure Labyrinth** that includes a maze of thousands of Thuja trees (CHF17, www.labyrinthe.ch). (Train: www.sbb.ch.)

⌂ **B&B Le Pernollet** ⊞ 4/7, CHF-/80/100/-, La Balmaz, 1902 Evionnaz, www.cafe-pernollet.ch, infoproprive@gmail.com, tel (0)24 485 3200.

After passing the center of town, cross the old GSB highway and take a narrow asphalt road behind a soccer pitch and **lumberyard** (**0.7km**). The road traces the right-hand edge of the valley floor as it meets the steep and forested mountain slopes. Veer right at the entrance to **La Balmaz** (**1.9km**, café, bar) to join a sidewalk of the old highway, which shares this narrow passageway between mountains with the new highway, the river and the train tracks. Divert off the highway to walk through the village of **Miéville** (**1.0km**). Continue either on the trail to the right just after La Cascade hotel (**0.7km**) with the 116m **Pissevache waterfall** (lit. 'cow piss' waterfall, as compared to its ruminant relative, the Pissechèvre Waterfall across the valley) cascading down the cliff just behind, or take the highway directly into **Vernayaz** (**1.1km**, food, groceries, train, ⌂ **Hôtel Camping La Cascade Pissevache**, www.cascadepissevache.ch). The two tracks rejoin at the far end of Vernayaz.

A roadside park offers views toward the 116m Pissevache waterfall at Vernayaz

After town follow the highway sidewalk around the cliffside and pick up a trail that begins just afterward, following it along the foot of the mountain as it gently undulates uphill. The path occasionally passes through fields of moss-covered boulders that have fallen off the mountain slopes above and becomes a pleasant and wide green trail, with orchards on the left and the steep mountains looming on the right. Just after a straight, gravel road takes off to the left, scramble up a very steep 5m high bank. Soon come to a chain-link fence that separates you from the sluice pipes and turbines of a **hydroelectric plant** (**4.0km**). After the plant a road joins from the right as you continue straight ahead.

Walk carefully along the roadway toward a parking lot in 400m, veering right to pick up a street beyond in the neighborhood of La Bâtiaz (**0.8km**, restaurants). At the end of the main street cross the covered, wooden **Pont de la Bâtiaz** bridge leading to central **Martigny**. Continue just a few blocks to the restaurants, cafés and bars on the central square and a block later to the Catholic parish of Notre Dame de la Visitation at stage end (**0.8km**).

11.0KM MARTIGNY (ELEV 472M, POP 18,301) 🍴 ⊕ 🛏 🅒 Ⓒ ⓞ ⓞ ⊕ ⊕ Ⓗ ❶ (1057.1KM)

This cosmopolitan, artsy town is our last stop on the Rhône proper and the largest city on the Via Francigena until Aosta. Called Octodurus by the Gauls, the Romans conquered the town in 57 BC as part of their plan to ensure control of the Great Saint Bernard Pass. A restored Roman amphitheater, temples and baths can be seen today. Martigny is also site of the first Catholic diocese in Switzerland, established in the 4th c. AD. In the Middle Ages Martin of Tours was honored as its patron saint and the town became known in French as Martigny. The **Château de la Bâtiaz** above town was built in 1260 and is the town's sole surviving medieval building (closed Mon/Tues, www.batiaz.ch). **Fondation Pierre Gianadda Museum** hosts painting exhibitions each year featuring important works, as well as Gallo-Roman treasures recovered from the surrounding region (CHF16, www.gianadda. ch). (Train: www.sbb.it as far as Orsières. Bus: €20 to Aosta www.savda.it.)

🛏 **Paroisse Catholique** 🅳🅾 🆁 🅺 1/6, CHF20/-/-/-, Rue de l'Hôtel-de-Ville 5, www. paroissemartigny.ch, secretariat@paroissemartigny.ch, tel (0)27 722 22 82.

🛏 **Paroisse Protestante** 🅳🅾 🆁 🅺 1/4, CHF20/-/-/-, Rue d'Oche 9, paroissep@ bluewin.ch, tel (0)77 269 7242. Room not available Mon & Wed.

🏠 **Hôtel de la Poste** 🅿🆃 🆁 🅱🆁 🅲🆃 🆉 34/68, CHF-/77/80/-, Rue de la Poste 8, www. hoteldelapostemartigny.ch, info@hoteldelapostemartigny.ch, tel (0)27 722 14 44.

🏠 **TCS Camping** 🅿🆃 🅳🅾 🆁 🅺 🆆 🆂 5/28, CHF21/-/65/-, Rue du Levant 68, camping.martigny@tcs.ch, tel (0)27 722 45 44. Dorm rooms and tent sites available. Open Apr–Oct. Breakfast CHF10.

STAGE 5

Martigny to Orsières

Start	Martigny, Parish of Notre Dame de la Visitation
Finish	Orsières, Église d'Orsières
Distance	18.3km
Total ascent	987m
Total descent	572m
Difficulty	Moderately hard
Duration	6hr
Percentage paved	45%
Hostels	Sembrancher 12.2km, Orsières 18.3km

Today you leave behind the Rhône River Valley and head up into the steeper mountainsides and narrower valleys of the Dranse River drainage. The stage rewards pilgrims with views of steep and tall mountains surrounding high, green pastures above valleys dotted with tiny hamlets. Many consider the Martigny-Croix to Sembrancher portion of this stage the most difficult stretch of the entire Via Francigena. Seasoned Alpine hikers will be unfazed by a stretch of narrow path between Martigny Croix and Le Be Bourgeaud, while people from the flatlands may be unnerved by that and the subsequent suspension bridge. Walking the road up the narrow valley would be too dangerous, so pilgrims with a fear of heights have only two choices: to walk the path with courage and agility, or skip the hardest portion with a 10-minute train ride from Martigny Croix to Sembrancher (hourly, CHF3, www.sbb.ch).

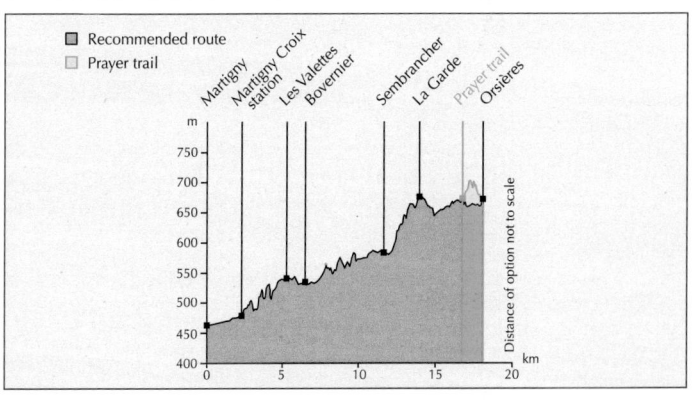

Follow the waymarks past the **Fondation Pierre Giannada** to charming, suburban **Martigny Bourg** (**1.5km**) with its shops, cafés and bars. After a soccer pitch on the right, come to **Martigny-Croix** train station (**0.8km**), last chance to skip the most difficult portions of today's stage by taking the train to Sembrancher. Otherwise, at the end of the gravel parking lot below the station take a makeshift stairway left and cross the tracks, picking up a gravel road on the opposite side that climbs gradually upward. After a brief time, cross back over the tracks and afterward cross again under an **arched railroad bridge**.

Here the steep and sometimes slippery stretch begins, and you search for steady footing among rocks and tree roots with an abrupt drop-off down a wooded bank to the river 20m below. You've made it through the most difficult section when you descend to a crisp and modern metal **suspension bridge** (**2.1km**) spanning the river. Cross again under the tracks through a single archway and head steeply up the hill on a wide gravel road. Meet the highway briefly and then cross under the highway bridge into the roadside town of **Le Bourgeaud**. Turn right before the gas station, heading uphill alongside a noisy stream on an asphalt driveway which leads toward **Les Valettes** (**1.1km**, café) where you can see many examples of the local, traditional building style of barns made from massive, unpainted timbers.

A pilgrim crosses the suspension bridge over the Dranse before Le Bourgeaud

The route continues through **Les Valettes** and then along an asphalt road that traverses the mountainside 15m above the highway. Cross the highway and tracks at the railway station (café, restaurant) of **Bovernier**, (**1.3km**, bar). After leaving town the route leads to a path alongside the highway for a couple of hundred meters. At a forestry and logging facility an asphalt road branches off to the right, eventually carrying you onto a single-track path through the forest which leads to the second challenge of the day. Clamber among the moss-covered boulders that have fallen over millenia from the mountainside above, watching carefully for the yellow diamonds painted on rocks and trees that guide the way.

After passing a **bench** and fire pit (**2.7km**) the hardest part of the day is behind you. As the highway to the left enters a brief tunnel, the path scrambles up the left

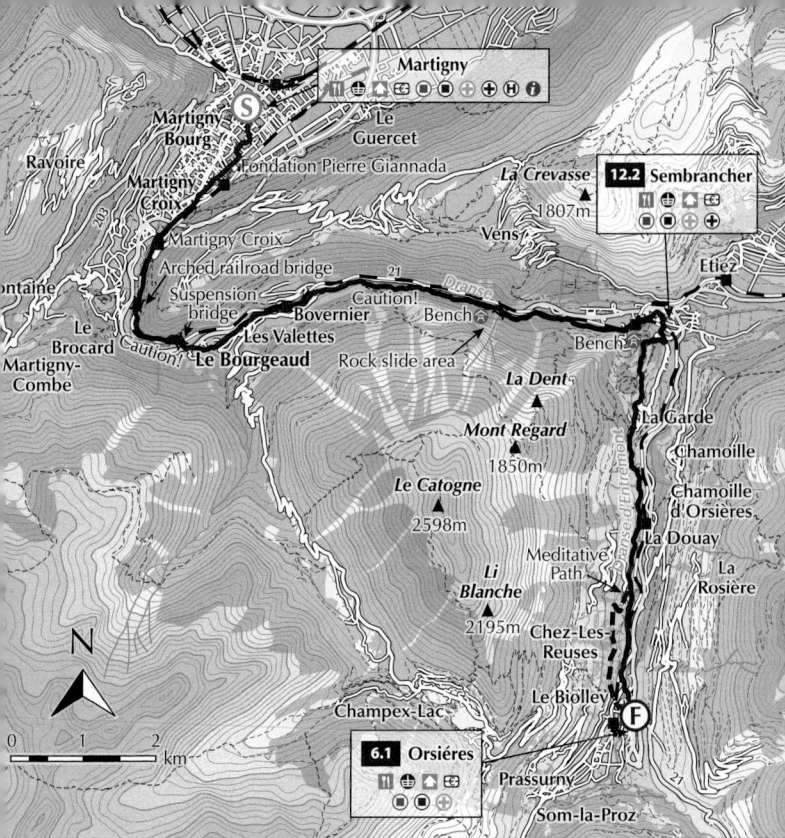

side of a rockslide and begins a series of steep ascents and descents where the footing is somewhat tricky, though not as challenging as what came before. Cross the stream bed on a wooden bridge and follow a wide gravel road above industrial estates that mark the entrance to **Sembrancher**, which you reach by crossing the rail tracks on a bridge (**2.8km**).

12.2KM SEMBRANCHER (ELEV 711M, POP 1042) 🍴 ⊕ 🏠 🅖 ◉ ◉ ⊕ ⊕
(1044.9KM)
Mentioned as early as the 12th c., Sembrancher lies at the junction of two river valleys. Our route leaves the Dranse behind and forks right into the Dranse d'Entremont toward the Great Saint Bernard Pass. (Train line ends at Orsières: www.sbb.ch. Bus: €20, daily to Aosta www.savda.it.)

After enjoying the charming, though quiet, downtown, head gradually uphill, crossing under the tracks and across two asphalt roads to find a steep, wide gravel road leading farther uphill. Traverse the hillside through green, sloping pastures until you come to a hairpin curve of an asphalt road. Take a narrow, asphalt driveway to the right of the road and find yourself in the scattered hamlet of **La Garde** (2.0km).

From here the track gradually descends while wide views of the valley open among green pastures. Descend steeply through the forest on a dirt path that becomes a dirt road, continuing the mountain traverse with views below of the hamlet of **La Douay**. After farm buildings appear, go straight, joining another dirt track that continues the traverse. Soon you see Orsières ahead, making it easy to miss a right turn back up the mountainside that carries the official track higher, along a steep and scenic 1km longer **Meditative Path**, punctuated by carvings of the Stations of the Cross. Either take this scenic path or simply continue along the road, briefly following the shoulder-less highway, then branching left to cross the river and find yourself at the Église d'Orsières in the heart of town (4.1km).

6.1KM ORSIÈRES (ELEV 887M, POP 3187) ⏹ ⊕ ⬆ ⒸⓄⓄ⊕ (1038.8KM)

The town is mentioned as early as 972 when St Majolus, abbot of powerful Cluny, was detained here and held for ransom by Saracen invaders. Archbishop Sigeric recorded it as Stage L Ursioris and the town's tall **Romanesque church tower** dates from the 13th c. Orsières is terminus of the train line from Martigny, and buses lead from here to the pass and beyond. If you are crossing Great Saint Bernard Pass in spring or fall, Alpine hiking gear is available at Cristal Sport (Place du Clocher 7, www.cristalsport.ch, tel 027 783 24 40), the last sports store until Aosta. (Train: www.sbb.ch. Bus daily to Bourg-Saint-Pierre and Aosta: www.savda.it, four times daily bus to Bourg-Saint-Pierre, www.postauto.ch, www.tmrsa.ch.)

⬆ **Gîte Accueil St-Bernard** ⓄⒹⓀ 1/8, CHF15/-/-/-, Ruelle de l'Église 2, www.saint-bernard.ch, info@saint-bernard.ch, tel (0)27 775 23 81. Ask for the access code at the tourism office, train station or rectory.

⬆ **Hôtel Terminus** ⓄⓅⒹⓇⒼⓌⓈⓏ 27/63, CHF39/75/89/123, Route de la Gare 25, www.terminus-Orsieres.ch, info@terminus-Orsieres.ch, tel (0)27 552 11 00. Low season room prices shown. Dorm price for pilgrims year-round. Laundry service available. Demi-pension CHF38.

STAGE 6
Orsières to Bourg-Saint-Pierre

Start	Orsières, Église d'Orsières
Finish	Bourg-Saint-Pierre, Église Bourg-Saint-Pierre
Distance	14.0km
Total ascent	989m
Total descent	239m
Difficulty	Moderately hard
Duration	5hr
Percentage paved	36%
Hostels	Liddes 8.3km (hotel), Bourg-Saint-Pierre 14.0km

Though this stage is only 14km, the elevation gain of 750m makes it seem longer. Most of the day is spent on slow and picturesque climbs through sloping green pastures bordered by steep, green mountains. In clear weather it is a beautiful day of pristine, Alpine scenery.

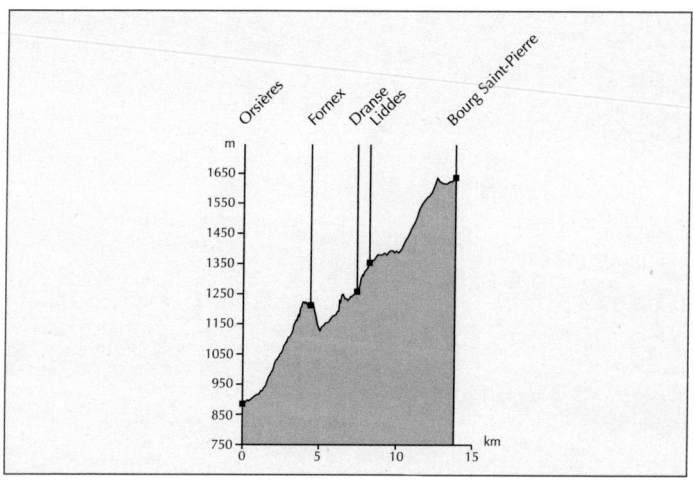

From central Orsières the route leads directly south toward the steep mountain marked by the long sluice pipe on its face. Here you cross a bridge (**1.3km**) to continue on the opposite side of the **Dranse d'Entremont** river, ultimately reaching its headwaters at the Great Saint Bernard Pass. Begin the long climb up the mountain face on the switchbacks of a wide, gravel road. After a long climb the road turns to asphalt and you enter the hamlet of **Fornex** (**3.2km**, no services). The asphalt road turns again to gravel and in 100m a steep dirt path takes off to the left. Join an asphalt road at the bottom and

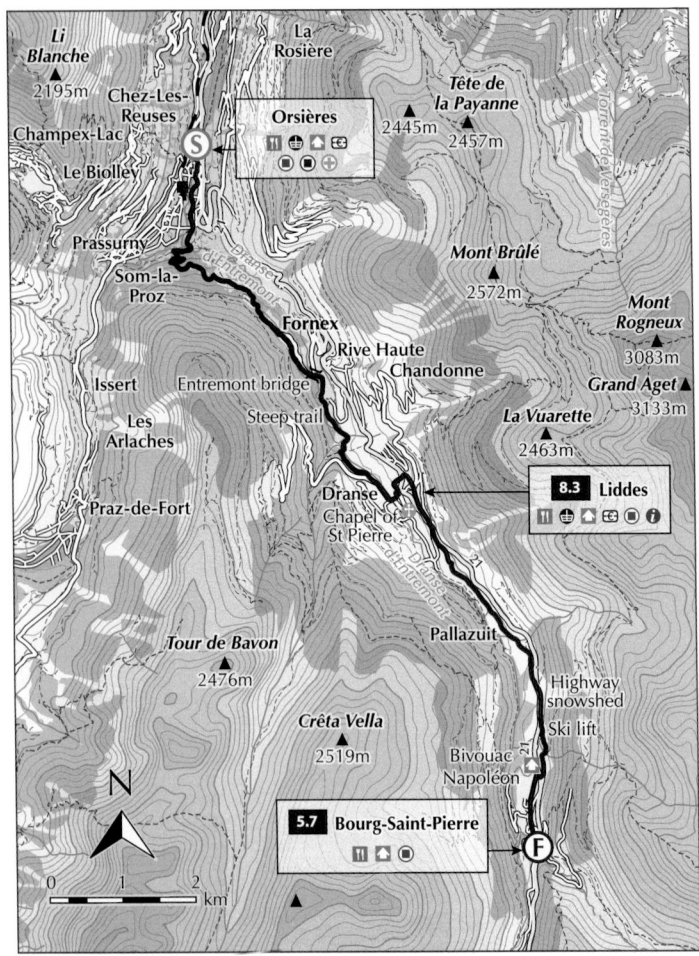

A pilgrim follows a track before Liddes

cross a second **Entremont bridge** (**0.6km**), turning right on a gravel road that climbs on the opposite mountainside.

At a hairpin turn, go straight until the gravel road ends and a very steep trail (**1.4km**) picks up on the left with frequent signs warning against flash floods caused by releases of water from upstream dams. At a barn, the gravel road becomes asphalt and you come to the outskirts of **Dranse** (**0.8km**). Before entering town, catch another Entremont bridge to the left and then find a grassy path between two farm buildings immediately ahead. Take this path, switching back up to the quiet road above where you turn left to find the entry (café, tourism office, cash machine) to **Liddes**. Follow signs to cross the E27 highway and continue one block, then turn right onto the Rue du Fond de Ville with its services clustered together a block from the church.

8.3KM LIDDES (ELEV 1353M, POP 720) 🏨 ⛪ 🏧 💶 🚌 ℹ️ (1030.5KM)
The first documentary mention of Liddes is in 1177, and the quiet center of the village is a Swiss Heritage Site. Liddes is a hub of the valley's dairy and sheep industries, and local farmers have recently invested in crops of potatoes and medicinal herbs. (Bus to Bourg-St-Pierre: www.sbb.ch.)

⛺ **Hôtel du Grand-St-Bernard** 🅿️ 🆁 🅶 4/8, CHF-/45/100/140, Rue du Fond de Ville 1, www.hotel-gd-st-bernard.ch, info@hotel-gd-st-bernard.ch, tel (0)27 783 13 02. Closed Tues.

After town, pass the lonely **Chapel of St Pierre**, and cross the highway, finding an asphalt road just below which you follow in the direction of **Pallazuit** (**1.2km**), a collection of farm homes in a small vale. Continue as the gradually ascending road turns to gravel and bisects the pastures between the river on the right and the highway on the left. When the E27 highway ducks into a **snowshed**, cross over it, continuing on the opposite side of the road. Follow alongside the road, turning left at the bottom of a **ski lift (2.8km)** to climb the ski run. At a road toward the top, turn right and come to the **Bivouac de Napoléon** hotel **(0.8km**, restaurant), the first buildings of **Bourg-Saint-Pierre**. Carefully cross the highway and continue through a parking lot one block further to the Rue de Raveire, then turn left to the center **(0.9km)**.

A Roman mile marker at the Bourg-Saint-Pierre church

5.7KM BOURG-SAINT-PIERRE (ELEV 1637M, POP 196) 🏠 📷 ⊙ **(1024.9KM)**
The 11th c. Romanesque church tower is the centerpiece of this historic village, last settlement before the Great Saint Bernard Pass. At the tower's base is a **Roman milestone** dating from the 4th c. bearing the words 'To the Emperor Cesar Valere Valere Constantin.' In the era of Charlemagne, a monastery dedicated to St Peter was built here and Archbishop Sigeric included the town as his Stage XLIX Petrecastèl. A plaque on one house recalls that **Napoleon Bonaparte** stayed here before crossing the pass in May 1800, signing a letter of debt for CHF40,000 to cover expenses for his 40,000 soldiers. The IOU is on display in the town hall. A pilgrim stamp is available inside the church door. (Bus to Great Saint Bernard Pass when road is open: www.postauto.ch. Bus to Italy via tunnel: €15, daily at 09:15, www.savda.it, www.tmrsa.ch.)

🛏 Maison St-Pierre ⓞ Pr Do R K S 9/61, CHF25/-/-/-, 1946 Bourg-Saint-Pierre, www.maisonstpierre.ch, tel (0)79 290 90 09 or (0)78 814 69 95. Adjacent to church priory in heart of village. Grand Maison for groups of 15–41, Petite Maison for 1–20 people. Book on website. Bag liner or sheet required.

🛏 ▲ Camping du Grand St Bernard Do R K C W S 1/4, CHF20/-/-/-, 1946 Bourg-Saint-Pierre, www.campinggrand-st-bernard.ch, reservation@ campinggrand-st-bernard.ch, tel (0)79 370 98 22. One dormitory with 4 beds plus tent sites. Open May–Oct.

🛏 Au Bivouac de Napoléon ⓞ Pr R Br Dr Cr S Z 22/70, CHF-/115/149/165, 1946 Bourg-Saint-Pierre, www.bivouac.ch/en, info@bivouac.ch, tel (0)27 787 11 62. Prices CHF55 double and CHF129 triple in high season. Restaurant with pilgrim menu. Spa.

🛏 Hôtel du Crêt ⓞ Pr Do R Br Dr Cr S Z 30/80, CHF25/60/80/-, Route Grand-Saint-Bernard 33, www.hotel-du-cret.ch, reception@hotel-du-cret.ch, tel (0)27 787 11 43. Breakfast CHR15, dinner CHF23.

STAGE 7

Start	Bourg-Saint-Pierre, Église Bourg-Saint-Pierre
Finish	Col du Grand-Saint-Bernard, Great Saint Bernard Hospice
Distance	12.4km
Total ascent	1062m
Total descent	224m
Difficulty	Hard (due to slippery footing, altitude and ascent)
Duration	5hr
Percentage paved	5%
Hostels	Great Saint Bernard Pass, 12.4km

This stage rewards the walker with incomparable above-the-treeline Alpine scenery in fair weather, and one of the world's most historic and atmospheric pilgrim hostels at day's end. The nonstop climb is often on narrow pathways whose slippery footholds require good traction. For about 9 months of the year the hiking trail from Bourg-Saint-Pierre to the Great St Bernard Pass is covered in deep snow, with the path to the summit reliably open only in July, August and September though the road is plowed and open for cars and walkers from early June. In shoulder seasons it is sometimes possible to surmount the pass either on pavement up the old highway when it is clear or by snowshoe on pathways, though this should be attempted only by experienced, well-equipped, and hardy hikers. For either option, check with the GSB Hospice to determine if weather and avalanche conditions are suitable for your walk. A daily bus from Bourg-Saint-Pierre uses the tunnel to bypass the summit, taking passengers to towns beyond the pass as far as Aosta (€15, daily at 09:15, www.savda.it).

At Bourg-Saint-Pierre church you have an important option – either fork right to follow the scenic trail on the west side of the valley or fork left to save energy by taking the gravel road up to the base of the Barrage des Toules dam. The two options converge at a series of switchbacks on the gravel road as it climbs to the top of the dam (**3.8km**), where the **Lac de Toules** reservoir spreads out before you. Just before a narrow ravine, where the gravel road heads right on a switchback, pick up a narrow dirt trail, crossing the ravine on a wooden bridge and then comfortably traversing the mountainside above the reservoir. Pass a **derelict mountain hut** (**1.2km**) on the left and soon see ahead the snow sheds and service buildings that mark the start of the **GSB tunnel**.

The narrow trail snakes its way uphill toward the pass

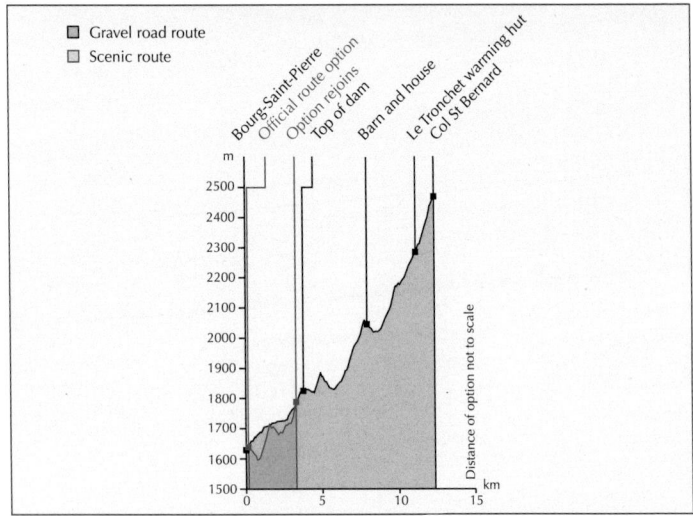

The path passes through two metal gates, veers right, and climbs a narrow trail on a wide and open slope between two mountains to reach a **farmhouse and barn** (**3.1km**). Crossing in front of them, find a gravel road that heads toward the old GSB highway and a ventilation tower of the tunnel far below. Cross the old GSB highway (**1.5km**), heading steeply uphill at the Torrin de Tchoiere, a strong stream shooting down the small valley ahead. The route continues to follow the highway, though now on rocky hills along the left side. Here the path shares its course with tiny rivulets, and the streams coursing down the mountain sometimes make the footing precarious. The

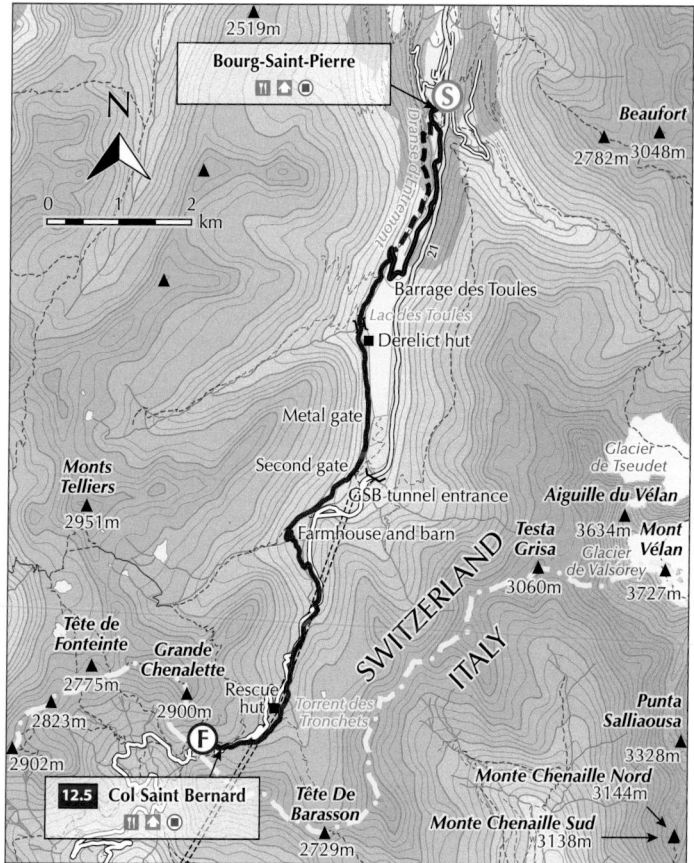

steep and rocky trail crosses a fairytale carpet of Alpine flowers, lichen-covered stones, and noisy brooks making their way down the mountain. A dramatic, stairway-like trail appears beyond a low, wooden bridge. At its top is a **rescue hut** (**1.7km**, stove and SOS phone) dedicated to Lucien Droz, a hiker who died here on 19 November 1951 and in whose honor the hut was erected.

Veering right again, with the highway above, the steepest ascent of the day begins. Soon the first buildings of the GSB hostel appear above. After an entire day of walking rugged Alpine paths, the last 60m ends in a slippery scramble straight up a dirt and gravel bank. Arriving at the **Col du Grand-Saint-Bernard**, to the left is the Mont Joux café, further on are two buildings joined by a skybridge: on the left, the Hospice with its chapel, and on the right the hotel with its gift shop and restaurant. Walking between the two buildings come to a viewpoint overlooking Lake Great St Bernard and beyond to the scattered buildings of the Italian side of the pass with dramatic, sharp, granite peaks as their backdrop (**1.2km**).

12.4KM COL DU GRAND-SAINT-BERNARD (ELEV 2478M, POP 10) ⃞ ⃞ ⃞
(1012.4KM)

This historic pass over the Alps sits at the border of Switzerland and Italy in a jagged saddle between Mont Blanc to the west and the Grand Combin to the east. Water that falls on the north side of the pass drains into the Rhône Valley through Switzerland and France, while water falling on the south side of the pass drains into the Dora Balthea and Po Rivers in Italy.

The Alpine crossing is first mentioned in historical documents describing the invasion of the Italian peninsula by Celts in 390 BC. An expedition sent by **Julius Caesar** in 57 BC attempted to take the pass, but it was not until a generation later that Augustus Caesar won the crossing for the Romans. In AD 43 Claudius completed a new Roman road through the pass and erected a temple to Jupiter at Plan de Jupiter on the Italian side. After the Roman period the pass continued to be used, though travellers were plagued by bandits and sudden storms. In 1049 Bernard of Menthon established a **monastery and hospice** here which has maintained uninterrupted, year-round service to travelers since its establishment. In May 1800, Napoleon Bonaparte crossed the Alps here. Leaving last after his 40,000 men, he is said to have slid down the snowfield on his backside.

St Bernard dogs were bred here and used for rescue operations, the most famous being 'Barry,' who is said to have saved 40–100 lives. The dogs are first recorded in the year 1690 in paintings by Salvatore Rosa and though they have been retired from service since the 1950s a small number are brought to the pass each year for the enjoyment of tourists. (Bus to Aosta Valley locations in season: www.postauto.ch, www.tmrsa.ch.)

⛰ **L'Hospice du Grand-Saint-Bernard** ⃞ ⃞ ⃞ ⃞ ⃞ ⃞ ⃞ ⃞ 6/80, CHF37/55/-/-, Col du Gd-St-Bernard 2, www.gsbernard.com, hospice@gsbernard.com, tel (0)27 787 12 36. Breakfast incl.; half board CHF75, full board CHF90. Rooms in adjacent hotel start at CHF119 (www.aubergehospice.ch). Hostel open year-round, but road and hotel are closed depending on weather Oct–June.

⛰ **Hotel Italia** ⃞ ⃞ ⃞ ⃞ ⃞ 14/28, CHF-/50/70/-, Colle del Gran San Bernardo 2, www.gransanbernardo.it, info@gransanbernardo.it, tel +39 0165 780063. On the Italian side of the pass.

SECTION 2: AOSTA VALLEY

The Aosta valley widens as the route passes the tower of Sant'Ilario in Gignod (Stage 8)

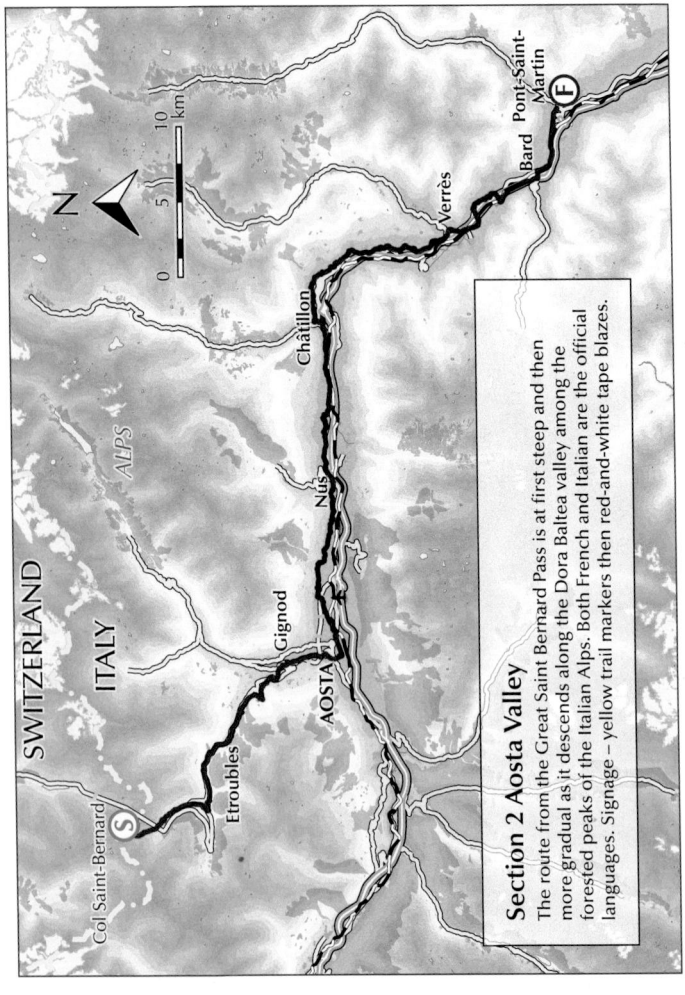

Section 2 Aosta Valley

The route from the Great Saint Bernard Pass is at first steep and then more gradual as it descends along the Dora Baltea valley among the forested peaks of the Italian Alps. Both French and Italian are the official languages. Signage – yellow trail markers then red-and-white tape blazes.

STAGE 8

Col du Grand-Saint-Bernard to Aosta

Start	Col du Grand-Saint-Bernard, Hospice
Finish	Aosta, Cathedral of Santa Maria Assunta
Distance	28.8km
Total ascent	455m
Total descent	2347m
Difficulty	Hard (due to distance and constant descent)
Duration	7hr
Percentage paved	63%
Hostels	Saint-Rhémy-Bourg 6.6km, Saint-Oyen 11.4km, Etroubles 13.1km, Echevennoz 15.1km, Aosta 28.8km

In the first few kilometers after Col du Grand-Saint-Bernard the downhill path is steep and footholds require care. The descent quickly carries you below the tree line onto a series of mountainside trails with stunning Alpine views until you reach lush pastures at the valley floor. After Echevennoz a wide path descends very gently beside the Ru Neuf irrigation canal. The charming cafés and shops of Aosta's pleasant center city offset the bit of highway walking and the final steep climb just before town. Blisters are the biggest danger to feet unaccustomed to unrelenting downhill terrain and if the distance seems too great, an overnight at Etroubles or Echevennoz can divide the stage.

Walking from the Swiss to the Italian side of the summit, the official TDC/103 markers point you to the right of the statue of St Bernard along a twisted trail to a highway crossing. Either choose that route or simply walk on the asphalt road to the left of Hotel Italia down the highway for a couple of hundred easy meters until the trail crosses the road in the midst of a steep, green valley surrounded by sharp, granite peaks. Head downhill on the TDC/103 or 13 path that at first follows just below the highway snow sheds and then switches back, pointing downward toward a three-storey stone building, **Il Rifugio del Pellegrino** (**2.5km**, ⌂ Casa Don Angelo Carioni Pt Do R Br Dr W S Z 12/82, €44/-/-/-, SS27 del Gran San Bernardo km30, info@prodomoimpresasociale.it, tel 335 6012847. Price includes breakfast and dinner), which you will pass on its right side as you again cross the highway. Now you are on a grassy path leading downhill on the left side of the valley toward the tree-covered mountains below. Soon you see far below you the service buildings for the Italian end of the **GSB tunnel**. The floor of the valley draws closer and not long after a parking lot on the valley floor the path ends at the **SS27** highway (**3.3km**).

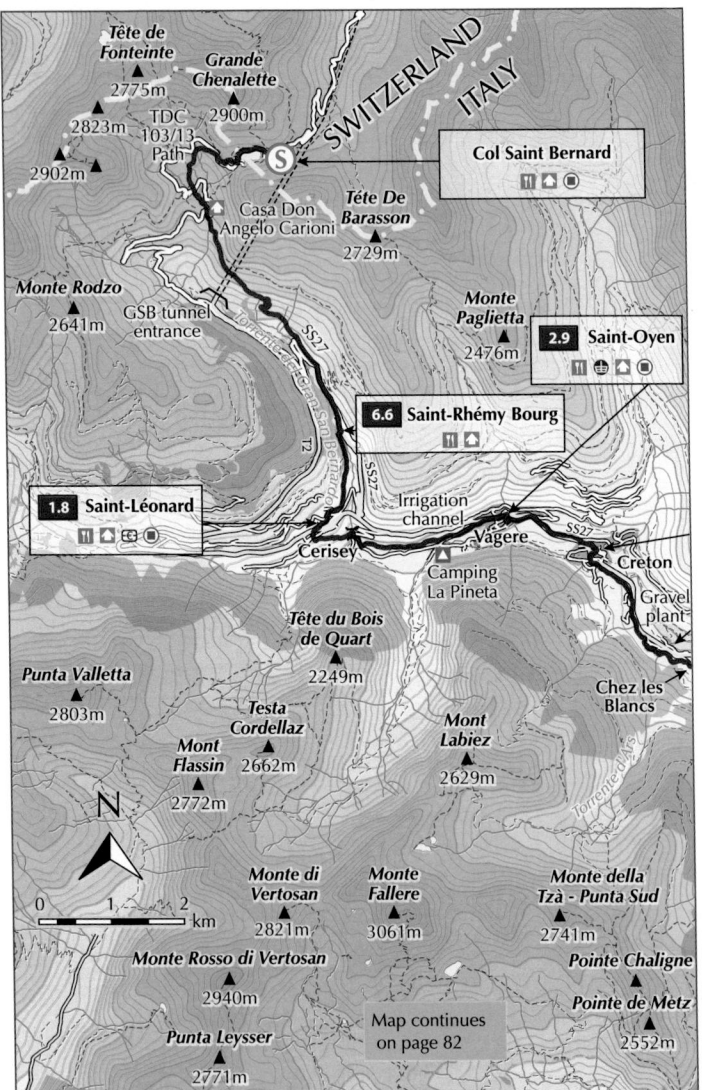

SWITZERLAND

ITALY

Tête de Fonteinte 2775m

Grande Chenalette 2900m

2823m

TDC 103/13 Path

2902m

Casa Don Angelo Carioni

Tête De Barasson 2729m

S

Col Saint Bernard

Monte Rodzo 2641m

GSB tunnel entrance

SS27

Monte Paglietta 2476m

2.9 Saint-Oyen

6.6 Saint-Rhémy Bourg

1.8 Saint-Léonard

Irrigation channel

SS27

Vagere

Cerisey

SS27

Creton

Gravel plant

Camping La Pineta

Tête du Bois de Quart 2249m

Chez les Blancs

Punta Valletta 2803m

Testa Cordellaz 2662m

Mont Flassin 2772m

Mont Labiez 2629m

N

0   1   2 km

Monte di Vertosan 2821m

Monte Fallere 3061m

Monte della Tzà - Punta Sud 2741m

Monte Rosso di Vertosan 2940m

Pointe Chaligne

Pointe de Metz 2552m

Map continues on page 82

Punta Leysser 2771m

Scattered buildings sit below the Tête de Fenêtre on the Italian side of the Great St Bernard Lake.

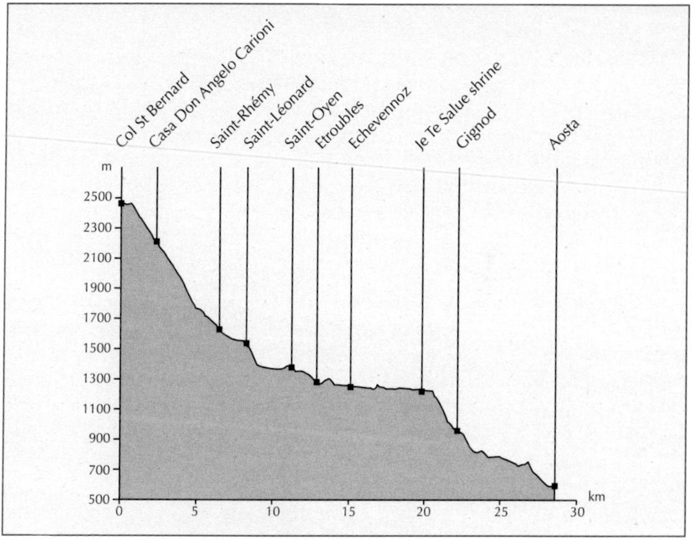

Follow the highway briefly then cross toward the right at a gap in the guardrail below a small dam where a path picks up between the highway and the stream. Before long, come to the quaint Alpine hamlet of **Saint-Rhémy-Bourg** (0.9km).

6.6KM SAINT-RHÉMY-BOURG (ELEV 1624M, POP 10) 🍴 🛏 (1005.8KM)
The hamlet of Saint-Rhémy-Bourg sits on the Gran San Bernardo stream in the larger municipality of Saint-Rhémy-en-Bosses and was a key outpost in Roman times for the transit across the pass. Sigeric identifies it as Stage XLVII Sancta Remei. Its **Church of San Lorenzo** dates from the 18th c.

🔺 Hotel Suisse **Pr R Br Gr** 8/15, €-/40/80/-, Fraz. St. Rhémy-Bourg 26, www.suissehotel.it/en, info@suissehotel.it, tel 0165 780901. Price incl. breakfast, half board €27. Open Jan–Apr, Jul–Nov. Restaurant.

🔺 Casa Cure de Saint-Rhémy **Do K** 12/46, €10/-/-/-, Località Saint-Rhémy 5, www.idscaosta.it, idsc@idscaosta.it, tel 0165 363589.

At a bridge in Saint-Rhémy-Bourg cross to the other side of the **Torrente del Gran San Bernardo** and follow a wide, gravel road, gradually arriving at **Saint-Léonard**. Follow waymarks toward the church and just afterward pass a round, outdoor stained-glass window depicting a blonde pilgrim overlooking the lake and hospice at the GSB.

1.8KM SAINT-LÉONARD (ELEV 1521, POP 182) 🍴 🛏 🄲 ◉ (1004.0KM)
The town serves as capital of the Saint-Rhémy-en-Bosses municipality. Next to the 19th c. Church of Saint-Léonard is the **castle of Bosses** from the 14th–15th c. The region celebrates its Jambon de Bosses prosciutto, famous throughout Italy and protected by strict production guidelines. Here a thoughtful welcome desk for pilgrims is marked 'Roma KM 1007' (Check online resources for available tourist accommodation. Bus to/from Aosta: www.savda.it, www.tmrsa.ch.)

Now begins a sometimes-steep dirt track heading down toward the river. Take a wooden bridge across the stream and enter the hamlet of **Cerisey (0.7km)**, searching out the track within this small settlement of homes. Then make your way farther down the narrow Artanavaz valley of lush, green pastures among tree-covered mountains to the sounds of cow bells and the enthusiastic river below. Soon an **irrigation canal** picks up on the left side. At **Vagere (2.1km)** the track joins the highway, continuing alongside it to reach **Saint-Oyen (0.2km)**.

2.9KM SAINT-OYEN (ELEV 1373M, POP 216) 🍴 ⊕ 🛏 ◉ (1001.1KM)
🔺 Château Verdun **O Pr Do R Br Gr W S Z** 36/80, €25/35/70/115, Strada Flassin 3, www.chateauverdun.com, info@chateauverdun.com, tel 0165 524968. Reservation required.

▲ **Camping La Pineta** ◎ ▯ ▯ ▯ ▯ ▯ ▯ ▯ €10/tent site, Rue de Flassin, www. campingbarpineta.it, campingbarpineta@gmail.com, tel 0165 78114. Tent sites only.

Drop below the highway briefly, then cross it to take a roadside path on the far side of the highway into **Etroubles** (**1.7km**).

1.7KM ETROUBLES (ELEV 1274M, POP 507) ▯ ▯ ▯ ◉ ⊕ ❶ (999.3KM)

Etroubles traces its roots to Roman times, when it was known as Restapolis and held a garrison that controlled the halfway-point between Aosta and the pass. The modern name derives from the local dialect, where *étrobbla* is the stubble straw left from the grain harvest. On 20 May 1800 Napoleon slept at the home of Abbot Léonard Veysendaz. In 1317 a pilgrim hospice was built in the village and was still functioning in the 19th c. (Bus every 4hr to Aosta www.savda.it.)

⌂ **Maison Julie** ◎ ▯ ▯ 4/16, €-/-/59/-, www.maisonjulie.it, erik.chentre@gmail. com, tel 329 231 7800. Four apartments in historic home.

⌂ **Col Serena** ◎ ▯ ▯ ▯ ▯ 15/30, €-/66/91/111, Rue des Vergers 5, www. hotelcolserena.com, info@hotelcolserena.com, tel 0165 78218.

Cross the Artanavaz on the Ponte di Legno covered bridge just below the highway and wind your way around a restaurant and cemetery to a wide, grassy path above the village. Come alongside a **gravel plant** and before long arrive at the village of **Echevennoz** (**2.0km**).

2.0KM, ECHEVENNOZ (ELEV 1251MM, POP 74) ▯ ▯ ◉ (997.3KM)

The tiny village is bisected by the SS27 highway.

⌂ **Dortoir-Punto Tappa Echevennoz** ▯ ▯ ▯ ▯ ▯ ▯ ▯ ▯ ▯ 3/14, €25/30/-/-, Frazione Echevennoz, ruffierdidier@libero.it, tel 0165 78225.Closed May–Oct. Half board incl.

On the far side of the village cross a stream to continue along a narrow gravel path next to an irrigation channel, the **Ru Neuf Canal**, on the right side. Pass the tiny settlement of **Chez les Blancs** and find the canal-side path. The Ru Neuf Canal has directed water from the Artavanaz drainage toward Aosta Valley farms since the early 15th c. After a time, come to the **hairpin curve** of an asphalt road (**3.7km**), and cross to find the path between the road's two arms. At a hard left turn in the path just after a cascading creek find the **Je Te Salue Grotto** (**1.2km**) with benches.

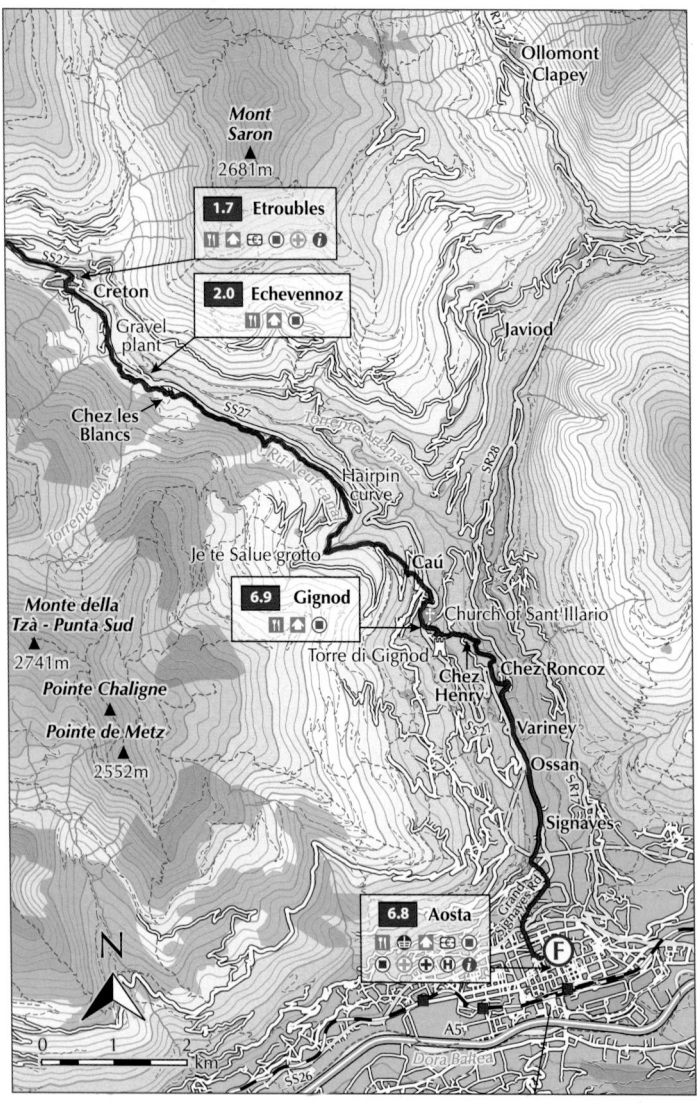

Ollomont
Clapey

Mont Saron
▲ 2681m

1.7 Etroubles

SS27

Creton

2.0 Echevennoz

Gravel plant

Javiod

Chez les Blancs

SS27

SR28

Hairpin curve

Je te Salue grotto

Caú

Monte della Tzà - Punta Sud
▲ 2741m

6.9 Gignod

Church of Sant'Illario

Torre di Gignod

Chez Roncoz

Pointe Chaligne

Chez Henry

Pointe de Metz
▲ 2552m

Variney

Ossan

Signayes

6.8 Aosta

Ⓕ

N

0   1   2
km

A5

Dora Baltea

SS26

82

A statue of the adolescent Jesus being guided by his mother at the Je Te Salue shrine

Engineers on the Ru Neuf Canal noticed the **grotto** alongside the official track of the Via Francigena and suggested to the village priest that a shrine be erected there. The artist Silvano Salto, originally from this area, was commissioned to create the white marble statue of the adolescent Christ with his mother, Mary, pointing the way. Water falling from the mountainside above is meant to represent the waters of baptism.

Follow the canal onward until you come to another road at a hairpin bend (**0.8km**). This time turn left and descend toward the valley floor, with views below of Montjoux and to the right the tall, slender stone tower of the Church of Sant'Ilario in Gignod. Cross a road and begin a steep descent, first through the village of **Caú** and then shortcutting through backyards and along gardens to the church tower in upper **Gignod**. After the church, head down to the highway and find a café and small campground in the lower village (**1.2km**).

6.9KM GIGNOD (ELEV 984M, POP) ▯▯ ▱ ◉ (990.4KM)
The tall bell tower of the **Church of Sant'Illario** was built from repurposed stones of the 12th–15th c. Castle of Gignod, located where the current church stands. In the lower village, the **Tower of Gignod**, built as early as the 12th c., was used by the feudal Gignod family as a lookout over the lower valley. Each year the town's residents make a procession to the 2608m Punta Chaligne peak to remember the area's survival from a plague in the 17th c., which killed two-thirds of the region's inhabitants. (Bus: www.savda.it.)

⌂ Hotel Bellevue ▯▯ ▱ ▱ 23/46, €-/30/40/80, Frazione La Ressaz 3, tel 0165 56392.

Cross the highway in the direction of the medieval castle tower, **Torre di Gignod**, and follow a gentle and quiet road leading downhill first through a string of Aosta suburbs beginning with Chez Courtill, then **Chez Henry** (**1.2km**), and **Chez Roncoz** (**1.3km**), where the road ends. Turn right here, picking up the sidewalk of the Strada Regionale, through the roadside villages of Petit Quart, **Variney** (**0.5km**) and **Ossan** (**0.8km**). Before the denser village of **Signayes** (**0.7km**) leave the SS27 highway, turning right after the village to climb up the Grand Signayes asphalt road that steers you into the vineyards above Aosta. A series of narrow and steep lanes bring you downhill on the Viale Ginevra. After the Archeological Museum veer left to come to the colorful façade of the Cathedral of Santa Maria Assunta in central **Aosta**, with central Piazza Chanoux just two blocks right after the cathedral's twin towers (**2.3km**).

6.8KM AOSTA (ELEV 586M, POP 125,666) 🔢 ⊕ 🅰 🅴 ⊛ ⊛ ⊕ ⊕ 🅷 *i* (983.6KM)
Surrounded by tall mountains and located at the confluence of roads leading from the Great Saint Bernard Pass and its quieter Alpine sister, the Little Saint Bernard Pass, Aosta has long served a strategic role in control of Alpine crossings. In 25 BC at the direction of Augustus Caesar, Roman troops vanquished the resident Salassi tribe and established the Roman colony of Augusta Praetoria Salassorum – now shortened as 'Aosta.' Many **Roman landmarks** survive, including the Roman city walls at the east (Porta Pretoria) and south gates, the façade of the Roman theater, a Roman bridge that once spanned the Buthier River, and the monumental Arch of Augustus, built in 35 BC to celebrate the Roman conquest of ten years prior. The **Leper's Tower** was originally a turret in Aosta's Roman walls but was rebuilt and maintained by the Order of Saint-Maurice as a charity hospice. A leper was imprisoned there in the 18th c., earning the tower its modern name. Post-Roman architecture includes the 11th c. **Cathedral of Santa Maria Assunta** and the Romanesque/Gothic **Church of Santi Pietro e Orso**, dedicated to the 6th c. Saint Ursus of Aosta, said to be of Irish origin. Sigeric lists Aosta as 'Agusta,' his Stage XLVII. A hundred years or so after his transit, the eminent theologian Anselm of Canterbury (1033–1109), born in Aosta, would also serve as Archbishop of Canterbury.

Modern Aosta is a recreational and commercial hub of the Aosta Valley and the Cogne Acciai Speciali steel plant near the train station dominates the skyline. The town hall stands at **Piazza Chanoux** in the heart of the old city, and running roughly east/west from the piazza is a rich warren of shops and restaurants on the Via Jean Baptiste, Via Porta Praetoria, and Via Sant'Anselmo making the town a relaxed and hospitable setting for shopping or strolling.

⌂ **Curra's House** 🅾 🅿🅡 🅡 🅚 🅦 🆂 1/2, €Contact, Via Avondo 3, sabrinaewp@ yahoo.it, tel 347 0704617 or 338 4871355. One apartment with max of 3 pilgrims.

⌂ **Albergo Mancuso** 🅾 🅿🅡 🅡 🅑🅡 🅒🅕 🅦 🆂 12/22, €-/45/70/90, Via Voison 32, info@albergomancuso.com, tel 0165 060333. Prices vary by season.

⌂ **Nabuisson B&B** 🅿🅡 🅡 🅑🅡 2/4, €-/75/120/-, Via Edoauard Aubert 50, www. bedbreakaosta.com.

The 12th–13th c. Tower of Gignod overlooks the valley above Aosta

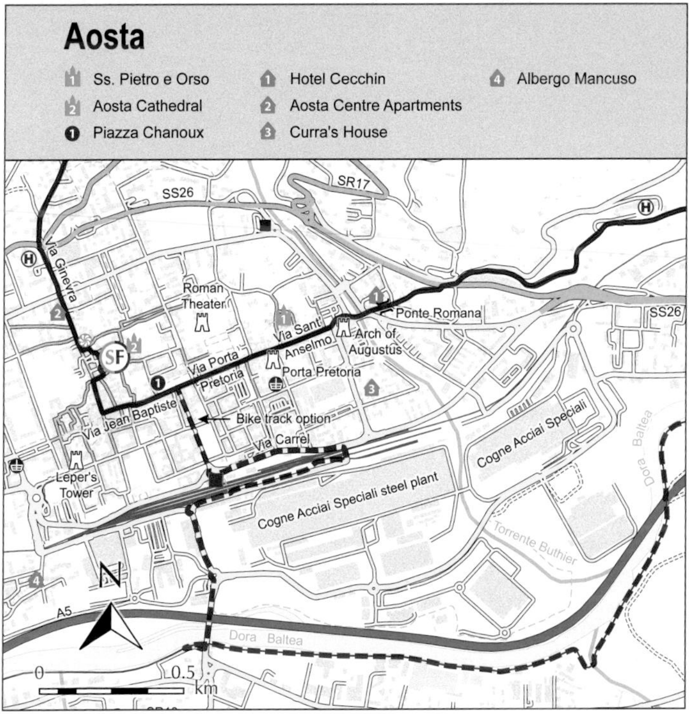

Aosta

🏰	Ss. Pietro e Orso	🏨	Hotel Cecchin	🏨	Albergo Mancuso
🏰	Aosta Cathedral	🏨	Aosta Centre Apartments		
●	Piazza Chanoux	🏨	Curra's House		

STAGE 9
Aosta to Châtillon

Start	Aosta, Cattedral di Santa Maria Assunta
Finish	Châtillon, Piazza Duc
Distance	27.8km (30.1km bike route)
Total ascent	1088m (259m bike route)
Total descent	1149m (388m bike route)
Difficulty	Moderately hard (Moderate for bike route)
Duration	8¼hr (7½hr bike route)
Percentage paved	69% (100% bike route)
Hostels	Nus (turn-off) 14.4km, Châtillon 27.8km

The official walking track follows mountainside trails for a long up-and-down day made pleasant by spectacular views of the Val d'Aosta in clear weather. With no services until Chambave at 22.5km (except by heading off the track at Nus) you will need to pack plenty of food for the day. The much flatter bike alternative on the south side of the Dora Baltea River (see map) also works for pedestrians, reduces the day's rigorous climbs, and gives an option to tour the Castle of Fènis.

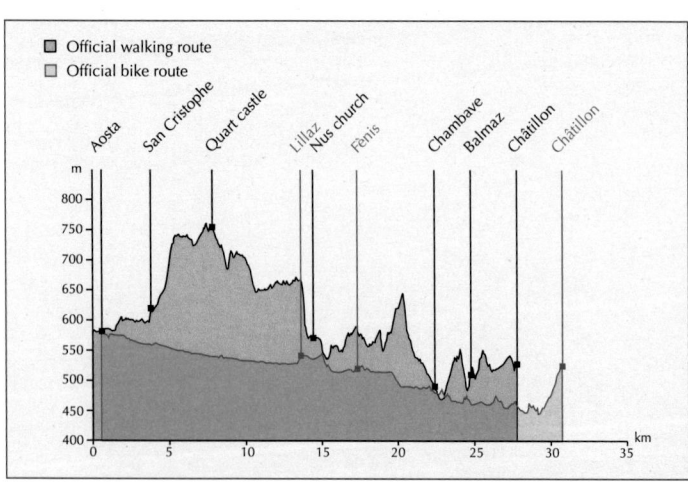

Via Sant'Anselmo leads out of Central Aosta, past the Arch of Augustus, and across the Roman bridge

Walk south from the cathedral to Piazza Chanoux and turn left onto Via Porta Pretoria, which you follow past the **Augustus Arch** and through the old neighborhood directly opposite, crossing the Roman bridge. This puts you onto an alleyway alongside the main road and leads up on a paved road that crosses in front of the **regional hospital** (2.3km). Following Trail 103 markings and VF red-and-white blazes, continue through **La Cretaz** and **Chaussod** to **Saint Christophe** (1.5km) whose Bar Castoro is the last food establishment until Chambave. Follow a cobblestone path up to the tall steeple of the church and town hall. A road slightly above takes you to the settlement of **Bagnere**.

Follow signs here that lead uphill alongside a noisy stream. Cross the stream on a bridge and continue up, finding soon a steep, two-track gravel road which you climb behind orchards. A pleasant dirt road traverses the mountainside before a left turn up a steep path takes you to another traverse on part of a regional trail system called the Rue Souverout. Continue along and cross an asphalt road, coming just afterward to the **Monastero Mater Misericordiae** (2.3km), housed in a modern building with white arched windows partly visible through the trees to the right. In a few minutes a canal joins on the left. When the path ends at an asphalt road, turn right and descend to a parking lot and, just beyond, **Quart Castle** (1.7km). Documents date construction of Quart Castle to 1185 when the Quart family moved here from Aosta. Fragmentary frescoes inside survive from as early as the 14th c.

Continue, with the best views of the castle now behind you, then cross the SR37 (0.9km) to a pathway that descends steeply among gardens of newish, two-storey homes past the small, 14th c. **Castle of La Tour-Povil**. Continue through the hamlet and come to an asphalt road that descends and begins its own traverse of the mountainside, first through the settlement of **Epillod** (0.5km) and then through the hamlets of **Imperiau** and **Seran** (0.7km).

The road begins to descend toward the valley floor, passing **Chetoz** (1.1km) as it continues, with stone walls and the canal running alongside, sometimes through woods and otherwise along sloping fields. A **narrow gravel road** forks to the right across the mountainside, at first above a large heap of construction rubble. After a time, it crosses

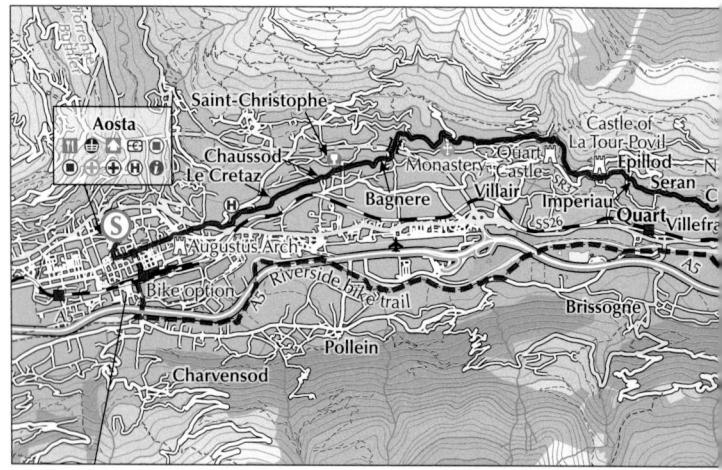
The 14th c. castle of La Tour-Povil overlooks the Aosta Valley

a green **pipeline** (**1.7km**) that descends from the mountain above. Farther on, the 3m-wide trail skirts a series of steep **cliffs** to the left and ends at a trail with a series of **slippery switchbacks** leading downhill toward the Saint Barthelmy **Church** above the town of **Nus** (**1.9km**). To access the town's services, take the stairs below the church and descend 5–6 steep blocks to the town center.

14.4KM NUS ELEV 568M, POP 2993) 🍴 ⊕ 🏠 € ◉ ◉ ⊕ **(969.2KM)**
The name Nus (unlike in French, the final 's' is pronounced) derives from the Latin
word *nonus* for 'nine,' since it was nine Roman miles from Aosta. The Roman governor **Pontius Pilate** is said to have stayed here on his journey to exile in Gaul.
From the 11th–16th c. the area was under the control of the Lords of Nus, who
built the **castle** above town in 1350. Nus's Church of Saint-Hilaire was built in
1153.

🏠 Hotel Florian 🅾 Pr R Cr S Z 13/24, €-/36/57/95, Via Risorgimento 3, www.
   hotel-florian.it, info@hotel-florian.it, tel 0165 767538 or 333 4645424.

After the church, cross the SR36 asphalt road and turn right on a gravel road that
becomes a gravel driveway as it descends slowly across the mountainside through
vineyards, with valley views to the right. The road becomes an asphalt drive which
zigzags downhill then finds the asphalt Via Frazione Plantayes to continue the traverse.
Come to the hamlet of **Rovarey** (**2.0km**) where you descend on a two-track gravel road
in trees with pleasant views back toward Nus.

Go through **Ronchettes** until the gravel road ends at Chevence Dessous, finding an asphalt road to continue along the mountainside. At Santa Lucia Church
at **Diemoz** (**2.4km**), turn right just after the church onto a steep path and descend
quickly to a road that continues on the mountainside at a lower elevation. The
asphalt road becomes a driveway and then a grassy path along the hillside, connecting to another property and a driveway that leads to another asphalt road. Cross

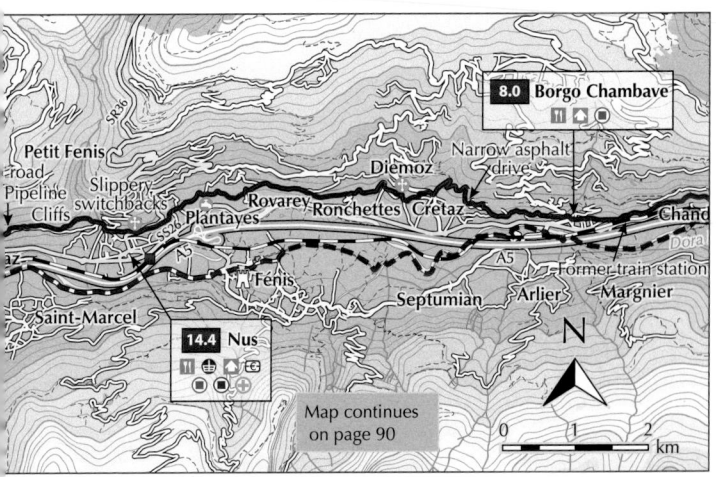

the SR42 (**0.7km**) and enter **Cretaz**, where you climb up an asphalt road leading to cliffs above.

Make a hard right turn down the hill on a dirt track between vineyards. The dirt track ends at a collection of homes and farm buildings – turn left on a **narrow asphalt drive** (**1.1km**) that continues to descend. A series of roads ultimately lead to **Borgo Chambave**, where you turn left on cobblestone streets to find bars and cafés (**1.8km**).

8.0KM BORGO CHAMBAVE (ELEV 490M POP 939) 🍴 🛏 ◉ (961.1KM)

Sited on the road over the Alps, Chambave was once an important market town in the mid-Aosta Valley. Since the 14th c. it has been famous for its Muscat de Chambave and Chambave rouge wines. (Bus: www.savda.it.)

🛏 I Tre Pini 🅿️ 🆁 🅱️ 2/5, €-/65/65/-, Via de Cly 15, https://beb.it/itrepinibnb/en, itrepinibnb@gmail.com, tel 328 4480833.

Follow the main street out of town, heading toward the former train station then turn uphill through the back alleys of the tiny hamlet of **Chandianaz** (**1.3km**), festooned with painted boards of mountain scenery. After the village, come to an overgrown, gravel path that descends through backyards and small farms to reach the ghost-village of **Barmaz** (**1.1km**), which you pass on a steep path to the left. The crumbling buildings of this 16th–17th c. village are all that stand of a once-prosperous agricultural settlement, ultimately abandoned due to lack of a reliable water source. Now you can clearly make out **Castello Gamba** and across the valley the **Castello di Ussel**, both

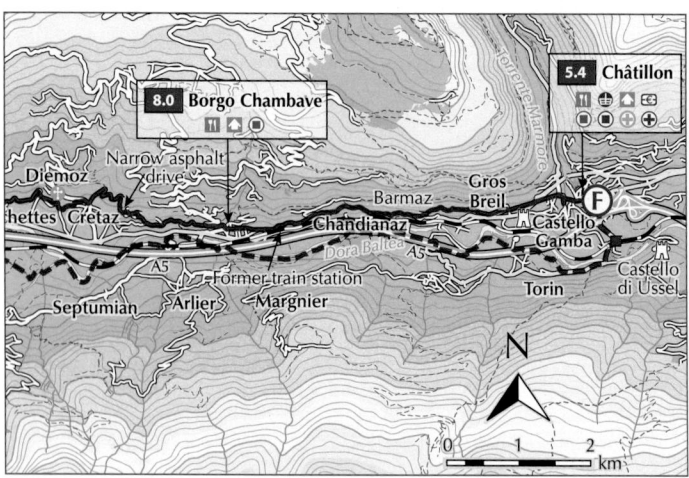

indications you are nearing Châtillon. Continue along stone walls that include bits of the blue/green granite of the cliffs of this mountain. At the hairpin turn of an asphalt road begin the final descent to the Menabrea highway (**1.8km**) on the outskirts of town. Turn left and follow signs into an underpass below the highway and then right onto cobblestone streets, across the bridge onto Via Emilio Chanoux into the town center of **Châtillon** (**1.2km**).

5.4KM CHÂTILLON (ELEV 527, POP 4966) 🍴 ⊕ 🏠 🏧 🅲 ◉ ◉ ⊕ ⊕ (955.8KM)
Châtillon sits at the junction of the Aosta Valley and the Valtournenche, a high valley that leads north up the Marmore River as far as the slopes of the Matterhorn. Châtillon was already inhabited in Roman times and in the Middle Ages was dominated by the Challant family, whose castles can still be seen scattered about the area. Much of Châtillon's center consists of homes built in the 16th and 17th c. A tall, single-arch bridge spans the Marmore and replaces an earlier Roman bridge whose foundations can still be viewed.

⌂ **Convento Frati Cappuccini** 🅾 🅿r 🆁 🆂 1/3, €Donation, Via Chanoux 130, chatillon@cappucinipiemonte.com, tel 0166 61471. In town center. Stefano can arrange low-cost meals at nearby restaurants.

⌂ **B&B Au Coin du Château** 🅿r 🅱r 🆂 2/5, €-/48/50/70, Fraz. Cret de Breil 47/A, aucoinduchateau@gmail.com, tel 340 4720974. Closed Nov.

A view back up the valley toward Nus and the high Alps beyond

STAGE 10
Châtillon to Verrès

Start	Châtillon, Piazza Duc
Finish	Verrès, Torrente Evançon Bridge
Distance	18.3km
Total ascent	803m
Total descent	955m
Difficulty	Moderately hard
Duration	5¾hr
Percentage paved	52%
Hostels	Saint-Vincent 5.1km, Verrès 18.3km

A day of castles, gorges and vistas, spent on paths and roads often high above the valley floor. Despite being relatively short, this stage offers some challenging climbs and descents, sometimes on tricky footing. The only easy-to-reach services are a couple of blocks off the route in Montjovet, so stock up before leaving Châtillon.

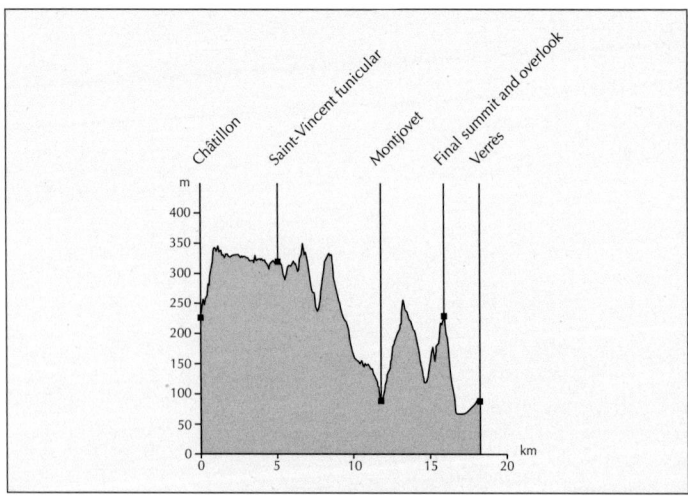

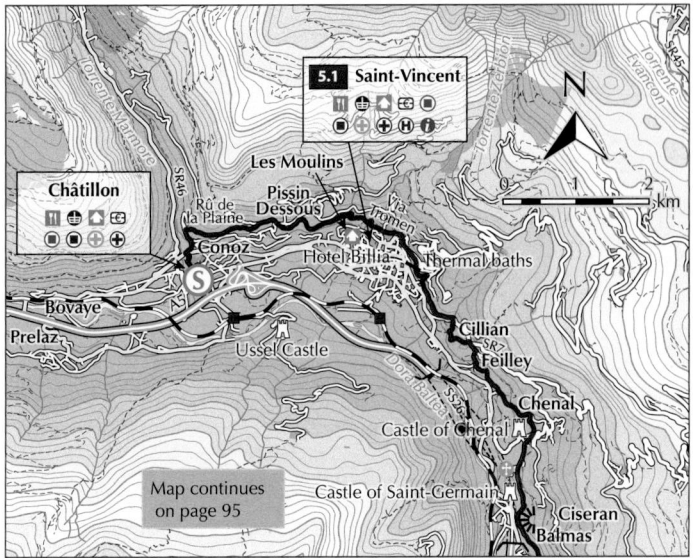

Climb up to the impressive Parish Church of San Pietro and then head left of the church's front door to climb further up, ultimately finding a flat, gravel, recreational path, the **Rû de la Plaine** (**1.0km**) above **Conoz**. Here begin a steady traverse of the mountainside, often with stone walls on the left and a sturdy, wooden fence on the right, always with views to the square Ussel Castle across the valley.

> **Ussel Castle**, built in the 14th c., is one of the first in the Aosta Valley to be built in a single structure. In the 18th c. it was used as a prison and then was abandoned. In 1983 Baron Marcel Bich donated it to the regional authority, which restored it for use as an exhibition center.

Cross now onto Rue de la Plein, a series of high trails above the environs of Saint-Vincent, with outdoor exercise equipment and sweeping views of the town and valley. Pass through **Pessin-Dessous** and then begin to see the profile of **Hotel Billia** and other buildings of the Saint-Vincent skyline below. The lovely path ends (**3.3km**) at Via Tromen in the suburb of **Les Moulins**. To reach central **Saint-Vincent**, turn right in two blocks on SR33 and follow it downhill, otherwise turn left on the cobblestone sidewalk in the direction of the **thermal baths** (Terme). A fork to the right brings you below the main door of the hot springs building and leads you to a path that crosses under the funicular (**0.8km**) coming up from central Saint-Vincent below.

5.1KM SAINT-VINCENT (ELEV 622M, POP 4584) (950.6KM)

Archeological finds place Saint-Vincent's roots in Neolithic times. Its 11th c. **Church of San Vincenzo** includes a museum of sacred art. Best known in modern times as home of the Casino de la Vallée, one of the largest in Europe, it attracts tourists to its posh **thermal spa** (www.termedisaintvincent.com), whose waters were first discovered in 1770. Saint-Vincent's micro-climate gives it mild winters and cool summers.

- **Hotel alla Posta** O Pr R Br Cr S Z 46/90, €seasonal, Via 28 Aprile 1, www.hotelpostavda.it/en, info@hotelpostavda.it, tel 0166 512250. Fairly posh hotel. Adjacent to St Vincent church.
- **Camping Village Paradise** O Pr R Cr W S Z 2/4, €-/-/90/-, Via Trieste, www.villageparadise.com, info@villageparadise.com, tel 0166 503534, 0166 62643 or 3687511015. Reserve early for 2 chalets. Tent sites also available (€9pp).

A new path picks up a canal on its left, followed by an asphalt road. Turn right and very soon left onto a path between houses, leading to an asphalt road below. Continue along the road to a bus stop, forking right to enter **Cillian** (**1.2km**). Pass the Chapel to the Holy Innocents, and wind your way through this charming mountainside village to a path on the opposite side. Climb up to a wide dirt track along the mountainside, coming to the SR7 roadway (**0.6km**) and soon beginning to descend toward homes. Turn right off the road before the town of **Feilley**, heading down a stone pathway alongside a rivulet before turning left onto another asphalt road. Join another path very soon and more views open to the right as you descend among dark woods, gardens and cow pastures.

After climbing steeply on a shale slope, turn right on a gravel road and come to the tiny village of **Chenal** (**1.5km**), with its picturesque church and castle ruin. Remains of the 13th c. Chenal Castle, originally designed to be in direct line of sight to neighboring Castello Saint-Germain, can be viewed in a 5-min detour off the path. Turn left immediately after the village church and descend on a path that spills out onto an asphalt road. Continue downhill past the castle and church of Saint-Germain (**0.9km**).

The 11th–12th c. **Castle of Saint-Germain** is in one of the most strategic locations of the Aosta Valley, perched on an outcrop above a narrow gorge of the Dora Balthea Valley. It was destroyed in 1661 in favor of nearby Bard Fortress.

After the castle and church the narrowest part of the gorge is behind you. Soon you can see the spillway pipes of a hydroelectric facility on the far side of the still-narrow valley. The road bends to the left and a dramatic vista opens of the now-wider valley ahead and below. At the tiny settlement of **Balmas** (**1.0km**) the road ends at a parking strip and a splendid, scenic path along the terraces soon opens up. Come to the

The path leads among terraced vineyards at Balmas

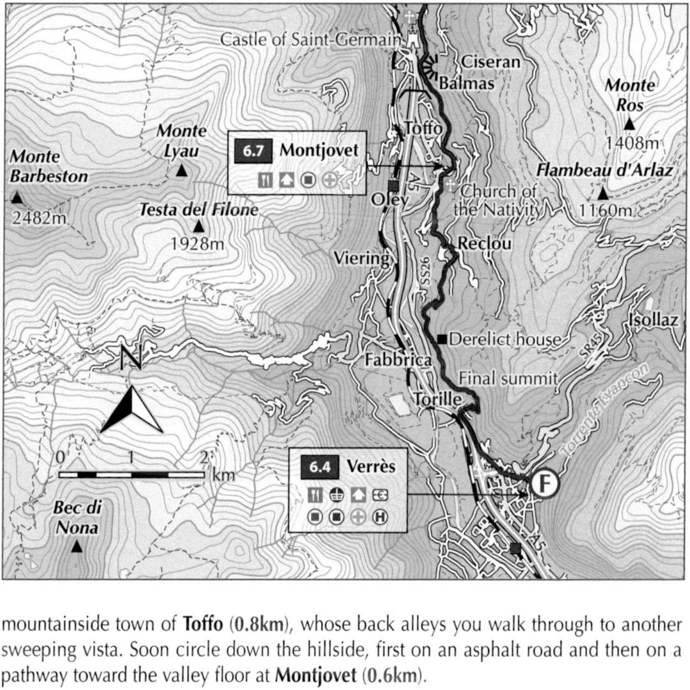

mountainside town of **Toffo** (**0.8km**), whose back alleys you walk through to another sweeping vista. Soon circle down the hillside, first on an asphalt road and then on a pathway toward the valley floor at **Montjovet** (**0.6km**).

6.7KM MONTJOVET (ELEV 395M, POP 1791) 🏨 🛆 ◉ ⊕ (943.9KM)

Settlement here dates to Neolithic times and it is possible the town got its name from a Roman temple to Jupiter – Mons Jovis – though no traces have been found. Historians theorize that a 13th c. landslide may have buried the original village of Publey, located here and identified by Sigeric as his Stage XLVI (Consult online resources for tourist accommodations. Bus: www.savda.it.)

Continue to the valley floor for a lunch stop at the bar on the old highway or climb up to the church steeple and pass between it and the 19th c. **Church of the Nativity of the Virgin**. After the church, turn left to find a pathway behind the village that carries you gently along the mountain slope. Just before an asphalt road where the path ends, climb steeply, then turn left and continue to climb on the road, passing through the hamlet of **Reclou (1.6km)**. Soon come to a long and well-graded gravel road that makes a long descent with occasional shortcuts to avoid the long switchbacks. A two-track gravel road picks up where this road ends and begins a steep climb up the mountainside.

At a **derelict house (1.8km)** the road becomes a single-track pathway that reaches a series of summits, sometimes with difficult climbs and tricky descents. At a final summit **(0.8km)** a sweeping view down the valley opens up and you realize you are standing a couple of hundred meters directly above the outskirts of Verrès. Begin a steep downhill, first on gravel, then on flagstones and finally on asphalt. Follow signs that shortcut through suburbs, aiming directly at the highway beyond in **Torille (0.8km)**. At the highway turn left and follow the brick sidewalk into **Verrès (1.5km)**, its east and west halves joined by a picturesque bridge across the **Torrente Evançon** river.

6.4KM VERRÈS (ELEV 393M, POP 2644) 🏨 ⊕ 🛆 🄴 ◉ ◉ ⊕ 🄷 (937.5KM)

Originally a settlement of the Salassi tribes, the Romans called the town Vitricium which suggests glass works in the area. The town of Verrès is dominated by its splendid 13th–16th c. **castle**, one of the most-visited sites in the Aosta Valley. Though built by the De Verretio family, it became property of the Challant family in 1372, who used it to control the Evançon Valley above and to the north of town. Each year on the last weekend of September a costumed festival celebrates Caterina di Challant, who descended to town to dance with its inhabitants. The 11th c. **Church of Saint Gilles** echoes the shape of the fortress. (Train: www.trenitalia.com. Bus: www.savda.it and www.vitagroup.it.)

🛏 Casa del Pellegrino 'Sant'Agostino' 🄳🄾 2/4, €Donation, Vicolo S. Egidio 13, www.francigenaverres.it, francigenaverres@gmail.com, tel 0125 929093. Open 1 Apr–31 Oct. Reserve at least 24hr prior. Check-in 3:30–4:30pm.

🛏 Solan 🄿🅃 🅁 🄱🅁 🅂 €-/40/55/90, Via Barme Solan 42, www.solan.it, info@bbsolan.it, tel 347 7103660.

STAGE 11

Verrès to Pont-Saint-Martin

Start	Verrès, Torrente Evançon bridge
Finish	Pont-Saint-Martin, Roman bridge
Distance	16.0km
Total ascent	289m
Total descent	338m
Difficulty	Easy
Duration	4½hr
Percentage paved	89%
Hostels	Hône 10.2km (hotel), Donnas 13.4km, Pont-Saint-Martin 16.0km

A short and easy stage that includes some epic landmarks – scenic bridges, Roman roads and medieval castles. The day's minor climbs and descents leave plenty of time and energy to tour the imposing Bard Fortress. The town of Donnas seems like a never-ending suburb leading to Pont-Saint-Martin itself, which is a collection of mostly modern buildings centered around an ancient bridge.

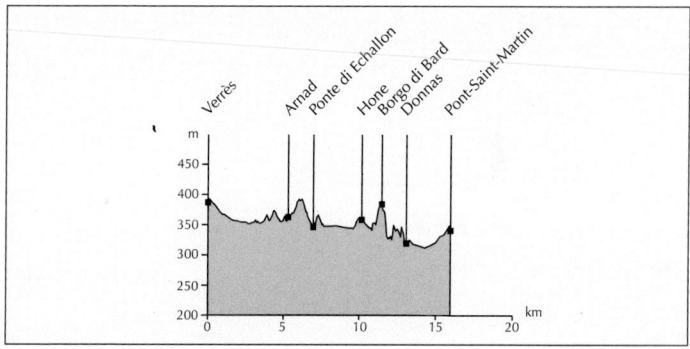

After the **Torrente Evançon** continue along the main street, turning right just after the San Rocco Chapel to come to the train station (**1.1km**), set in a deserted neighborhood of otherwise bustling Verrès. Soon the route takes you across the railway tracks and then left on a quiet road for a walk along the left bank of the **Dora Baltea River**, our first direct encounter with this major waterway. At a bend in the river the road turns back to the left side of the valley and crosses a bridge over the railroad tracks and A5

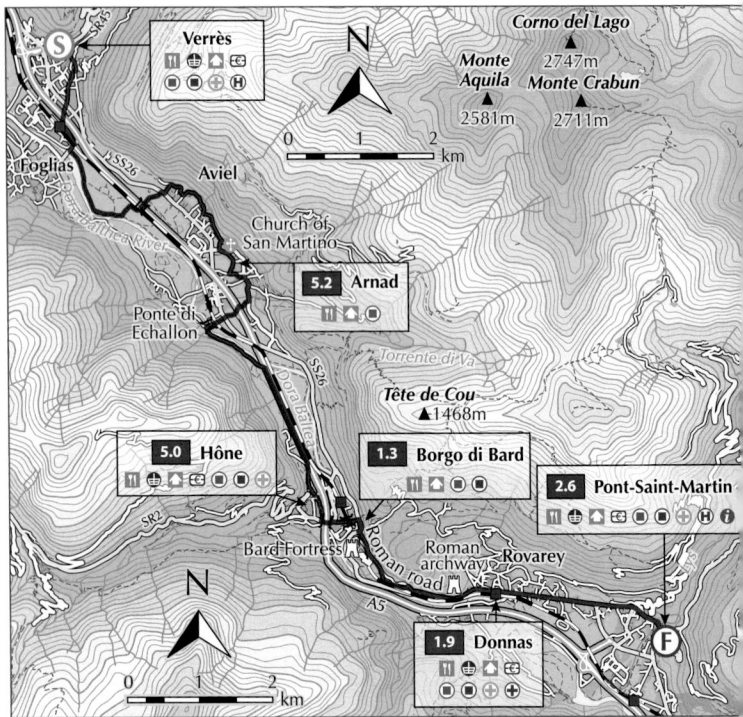

motorway. Once beyond, carefully cross the **SS26** highway toward the small villages huddled at the foot of the steep mountainside. Pass a medieval wine press in the first of several hamlets and continue on to **Arnad** (4.1km).

5.2KM ARNAD (ELEV 363M, POP 1269) 🏨 🏠 ⊙ (932.2KM)
The **Church of San Martino** was once the chapel of a monastery built on this site. It was rebuilt in the 11th c. when a flood destroyed the town's original parish church. The current building is decorated with 15th c. frescoes inside and out, painted by an anonymous artist. The parish keeps a museum of sacred artifacts, including a 13th c. crucifix. (Bus: www.savda.it.)

🛏 **Hotel Armanac** 🄿🅁 🄱🅁 🄳🅁 10/40, €Call, Frazione Clapey 21, www.larmanac. it, mail@larmanac.it, tel 0125 966939.

The graceful arches of the 18th c. Ponte di Echallon span the Dora Baltea River

After Arnad the route takes you back uphill a small distance to cross a water drainage channel, but returns once more to the bottom of the valley to cross in turn the **A5** highway, the old SS26, the train tracks, and finally the river itself. This last crossing is on the beautiful and historic **Ponte di Echallon** (**1.8km**). The scenic Ponte di Echallon was thought to be of Roman origin, though modern scholars attribute it to the mid-18th c. After the bridge, turn left onto a quiet asphalt roadway that continues at a flat gradiant along the right side of the river. When the road turns left at a highway underpass, turn right onto a two-track gravel road that continues alongside the A5 highway, offering excellent views of Bard Fortress. An archway alongside the Church of San Giorgio marks the entry to **Hône**, and the gravel turns to cobblestone as you reach the back streets of the pleasant medieval village (**3.2km**).

5.0KM HÔNE (ELEV 358M, POP 1142) 🍴 ⊕ 🛄 Ⓒ ◉ ⓞ ⊕ (927.3KM)
While Bronze and Iron Age relics have been found here, there is no sign of Roman habitation in Hône. In the Middle Ages it was subject to the Lords of Bard, who were vassals of the Vallaise families and the House of Savoy. Prominent buildings include the 17th c. **Palazzo Marelli** and the nearby 18th c. **Church of San Giorgio**, whose bell tower is visible throughout the territory.

🛏 Hotel Bordet 🄿🅃 🅁 3/8, €-/45/65/90, Via Chanoux 82, tel 0125 803116.

A medieval theme is celebrated at Borgo di Bard

The cobblestone street ends at the Via Chanoux, a wide boulevard with a pedestrian bridge ahead. Instead of crossing the bridge, turn left under the highway, and cross the railroad tracks and then the Dora Baltea bridge. Turn right and go uphill to find **Borgo di Bard** village and the entrance to **Bard Fortress (1.3km)**.

1.3KM BORGO DI BARD (ELEV 404M, POP 117) 🍴 🏠 ⊙ ⊙ (926.0KM)

In the early 6th c. Roman soldiers were garrisoned at Bard and from at least 1034 a medieval castle stood at this site, a key choke point in the lower Aosta Valley. In 1242 the Savoys controlled Bard and used the fortress to levy tolls on travelers. In May 1800 it took Napoleon's 40,000 soldiers over two weeks to dislodge the 400 Austrian soldiers defending it. After capturing the fortress, he dismantled it to protect his rear flank and supply lines. Beginning in 1830 the fortress was rebuilt, though it began to deteriorate later in that century and ultimately was used as a prison, a military depot, and now as a museum and exhibition center (€3 battlements, extra for museums and shows, www.fortedibard.it). The single street of the Borgo (village) di Bard features medieval-themed eateries and shops. (Bus: www. savda.it. Train: www.trenitalia.com.)

🔺 Vecchio Torchio 🄿🄿 🅁 🄱🄻 3/6, €-/46/76/-, Via Vittorio Emanuele 28, www. vecchiotorchio.com, info@vecchiotorchio.com, tel 0125 809860.

A funicular carries passengers from Borgo di Bard up to the fortress

Continue on the main street as it begins to descend, ultimately very steeply, toward the valley floor, briefly on the original Roman road. Veering left just before Donnas come to a section of Roman road hewn from the solid rock of the mountainside. The road ends just after an **archway** (**1.5km**), carved by the Romans directly into the stone. Afterwards, continue through the pleasant, backstreet neighborhood of **Donnas**, passing the parish church and its pilgrim hostel (**0.4km**).

1.9KM DONNAS (ELEV 323M, POP 2683) 🏨 ⊕ 🛆 € ⊚ ⊚ ⊕ ⊕ (924.1KM)

From Roman times Donnas was an important transit stop on the road over the GSB pass, and a milestone indicates it was XXXVI miles from Aosta. The charming old district of Donnas, entered through its medieval gateway, includes the 17th c. **Palazzo Enrielli**. The 'Donnas' red wine hails from the terraced vineyards above and is celebrated annually on the second Sunday of October in the town's wine festival.

🛏 Parrocchia San Pietro in Vincoli ⊙ Ḋ ℞ Ⓚ 1/6, €Donation, Via Roma 81, tel 0125 807032. Next to church. Very basic accommodation.

After the older section of Donnas, continue on sidewalks of the commercial arterial road until it calms at a roundabout and you enter the quiet and more scenic heart of **Pont-Saint-Martin**. Come soon to the **Lys River**, spanned by a modern bridge and the town's Roman bridge just to the left (**2.6km**).

The Parish of San Pietro in Vincoli at Donnas hosts one of many parish hostels on the Via Francigena

2.6KM PONT-SAINT-MARTIN (ELEV 344M, POP 3730) ⊞ ⊕ ⌂ ⓒ ◉ ⊕ ⋒ ⓘ (921.5KM)

Legend says that in the 4th c. St Martin of Tours won a bet with the devil to build a bridge in one day if the devil would leave the town's inhabitants alone. Recent archeology suggests that Pont-Saint-Martin's eponymous **Roman bridge** is actually about three centuries older than the saint. The bridge has served the town well for nearly 2000 years, though in the 19th c. the nearby modern span was built to accommodate additional traffic. The **ruined castle** above town was built in the 12th–14th c. but was already in ruins by the 16th c. The **Via Emilia Chanoux** that runs through the town's charming center is an excellent place to have a drink and take a photo of the bridge and castle.

⌂ Ostello Saint Martin Ⓞ Ⓓⓞ Ⓡ Ⓩ 12/58, €15/-/-/-, Via Schigliatta 4, info@comune.pontsaintmartin.ao.it, tel 0125 804433 or 347 2232039. Reservation required. Book at least 1 day prior.

⌂ Hotel Crabun Ⓞ Ⓟⓡ Ⓑⓡ Ⓓⓡ Ⓢ 28/56, €-/72/88/96, Via Nazionale per Donnas 3, www.crabunhotel.it, info@crabunhotel.it, tel 0125 806069.

SECTION 3: PIEMONTE

The well-preserved 12th c. Chiesa di Pietro outside Bollengo (Stage 13)

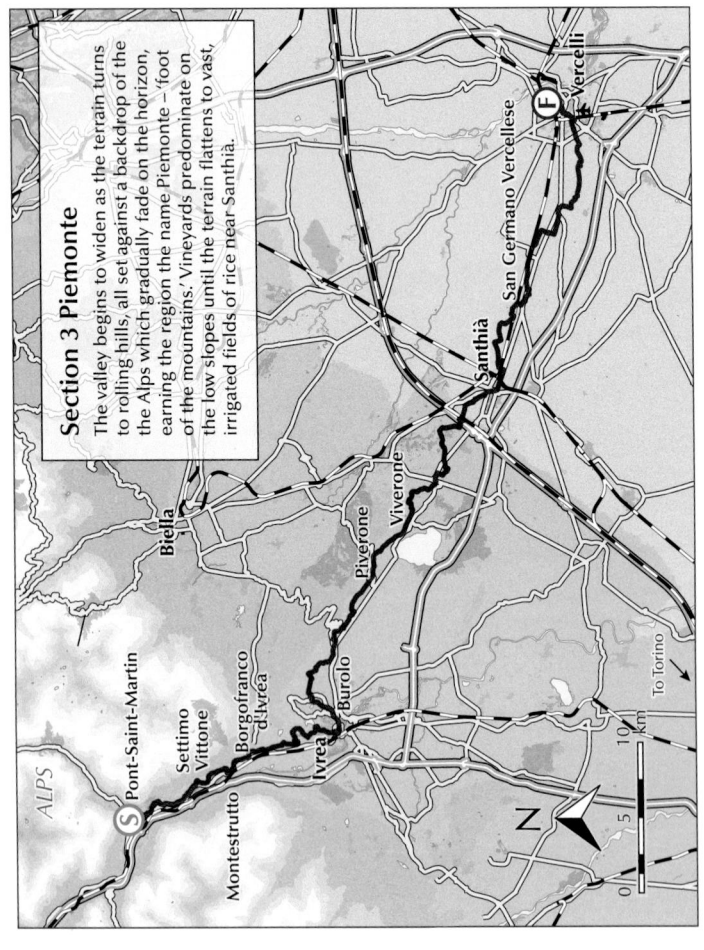

Section 3 Piemonte

The valley begins to widen as the terrain turns to rolling hills, all set against a backdrop of the the Alps which gradually fade on the horizon, earning the region the name Piemonte – 'foot of the mountains.' Vineyards predominate on the low slopes until the terrain flattens to vast, irrigated fields of rice near Santhià.

Vercelli

San Germano Vercellese

Santhià

Viverone

Piverone

Biella

Borgofranco d'Ivrea

Burolo

Ivrea

Settimo Vittone

Montestrutto

Pont-Saint-Martin

ALPS

To Torino

N

0   5   10
km

STAGE 12

Pont-Saint-Martin to Ivrea

Start	Pont-Saint-Martin, Roman bridge
Finish	Ivrea, Piazza Ferruccio Nazionale
Distance	23.1km
Total ascent	570m
Total descent	655m
Difficulty	Moderate
Duration	6½hr
Percentage paved	68%
Hostels	Settimo Vittone 7.9km (hotel), San Germano 12.3km, Borgofranco d'Ivrea 14.3km (B&B), Ivrea 23.1km

This could be a melancholy day as you say goodbye to the beautiful mountains of the Aosta Valley and enter the flatter region of Piemonte, except that a few castles and interesting villages add more than a little delight. Footing can be treacherous on the way into Carema, and around Montestrutto.

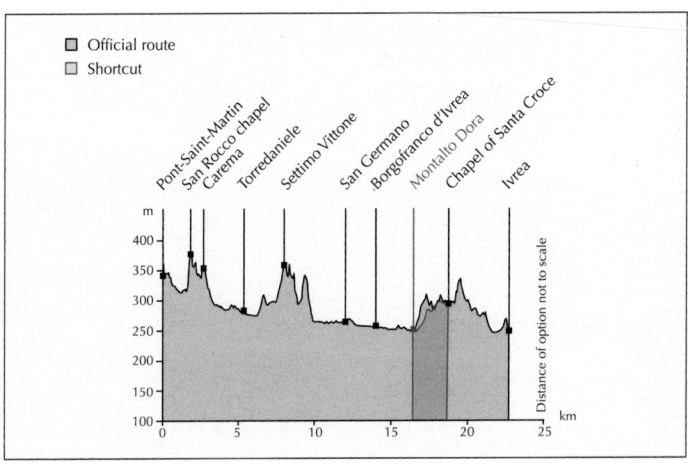

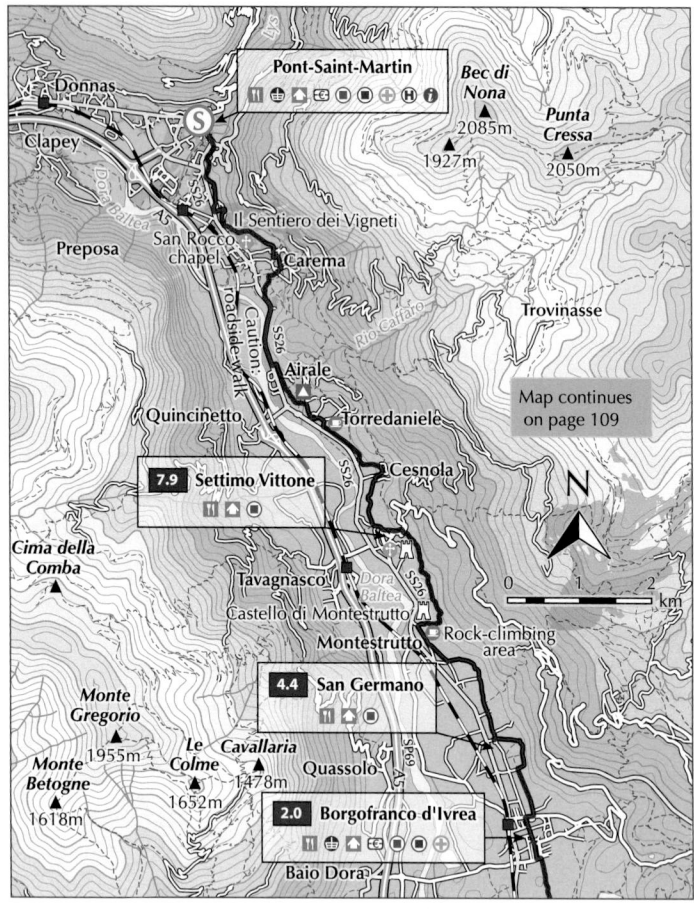

From the bridge in central Pont-Saint-Martin continue briefly along the main road and then find a side road that branches off to the left. The route keeps to the edge of the hillside among vineyards and under grape arbors rather than following the SR44 and SS26 roads. It briefly touches the **SS26** twice, the second time entering the Regione Piemonte, when it turns uphill to **Il Sentiero dei Vigneti** (Trail of the Vineyards). This goat-like trail aims at the 17th c. **San Rocco Chapel** (**1.9km**) on the hillside above, with splendid views of lovely **Carema** (**0.8km**), nestled against the mountainside below.

The path brings pilgrims down the mountainside above the church tower of Carema

Carema's name derives from *cameram* for 'customs' due to its historic role as the **border town** between the regions of Piemonte and Aosta. Wine terraces here are famous for production of the Carema wines. The central fountain was built in 1571 and the Latin inscription in English means 'If anyone is thirsty, come to me and drink.'

The downhill is intense, with tricky footing, though at least in the most difficult portion there is a rope handhold fastened to the cliffside. After Carema, the vineyard route continues on the mountainside, while our route instead heads down to the valley floor, joining the SS26 highway for a hazardous roadside walk until just before **Airale** (**1.9km**), where it forks left off the highway. Pass a large campground and cross a bridge to enter the next village, **Torredaniele** (**0.9km**, café). Walk between the Church of San Pietro and its tall tower within the tight, medieval confines of the village. Local tradition says the tower was built here in the 6th c. to defend a Benedictine monastery at this location and was named after the founding abbot.

Now turn onto a grassy farm road, keeping away from the SS26 as well as the forested mountains to the right which are the last of the Alps we will see up close on this walk. A hard left leads up the hillside to **Cesnola** (**1.3km**), before picking up a pleasant

concrete lane among terraces and orchards which then becomes a grassy path just
before the outskirts of **Settimo Vittone** (**1.3km**). Turn right on the SP72 to enter town.

7.9KM SETTIMO VITTONE (ELEV 318M, POP 1535) � ▲ ◉ (913.6KM)

Set at the entrance to the Canavese plain, Settimo Vittone traces its roots back
to a Salassi settlement at this location. After conquest by the Romans, Settimo
Vittone's name ('seventh') was changed to reflect its distance of seven Roman
miles up the road to Aosta. Local lore says that **Ansgarde, Queen of Burgundy**,
repudiated by her husband, returned here in the 9th c. to live with her brother
Attone Anscario, Lord of Settimo and that at her death in 889 she was buried in
the castle's former baptistry.

🏠 Il Falco e la Volpe **Pr** **R** **Br** **Dr** 6/13, €-/65/100/-, Via Settimo-Cavalgrosso 69,
   www.ilfalcoelavolpe.com, tel 0125 658470. Attached restaurant and enoteca.
   Closed Wedns.

   Continue along the route as it heads toward the church in the upper part of the
town. To the left are the 9th c. **baptistry and castle**. A small, stone stairway leads down
from the castle and becomes a footpath across a small field and vineyard. Soon the
path plunges into a dark wood, emerging briefly onto an asphalt road then becoming
a narrow and steep trail as it crosses a granite spur of the mountain. The **Castello di
Montestrutto** looms on the right and you descend through thick forest among boulders, rounding a spur of the mountain with a zip line course overhead. Come out of
the woods at **Montestrutto** (**2.2km**). As you continue through town come alongside a
rock-climbing area (café), source of the zip line route. The path continues along the
foot of the mountain, on mostly asphalt roads among orchards and large houses to
reach **San Germano** (**2.2km**).

4.4KM SAN GERMANO (ELEV 265M, POP 50) ⧉ ▲ ◉ (909.2KM)

What appear to be small houses stretching along the mountainside are in fact
balmetti, **wine cellars** that take advantage of currents of cold air from deep in
the mountain to keep a constant temperature of 8–10°C (46–50°F) year-round. In
June each year the *balmetti* are open to the public.

🏠 Ostello di San Germano **Pr** **Do** **R** **K** **Br** **Gr** **W** **S** **Z** 3/21, €18/44/56/68, Piazza
   Pertini 3, www.ostellosangermano.it, ferrandopatrizia64@gmail.com, tel 348
   6705143 or 347 4278351. Reservations recommended. Can arrange visits to
   the nearby *balmetti* for wine sampling.

   Continue along the foot of the mountain through the village of Cune to meet an
asphalt road where you turn right into **Borgofranco d'Ivrea** (**2.0km**).

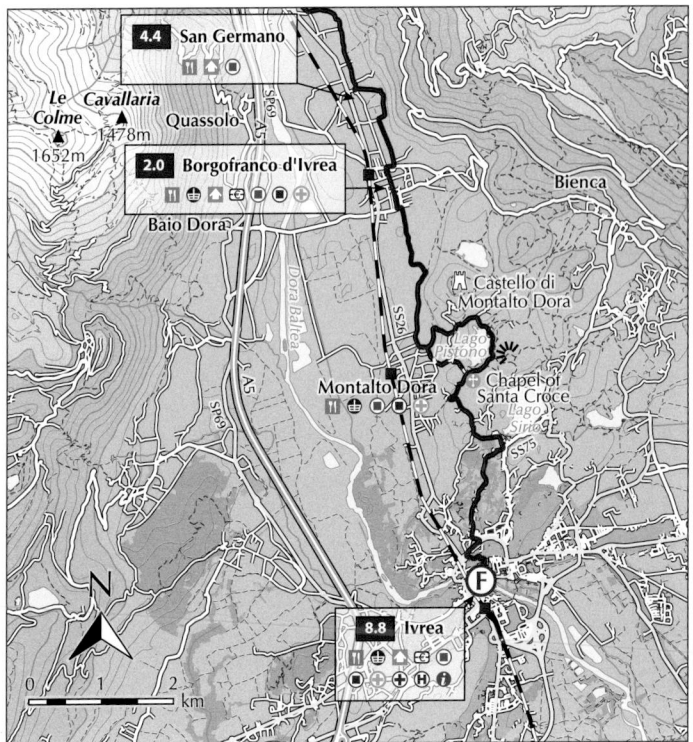

2.0KM BORGOFRANCO D'IVREA (ELEV 258M, POP 3740) ▯ ⊕ ⌂ ⓒ ◉ ◉ ⊕
(907.2KM)

In the 13th c. the three towns of Quinto, Monbueno and Buó merged to form Borgofranco. Fortifications were built after disputes with nearby Ivrea and soldiers from Vercelli, but the only surviving remnant is the **Torre Campanaria** bell tower at the entrance to the old town. The parish church was finished in 1663.

⬤ I Tre Ciliegi 🅿 ℝ €-/-/-/-, Via dei Mulini 24, tel 0125 752216.

Pass through the arch at the base of the church tower adjacent to the large, yellow church and continue as the road spills out onto a gravel track aiming toward the

109

last mountain on the left. For a time, the road continues under trees, then it opens up as it comes to the back streets of **Montalto Dora** (**2.4km**, restaurant, groceries, bus, train, pharmacy). Following the signs, the route now makes a hard left up toward the mountains. In just two blocks comes an option. A right turn takes you to the south of **Lago Pistono**, saving you 1.4km, and rejoins the route at the Chapel of Santa Croce. On the official route come first to the San Rocco Chapel (**0.5km**), and then further up the mountain you can see the picturesque 12th–17th c. **Castello di Montalto Dora** alongside serene Lago Pistono. The best view of the castle is found on the far side of the lake, where a footpath leads you to a wide, gravel drive and the **Chapel of Santa Croce** (**1.8km**).

The gravel road ends and a dirt footpath under trees picks up. Just as you think you are heading straight downhill toward town a path takes off on the left carrying you steeply uphill on sometimes jagged gravel. Finally come to the **SS75** highway (**1.8km**) where you turn left in the direction of 'Milano' and after a time find a narrow, asphalt road on the left between stone walls that leads you to the outskirts of **Ivrea**. Above and ahead you see the tall, brick turrets of the Castle of Ivrea and the smaller white towers of the Cathedral of Ivrea. Enter town with a right turn on the Avenida di Circulazione (**1.6km**) and then turn left into a small piazza at the base of the castle walls. Double back under a yellow arch to climb to the castle and cathedral, or simply continue around the piazza to find the main, pedestrian street and Piazza Ferruccio Nazionale at the center of the old city (**0.6km**).

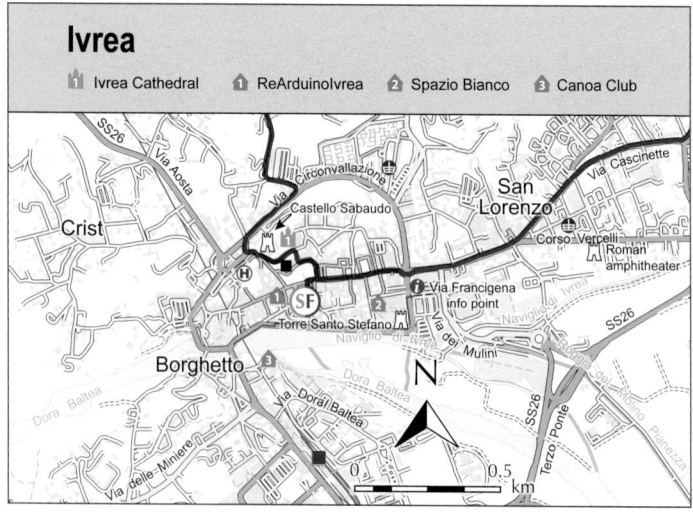

The Castello di Montalto Dora stands on a hill behind Lago Pistono above Ivrea

8.8KM IVREA (ELEV 258M, POP 23,599) 🍴 ⊕ 🏠 🅲 ⊙ ⊙ ⊕ ⊕ ⊕ ❶ (898.4KM)
Settled by Celts from around the 5th c. BC, Ivrea first appears in documents as a
Roman outpost called Eporedia. Remains of a **Roman amphitheater** lie just east
of the city center. After the fall of Rome, it was variously under control of the
Lombards, Franks, and the House of Savoy. Sigeric stayed here, noting its name
as Everi, his Stage XLV. The 11th c. **Cathedral of Ivrea** was rebuilt in 1785 in
Baroque style above town, and the nearby tall, brick Castello Sabaudo of Ivrea
was built in 1357 by Amadeus VI of Savoy. The **Romanesque Tower of St Stephen**
in the SE center city was built in 1041 for a Benedictine abbey located at its base.

Ivrea was headquarters of the once-mighty Olivetti typewriter company, and
in 1970 the town swelled with 90,000 industrial workers. On the last three days
of Carnival each year, the **Battle of the Oranges** is waged. According to legend,
the festival arose when a miller's daughter refused to grant the local duke his
'right' to spend a night with her before her wedding. Instead she chopped off
his head. During the festival townspeople throw some 265,000 oranges at actors
representing local nobility.

🛏 Ostello Canoa Club 🅾 🄿 🄳 🅁 🄺 🄱 🄲 🅆 🅂 5/25, €15/-/50/-, Via Dora
Baltea 1/d, www.ostelloivrea.it, info@ostelloivrea.it, tel 371 5780055. Closed
Jan. Reservation required. Riverside location across from city center.

🛏 B&B La Gusteria 🄿 🅁 1/3, €-/50/65/95, Via IV Martiri 5, tel 0125 45903.

🛏 Spazio Bianco 🅾 🄿 🅁 🄺 🄱 🄲 🅆 🅂 🅉 9/18, €-/80/95/-, Via Patrioti 17, info@
spaziobiancoivrea.it, tel 0125 1961620.

STAGE 13

Ivrea to Viverone

Start	Ivrea, Piazza Ferruccio Nazionale
Finish	Viverone, Town Hall
Distance	20.2km
Total ascent	401m
Total descent	355m
Difficulty	Easy
Duration	5½hr
Percentage paved	81%
Hostels	Burolo 6.4km, Piverone 15.2km, Viverone 20.2km (B&B, rooms)

The stage crosses the Serra Morenica d'Ivrea, an area of moraines that makes for a gently undulating walk marking the transition from Alpine foothills to Po Valley flatlands. Pass two 11th c. churches as you alternate between woods and vineyards to end at the lakeside town of Viverone.

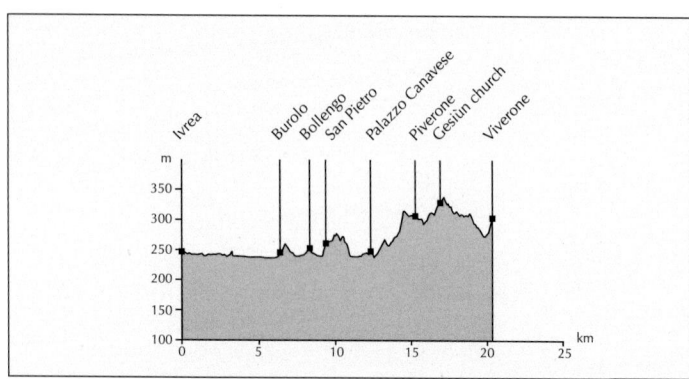

With your back to Ivrea's town hall, turn right and head down the quiet, main pedestrian street, the Via Palestro. This ends at a roundabout, where on the right side you will find a Via Francigena information point with maps and brochures. Follow the SS26

Azeglio sits above Lago di Viverone with the Alps in the background

straight ahead, forking left onto Via Cascinette and continuing until a narrow asphalt path forks left toward **Lago Campagna**, a quiet lake where a briefly steep path takes you along the shore. A left turn after a picnic area (**3.2km**) leads you to a series of gravel farm roads among cornfields and tree plantations, zigzagging before the green ridge straight ahead. Pass below **Burolo** (**3.2km**), a town of new, white stucco homes with red tile roofs above on the ridge.

Follow the **SS76** briefly before forking left to climb along the lower slope of the ridge. After a cemetery and pilgrim rest area (**0.8km**) come to the historic center of picturesque **Bollengo** (**1.1km**, café, groceries). Continue on the quiet **SP263** asphalt road along the foot of the forested ridge. Turn left off the road to come to the 11th-12th c. **Chiesa di San Pietro** (**1.0km**, picnic tables), a fine example of Romanesque architecture whose parish has long since disappeared. The road then sits on a terrace along the ridge, with a tall stone wall on the left and a similar stone wall below to the right. A switchback leads down to the valley floor and soon you see signs for **Palazzo Canavese** (**3.0km**).

12.3KM PALAZZO CANAVESE (ELEV 244M, POP 843) 🇮🇹 Ⓒ ◉ (886.0KM)

In the 12th and 13th c. this town of Roman origins found itself caught in **continual battles** between Ivrea and Vercelli. The distinctive tall brick clock tower with a pointed roof and four archways at its base presides over a large piazza with benches. The architecture is typical of Canavese villages – stucco-covered brick two-storey houses with balconies often covered by wide wooden eaves below roofs of red clay tiles. (Bus 351 to Viverone www.atapspa.it.)

⌂ **Il Granello di Senape** 🄿🅃 🅁 🄺 1/3, €-/-/-/55, Via Carlo Alberto 5, tel 366 4906064.

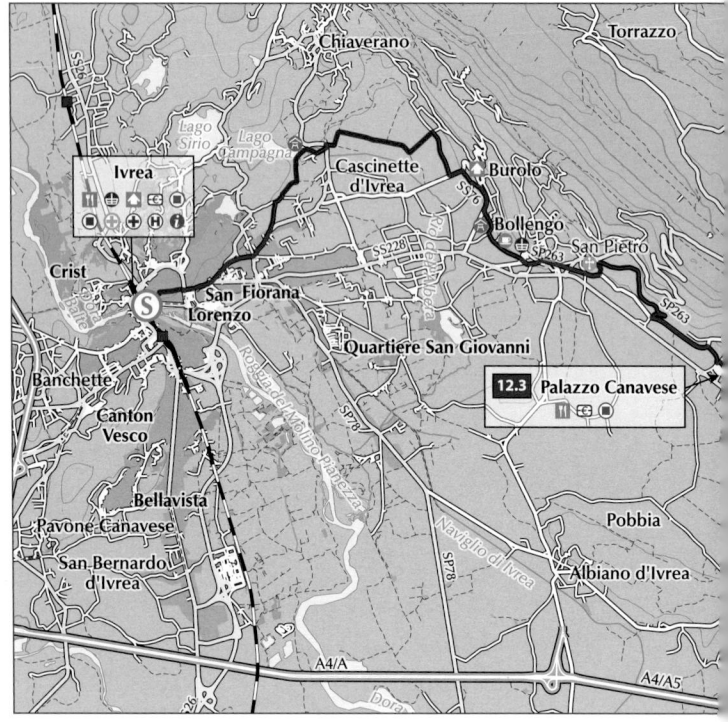

Turn left before the tower and follow Via del Castello down and around, exiting town down steps and soon following the **Via Piverone** highway. Come to a summit followed by signs indicating you are entering **Piverone**.

2.9KM PIVERONE (ELEV 305M, POP 1381) 🍴 🛏 ◉ (883.2KM)

Piverone's name, rather than being a variant of nearby Viverone, is said to come from the 'peppery' character of its residents (*peperone* tr: 'pepper'). In the 13th c. the ruling magistrate of Vercelli fortified the town with a bastion of three towers, one of which remains at the entrance to the old town as its squat clock tower. A tower of the former **Church of San Pietro** remains as well.

🛏 **Ostello la Steiva** ⊙ 🅳 🅡 🅚 4/30, €15/-/-/-, Via Giovanni Flecchia, ostellolasteiva@gmail.com, tel 339 7219024.

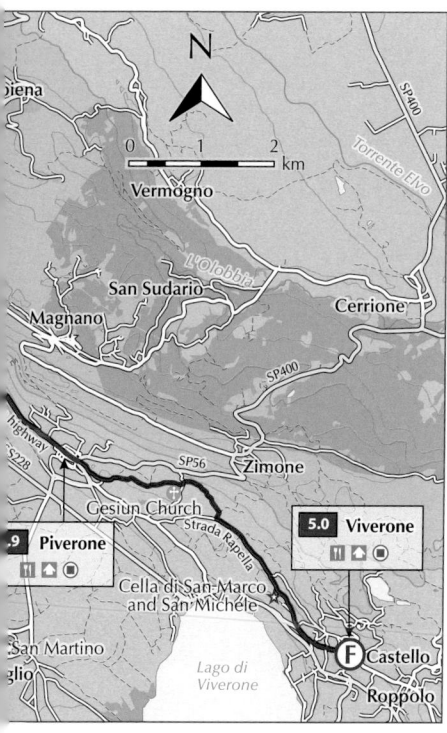

At the end of the old city, go straight onto Strada Novello and just after passing through town see your first glimpse of **Lago di Viverone** on the right, with lakeside Azeglio on the opposite shore and, on a clear day, a view of the Alps behind. A left turn takes you among pleasant vineyard roads to the ruins of tiny **Gesiùn Church** (**1.7km**). This 11th c. church is an important example of the Romanesque Canavese architectural style. It was once center of an active village and parish. Continue on the gravel road behind farms and among vineyards and woods until a left turn puts you on the asphalt **Strada Rapella**. As you near Viverone a tall tower on the right marks the site of the one-time monastery, **Cella di San Marco and San Michele**, now a winery. The road turns to cobblestones as it climbs to the center of **Viverone** (**3.4km**).

5.0KM VIVERONE (ELEV 302M, POP 1404) 🍴 🛏 ◉ **(878.2KM)**
Archeologists discovered Bronze Age artifacts from a prehistoric lakeside settlement under nearby **Lago di Viverone**, earning it status as a UNESCO World Heritage Site. Along the lake is a pleasant promenade, with a restaurant and hotel. As you leave town, pass the distinctive brick façade of the 18th c. **Church of San Rocco**, pilgrim saint.

🛏 La Locanda di Sant'Antonio Abate ◉ Pr R K Br W S 3/9, €-/60/70/100, Piazza Zerbola 2, info@bbsantantonio.eu, tel 349 4161428.

🛏 ▲ Camping La Rocca ◉ Pr Do R K Br W S 1/4, €-/65/65/90, Via Lungo Lago 35, www.la-rocca.org, laroccaviverone@hotmail.com, tel 347 7107146 or 0161 98416. Closed Nov–Feb. Reservation required. Tent camping plus caravan and apartment rental. Swimming pool. Lakeside location.

STAGE 14
Viverone to Santhià

Start	Viverone, Town Hall
Finish	Santhià, Town Hall
Distance	16.4km
Total ascent	150m
Total descent	268m
Difficulty	Easy
Duration	4½hr
Percentage paved	65%
Hostels	Roppolo 1.2km (B&B), Cavaglià 5.0km, Santhià 16.4km

After crossing the last of the Serra Morenica d'Ivrea you come to the first stretches of the Po Valley. Here canals separate fields mostly of corn, peas and beans. The vast agricultural territory is dotted by sparse towns and the most dramatic landscape features are the superhighway and high-speed train viaduct.

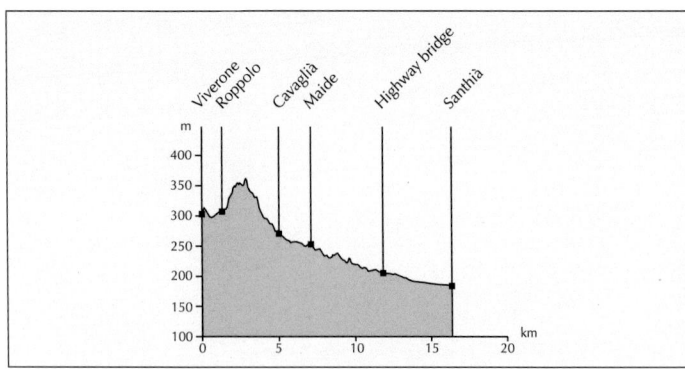

Continue along the main street, climbing through the narrow lanes and compact homes of central Viverone to pass the tall brick Church of San Rocco and head straight out onto the asphalt **SP419**. Pass a **cemetery** (**0.6km**) with a white church at its core and soon come to the white church tower of tiny central **Roppolo** (**0.7km**)

1.2KM ROPPOLO (ELEV 306M, POP 877) ⬛⬛⬤ (876.9KM)

Roppolo is an agricultural settlement that traces its roots back to Ligurian tribes in the first millennium BC. The 10th c. **Castello di Roppolo** was built on Roman foundations during ongoing wars against Ivrea. In the mid-15th c., Bernardo di Mazzè, a knight wounded in battle, disappeared after entering the castle under the care of Ludovico di Valperga, Lord of Castello di Roppolo. In 1459 Ludovico was found guilty of the knight's murder, but the victim was not found until castle renovations in 1800, when the body of a knight dressed in full armor was discovered entombed in a castle wall. (Bus to Piverone and Cavaglià: www.atapspa.it.)

⬛ **La Casa del Movimento Lento** Pr Do R Br W S 2/7, €22/50/62/81, Via Al Castello 8, www.casa.movimentolento.it/en, casa@movimentolento.it, tel 335 7979550 or 0161 987866. Linens €5 per person. Closed 1 Nov–2 Feb. €12 dinner avail. at nearby restaurant Wed–Sun, otherwise by delivery.

The route points you up the hill toward the château-like **Castello di Roppolo** above town but turns a few hundred meters shy of it at the pink Casa Maria Ausiliatrice church (**0.9km**). In a wood after a cemetery a right fork takes you down

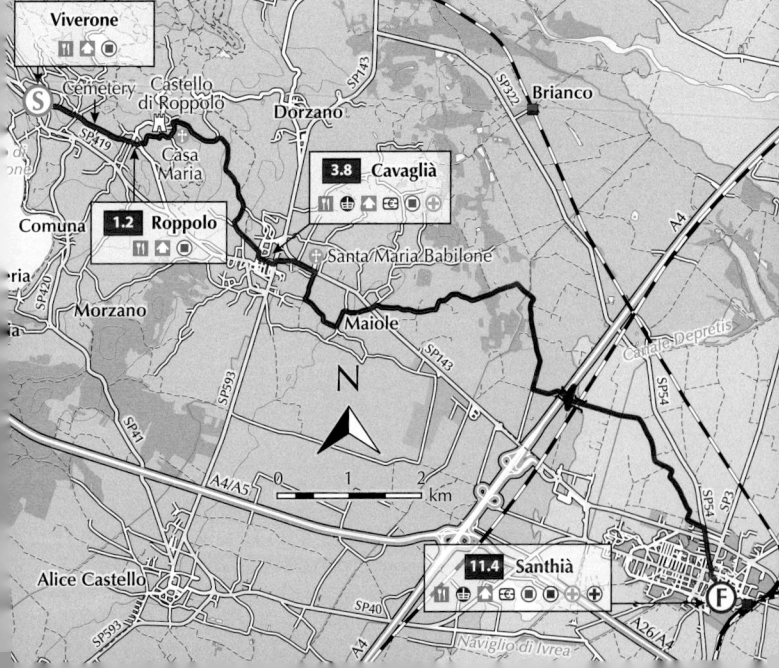

fairly steeply on a shady gravel road. After a community sports field come to the outskirts of colorful **Cavaglià** (**2.9km**).

3.8KM CAVAGLIÀ (ELEV 270M, POP 3641) ⚏ ⊕ ⚠ Ⓒ ⊚ ⊕ (873.1KM)

Last of the towns on the Serra Morenica d'Ivrea before the flat fields and farms of the Po Valley, Cavaglià rests at a crossroads between the Biella and Po Valleys. This location has led some to believe the town's name derives from its use as a horse station by the Romans (Latin: *caballo*, Italian: *cavallo*). The 18th c. brick **Castello Rondolino** was restored to its medieval style in the 19th c. Most unusual of landmarks is the grand, round 18th–19th c. **Church of San Rocco**, with a depiction of the pilgrim saint above the entrance.

🛏 Ostello comunale ◎ ◻ 1/7, €Donation, V. Generale Salino, urp.cavaglia@ ptb.provincia.biella.it, tel 0161 967016, 320 073 6509 or 0161 96033. Keys at townhall or children's nursery Il Salotto d'Argento. By reservation only.

Leave town on pink cobblestones toward the bright cupola of the cemetery church, **Santa Maria di Babilone**, veering off the highway before the church toward the farms and cornfields. Here see for the first time what will be common in the Po Valley – a field of corn (or rice or peas or another grain) with an irrigation canal beside it. The route turns into a pleasant asphalt road, often lined with trees, that comes first to the outskirts of **Maiole** (**2.1km**, no services), then meanders through the countryside in pleasant and flat farmland, sometimes among trees.

After a time, the road turns to gravel and the vastness of the flat terrain begins to be clear. Turn left onto another gravel road toward the A4 highway and railway viaducts (**4.7km**), which you cross. Now a series of cornfields begins, each bounded by an irrigation canal, until you reach houses and finally the asphalt **SP54**. Follow this to

The Church of Santa Maria di Babilone with the last peaks of the Alps in the distance

the right toward the main piazza of **Santhià**, which is one block to the left just before the main pedestrian street, Corso Nuova Italia.

11.4KM SANTHIÀ (ELEV 183M, POP 8457) ⬛ ⬤ ⬛ Ⓒ ⓞ ⬤ ⊕ ⊕ (861.8KM)

The town's first name was Victumulus, derived from the name of its inhabitants, the Ichtumuli. Romans called this town Vicus Viae Longae – Vicus of the Long Road – but in the Lombard period it was dedicated to the 3rd c. martyr Saint Agatha, which is root of its current name. Sigeric visited here as his Stage XLIV Sancta Agatha. With few natural defenses, Santhià was frequently subject to invading armies. In the Renaissance period it had extensive battlements, which have now completely disappeared. The current orientation of the town shows its historic connection to the trade routes over the Alps, with its central road on a line between the Alps and the road's next major stop at Vercelli. Santhià's oldest edifice is its 12th c. **Romanesque bell tower**. At the adjacent **Collegiate Church of Saint Agatha** is a prized 10-piece polyptych by the 16th c. artist Gerolamo Giovenone. In 1997 Santhià received a bronze medal for military valor in the Partisan struggle during WWII.

🏠 **Ostello Amici della Via Francigena di Santhià** Ⓞ Ⓓⓞ Ⓡ Ⓢ Ⓩ 5/20, €10(+€15+ in winter)/-/-/-, Via Madonnetta 2/Corso Nuovo Italia 134, www.santhiasullaviafrancigena.it, info@santhiasullaviafrancigena.it, tel 388 6333865. Adjacent to cathedral, with shops and restaurants nearby. Keys at Café della Piazza or city police.

🏠 **Bed and Breakfast La Sosta** Ⓟⓡ Ⓡ Ⓑⓡ Ⓦ Ⓢ 2/6, €-/35/60/75, Strada Vecchia di Biella 6, www.eng.lasosta.eu, gabry.corti@gmail.com, tel 335 481452. Closed winter. Reservation required.

STAGE 15
Santhià to Vercelli

Start	Santhià, Town Hall
Finish	Vercelli, Piazza Cavour
Distance	27.5km
Total ascent	85m
Total descent	137m
Difficulty	Moderate
Duration	7hr
Percentage paved	33%
Hostels	San Germano Vercellese 8.5km, Vercelli 27.5km

A straightforward day of zigzagging among rice paddies, with the occasional surprise field of corn or soy. After the pedestrian bridge over the train tracks at Santhià there are few structures above the horizon until you reach Vercelli, whose compact and atmospheric center makes up for any lack of scenery getting there. Pack plenty of food and water for a 19km stretch without services between San Germano and Vercelli.

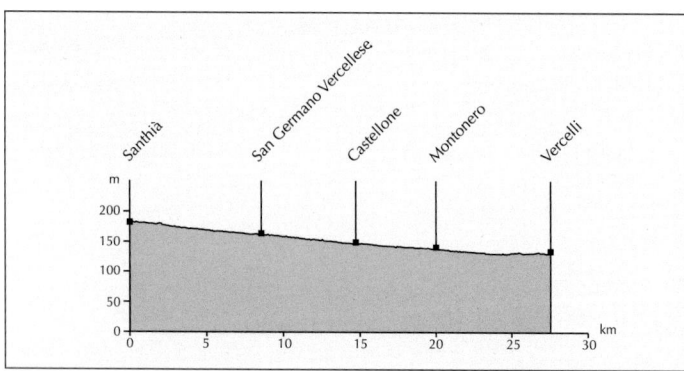

A block south of the town hall is the Corso Nuovo Italia, which you follow left in the direction of the train station, crossing the tracks out of town. A left turn puts you on a road toward the highway, which you reach just after the **Chapel of San Rocco**. Join

Looking back over fields of rice to San Germano Vercellese

the highway very briefly before turning left onto an asphalt road that crosses the train tracks on a bridge. From the bridge there is a good vantage point over the vast, flat, agricultural terrain of the valley. After passing a pilgrim rest area at a farm (**3.8km**), turn right and begin to see in the distance the tall dome of San Germano's parish church. Cross a wide canal, **Canale Cavour**, on a three-arch bridge, pass a small **shrine** (**0.6km**) to saints Grato and Appolonia, zigzag through fields, then turn right onto the **SP52**. Cross under the railroad tracks at the train station of **San Germano Vercelese** (**2.2km**) and go straight ahead to the center of town.

8.5KM SAN GERMANO VERCELLESE (ELEV 161M, POP 1734) 🍴 ⊕ 🏠 ◉ ◉ (853.3KM)

The 18th c. **San Germano church** is the town's most conspicuous monument, its slender dome reaching a height of 90m from its base. The church holds a working 1775 Serassi pipe organ, finest in the region. A bell tower is all that remains of the Renaissance-era fortifications.

🛏 Ostello Pellegrini Lungo la Via Francigena 🄳ₒ 🆁 🅺 🄱ᵣ 🆆 🆂 🆉 2/5, €15/-/-/-, Corso Giacomo Matteotti 60, segreteria@comune.sangermanovercellese.vc.it, tel 0161 95134. Open Apr–Oct. Reservation required.

Following signs, cross through a park with a WWI memorial and then cross a bridge at an unusual confluence of two canal channels. The route follows the south side of the SP11, then quickly crosses to the opposite side of the highway where you follow alongside the train tracks (**3.5km**) for a while before turning right at a small **marsh** (**1.3km**). The rice fields around Vercelli host a lively assortment of waterfowl, including mallard, tufted ducks, bitterns, kingfishers, cormorants, pochards, grey herons, coots, moorhens, egrets, night herons and the very rare red herons. Turn back toward the highway just before the large, yellow brick prison-like farm complex of **Castellone** (**1.5km**).

Castellone is an example of a *cascina a corte*, a centralized, sometimes-fortified farm characteristic of the Po Valley since at least the 13th c. In these walled clusters, family groupings of *contadini*, or peasants, lived and worked their entire lives under control of the manor owner. Bernardo Bertolucci famously depicted the 20th c. decline of Po Valley *cascine* life in his epic movie *1900*.

Continue across the SP11 to more rice paddies, along with occasional fields of soy. Vercelli is now visible on the horizon to the left. Go through a rusted gate to continue among the fields, returning briefly to the highway and passing the derelict **Cascine Strà** (**3.2km**). Zigzag on sometimes-ragged gravel roads to the farm

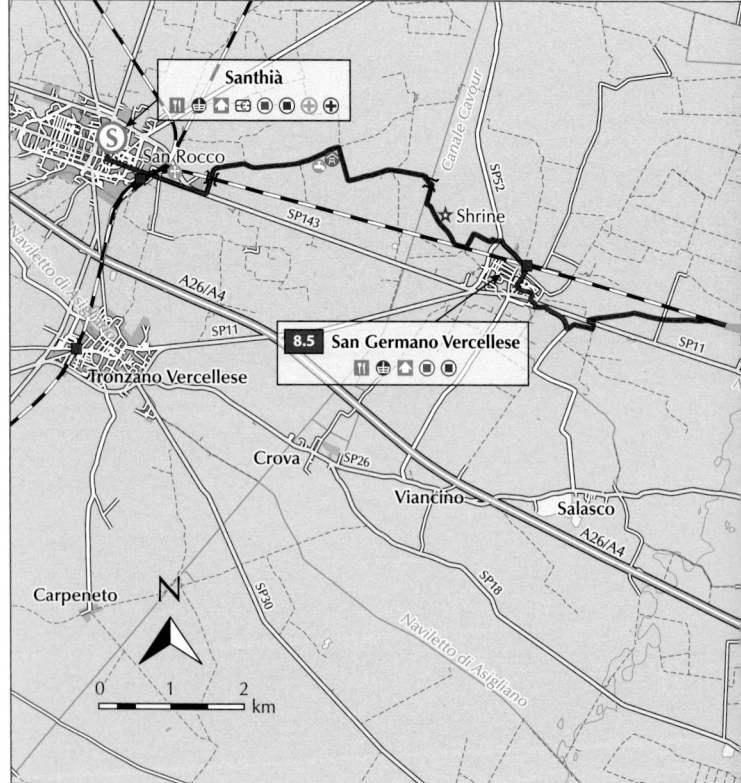

settlement of **Montonero** (**2.0km**, water fountain, ⬥ **B&B Montonero**, mritabaloss-ino@hotmail.com, 346 233 9585, €20 per pilgrim) with its small church and nearby *cascina*. Continue among rice fields and thread through a canal gate structure to meet the busy **Tangenziale Ovest** highway (**4.5km**), which you carefully cross before heading straight into town.

A right on Via Lager takes you to Via Trino. Turn left, following the road across the train tracks and then turn right on busy Largo Cagliari. Come to Piazza Vittorio Emanuele where you cross the park and follow Corso Libertà, the main pedestrian street of **Vercelli**, for a half dozen blocks until you see the cafés of spacious Piazza Cavour (**3.1km**), a block to the left.

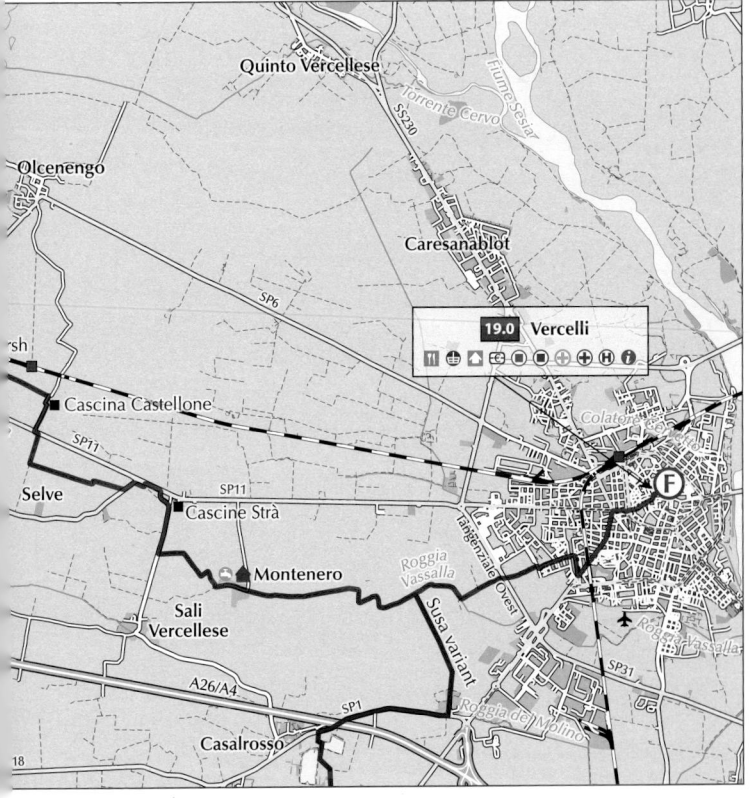

A statue of the Risorgamento figure Camillo Cavour
stands in the central piazza of Vercelli

The brick towers of Vercelli's Sant'Andrea Basilica

19.0KM VERCELLI (ELEV 131M, POP 46,552) ⏹ 🌐 ⬆ 🅒 ⏺ ⏺ ⊕ ⊕ ⊞ ❶
(834.3KM)

Vercelli is an important agricultural center. Sometimes called 'The Rice Capital of Europe', the crop has been grown here since the Renaissance era. Vercelli traces its roots to 600 BC when it was a key settlement of the Libici, a Ligurian tribe. Called Vercellae by the Romans, Gaius Marius defeated the Cimbri and Teutones nearby in the Battle of Vercellae in 101 BC and here 500 years later Flavius Stilicho annihilated invading Goths. Many Roman ruins can be found in the area, including an amphitheater and hippodrome. Fortress walls surrounded the town in the Middle Ages, when it was first a possession of the Lombards and later the Milanese, the Marquesses of Monferrato and the House of Savoy. Sigeric visited here as his Stage XLIII Vercel.

The imposing 17th–18th c. **Vercelli Cathedral** was built over much earlier predecessors, and its library contains the 10th c. Vercelli Book, one of the most important Old English manuscripts. The 13th c. brick **Romanesque Sant'Andrea Basilica** is preserved largely intact and is a fine example of plain but elegant Cistercian architecture. Its adjacent bell tower is from the 15th c. and the Cistercian monastery cloister dates from the 16th. Vercelli's cozy and atmospheric city center and volunteer-run hostel make it a pilgrim favorite.

🛏 Hospitale Sancti Eusebi ⏹ 🅳🅔 🅡 🅚 🅓🅻 🆆 🆂 4/23, €Donativo, Vicolo degli Alciati 4, info@amicidellaviafrancigena.vercelli.it, tel 334 2386911. Near Church of Santa Caterina in city center. Open 21 Mar–31 Oct. Check-in 14:00–19:00.

🛏 La Terrazza 🅟🆃 🅡 🅱🅵 6/12, €-/56/65/-, Via San Paolo 18, www. laterrazzavercelli.it, info@laterrazzavercelli.it, tel 347 8559521.

VARIANT
Val di Susa to Vercelli

Start	Montgenèvre or Mont Cenis
Finish	Vercelli
Distance	194.8km (Mont Cenis option 175.0km)
Duration	7–8 days (Mont Cenis option 6–7 days)

An ancient manuscript, the *Itinerarium Burdigalense*, recounts the oldest known Christian pilgrimage, the journey of an anonymous pilgrim who rode on horseback from Bordeaux to the Holy Land and back in the years 333–334. The portion of his or her route that crosses the Susa Pass over the Alps and meets the Via Francigena at Vercelli is preserved in the official Susa Valley Variant, an alternative to the Great St Bernard Pass that is especially useful for pilgrims from southeast France.

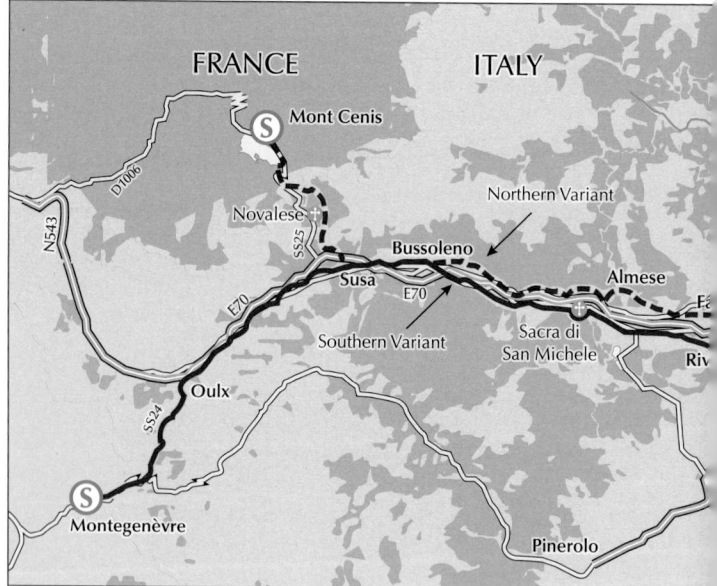

Two mountain passes cross the Alps west of Susa – one at Mont Cenis in the north and the other at Col de Montgenèvre to the south. From France, the Mont Cenis route is approached via Modane in the Arc valley and Montgenèvre is approached from Briançon. The two options converge in Susa, an ancient hub for travelers crossing the Alps. The path divides in two once again at Bussoleno – splitting to traverse either side of Riparia River. They join back together at the confluence of the Dora Riparia and Po rivers in metropolitan Turin, capital of Piemonte and one of Italy's important cultural, historic and economic centers. The town holds many cultural and historical delights. Soon after Turin paths follow the familiar agricultural topography of the Po Valley as it joins the Via Francigena at Vercelli.

Alps to Susa

Stage 1a: Mont Cenis to Susa (26.9km) Visit the Novalesa Abbey, an active Benedictine monastery founded in 726 with several adjacent chapels of 8th–11th c. origin.

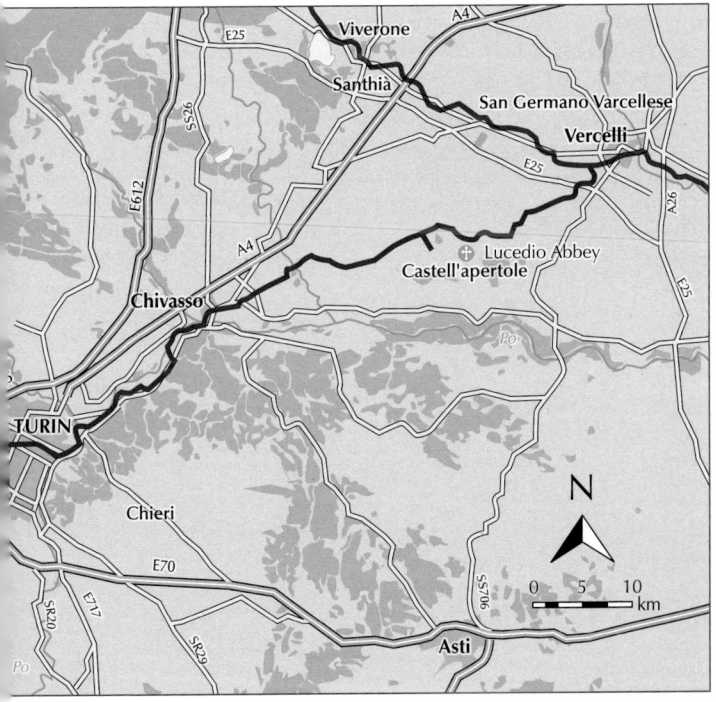

Stage 1b&c: Col de Montgenèvre to Oulx (19.4km) and Oulx to Susa (27.2km) Walk forested trails amidst Alpine scenery to the city of Susa, an ancient mountain gateway city.

Susa to Turin: Southern Variant

Stage 2a: Susa to Sacra San Michele (29km) Atop Monte Pirchiriano, the setting of this 10th–13th c. monastery is one of Italy's most spectacular. Sacra San Michele holds a masterpiece of 12th c. sculpture, the Porta dello Zodiaco.

Stage 3a: Sacra di San Michele to Rivoli (16.1km)

Stage 4a: Rivoli to Fabbrichetta (7.9km) to Turin (6.2km) While Turin is a modern, industrial metropolis, its center city features Baroque architecture from the Savoy period. Adjacent to the 15th c. Turin Cathedral is the Chapel of the Holy Shroud, where the Shroud of Turin currently resides but is available for viewing only on special occasions.

Susa to Turin: Northern Variant

Stage 2b: Bussoleno to Almese (25km)

Stage 3b: Almese to Turin Fabbrichetta (22.5km)

Stage 4b: Fabbrichetta to Turin (6.2km)

Turin to Vercelli

Stage 5: Turin to Chivasso (29.5km) Now fully in the Po Valley the scenery quickly turns to vast agricultural fields, while Chivasso holds the statue-adorned 15th c. Collegiate Church of Santa Maria Assunta.

Stage 6: Chivasso to Castell'Apertole (29km) Though Castell'Apertole is a small farming village, just 7km away is Lucedio Abbey, a former Cistercian monastery founded in 1124.

Stage 7: Castell'Apertole to Vercelli (30.4km) The route travels through farmland to arrive in Vercelli from the southwest.

For more information on this variant see: www.turismotorino.org/en/experiences/francigena-routes-piedmont and www.viefrancigene.org/en/mappe/#itinerarioValleSusa

SECTION 4: LOMBARDIA

A few stands of trees break up the fields of rice between Vercelli and Robbio (Stage 16)

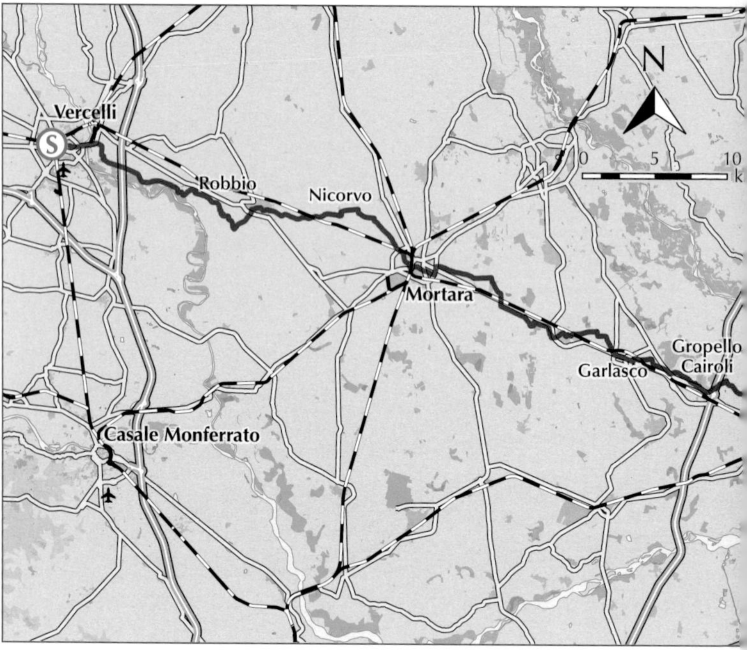

Two pilgrims walk along the Ciclovia del Po after Corte Sant'Andrea (Stage 22)

Section 4 Lombardia

Although modern and cosmopolitan Milan is capital of Lombardia (Lombardy in English), the route feels centuries removed from the modern world as it travels through grainfields of the flat and fertile Po Valley. Remnants of the traditional economy that predominated here for centuries are still visible in the walled farming villages, and contrast with the youthful energy of the university town of Pavia.

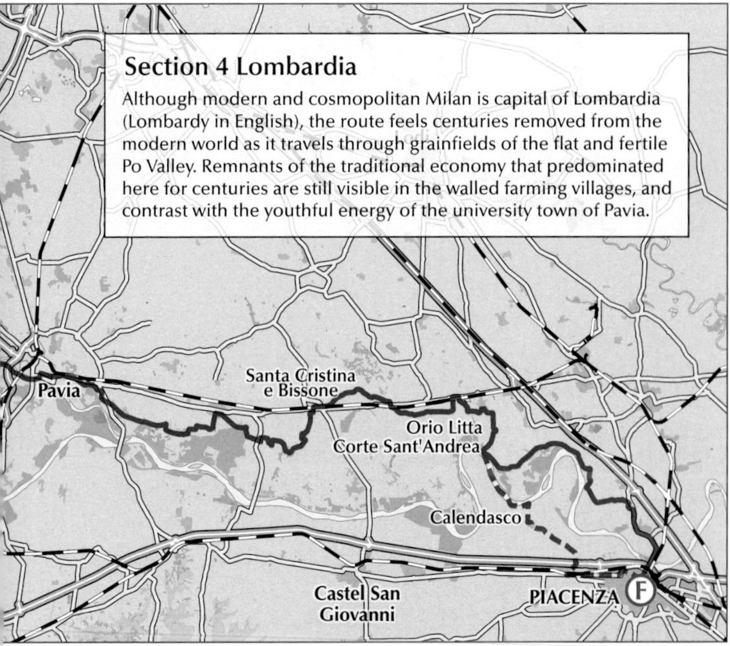

Pavia

Santa Cristina e Bissone

Orio Litta
Corte Sant'Andrea

Calendasco

Castel San Giovanni

PIACENZA **F**

STAGE 16
Vercelli to Robbio

Start	Vercelli, Piazza Cavour
Finish	Robbio, Church of San Pietro
Distance	18.6km
Total ascent	195m
Total descent	208m
Difficulty	Easy
Duration	5hr
Percentage paved	31%
Hostels	Palestro 11.0km (B&B), Robbio 18.6km

Small rice fields are sprinkled among larger rice fields separated by narrow canals or wide canals in this flat stage that may inspire dreams of risotto. The town of Palestro offers a mid-stage respite. Prepare for morning and evening mosquitoes after damp weather.

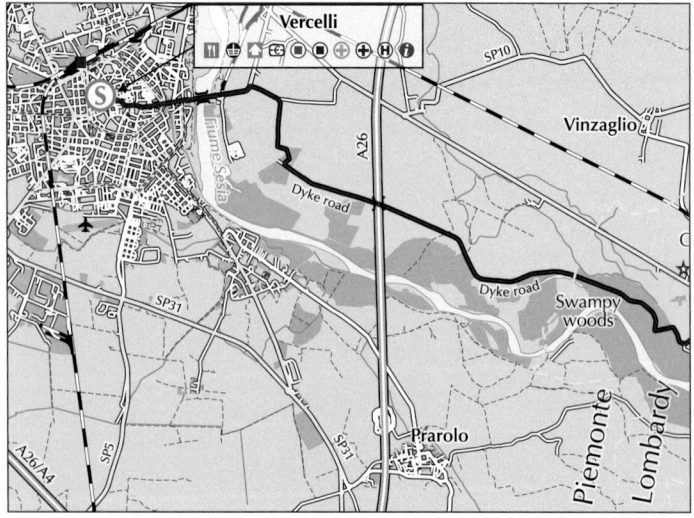

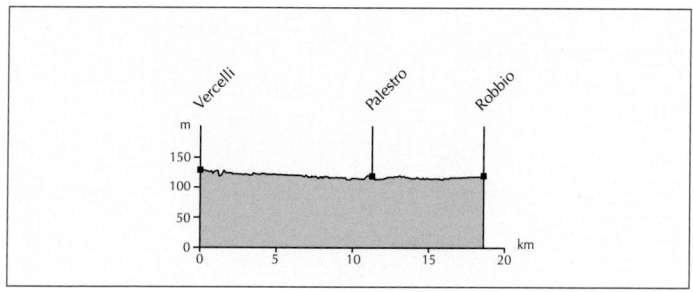

Beginning in Piazza Cavour, face the statue of Emilio Cavour and veer ahead to the right to pick up Vercelli's main pedestrian street, Corso Libertà. Continue as the street becomes a highway which then crosses the **Sesia River** (**1.1km**). Remain on the highway another few hundred meters until a road branches off on the right after a curve. Now enter a few fields of corn, but before long find yourself almost exclusively among fields of rice. Just before a tree plantation turn left onto a tall **dyke** (**2.4km**), and follow it under the low **A26** highway viaduct and through swampy woods. Here you cross from the Italian region of Piemonte into Lombardia. As the dyke ends turn left into **Palestro**, whose services are clustered around the yellow-towered Church of San Martino di Tours on the SS596, two blocks north of the route.

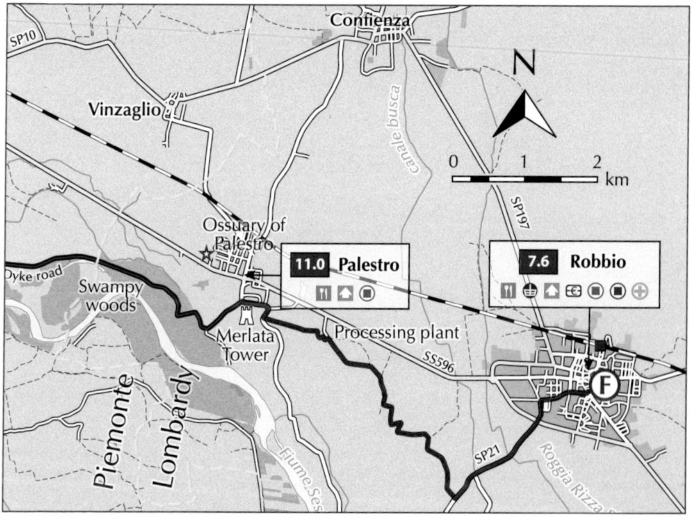

133

A WWI monument stands below the San Martino Church in Palestro

11.0KM PALESTRO (ELEV 120M, POP 2022) 🍴 ⛺ ◉ (823.3KM)
Though the area was settled in prehistory, Palestro is first mentioned in documents from the year AD 999, when it was given by the bishops of Vercelli to Emperor Otto III. In 1859 it was site of the Battle of Palestro in which the French and Italian forces defeated a portion of the Austrian army. In this clash King Victor Emmanuel II of Italy is believed to be the last European monarch to ride into battle. The tall and stately **Ossuary of Palestro** contains remains of the casualties and commemorates the battle, which is remembered each year on the last Sunday of May. The crenellated **Tower of Merlata** is what remains of the town's fortifications, which at one time included a pilgrim hospice.

⌂ **B&B Ospitaliere La Torre Merlata** 🅿 🆁 🅱 🅳 🅆 🆂 2/3, €-/50/70/100, Via Vodano 5, www.latorremerlata.it/english, castellaniambra@gmail.com, tel 349 7909044. Located in 12th c. tower. Closed Nov–Mar. Camping available. Reservation required.

A left turn just after town puts you onto sometimes-overgrown narrow roads and pathways among rice fields for the next few kilometers. Here you zag and zig at right angles among the fields, while admiring the much more direct SP596 that efficiently connects Palestro with Robbio. After nearing the highway at a **processing plant**, come

Intricate brickwork adorns the structure of the 12th c. Church of San Pietro in Robbio

to a complex intersection of canals that you cross on a series of tricky, small bridges. Continue along the rice paddies until the final gravel road (**2.5km**) ends at a narrow **SP21** asphalt road (**2.5km**). Turn left here and follow the road into **Robbio**, turning right onto Via Rosasco, then veering right onto Via Cernaia, which leads directly to the Church of San Pietro (**2.6km**), with the cafés of central Piazza 1 Maggio just two blocks to the left.

7.6KM ROBBIO (ELEV 118M, POP 6161) ⏹ ⊕ ⛺ 🄴 ⓜ ⓟ ⊕ (815.7KM)
Evidence of habitation here goes back to Neolithic times, and archeological expeditions unearthed a storage chamber filled with Bronze Age axes. Romans knew Robbio as Redobium and in the 11th c. it became property of the De Rodobio family. Prized among its buildings is the 12th c. **Church of San Pietro**, in the brick Lombard Romanesque style. The church houses 16th c. frescoes by Tommasino da Mortara. Adjacent to the church at one time was a pilgrim hospital. The Gothic-era **Church of San Michele** holds frescoes from the 15th c. and the **Church of Santo Stefano** has an elaborate wooden choir and richly detailed mosaic floor.

⛺ **Ostello Comunale** 🅳🅾 🆁 🅺 🅒 🆂 1/4, €Donation, Piazza Martiri della Libertà 2, tel 339 1265426 or 348 5538337. Located in the city hall. Closed Nov–Apr.

STAGE 17
Robbio to Mortara

Start	Robbio, Church of San Pietro
Finish	Mortara, Piazza della Libertà
Distance	14.5km
Total ascent	49m
Total descent	59m
Difficulty	Easy
Duration	3¾hr
Percentage paved	56%
Hostels	Nicorvo 6.5km, Mortara 14.5km

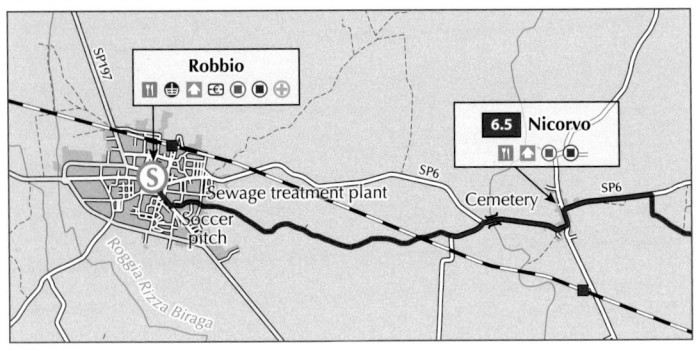

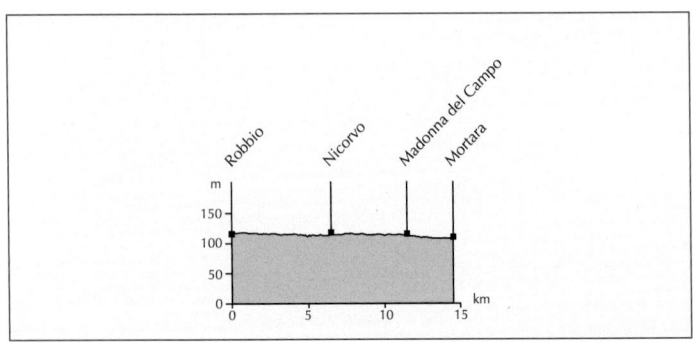

A walk among rice and grain fields, with vast distances between buildings and trees. Nicorvo offers the only hope of a mid-stage café, but the vagaries of its opening times suggest it's best to come fully equipped with food for the entire distance.

From the Church of San Pietro, follow the Via Mortara straight out of town. In three blocks turn left onto the Via Roggetta that leads among the workshops and small factories of the industrial district of Robbio. Pass a **soccer pitch** on your right and follow the asphalt road as it leads out among rice fields and small warehouses. The road turns to gravel after the **sewage treatment plant** and buildings become sparse. At first a large cornfield suggests you are nearing the southern limits of the water-thirsty rice region, but soon rice once again predominates. The road is well-graded and flat and continues on, crossing the train tracks (**2.6km**). Not long afterward the gravel becomes asphalt. Go straight through an intersection, crossing two canals in rapid succession before

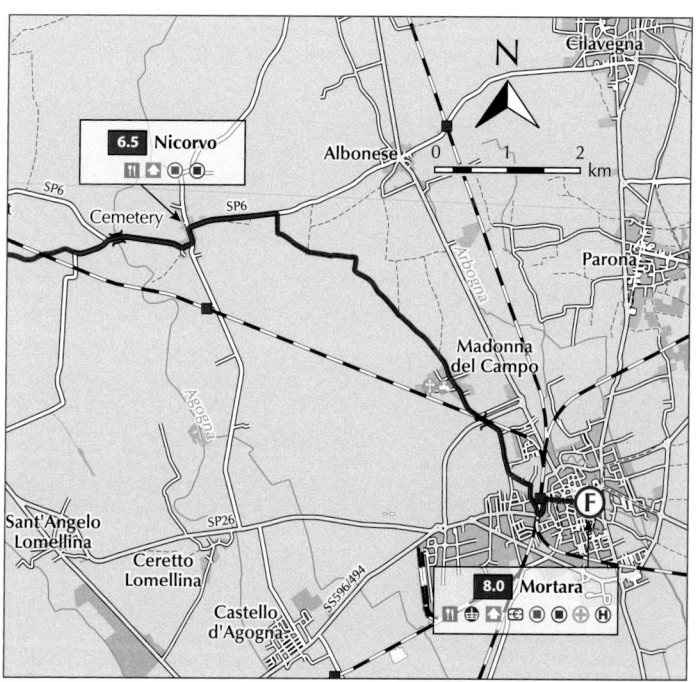

turning right on the narrow **SP6** highway. Walk carefully as the road narrows before crossing the **Agogna River** (**1.1km**) and pass a **cemetery** before turning left to arrive at the heart of **Nicorvo** (**1.3km**).

6.5KM NICORVO (ELEV 114M, POP 370) ⓘ ⌂ ◉ ◉ (**809.2KM**)
The first documented mention of Nicorvo comes from the year 960. Its **Church of San Terenziano** holds 20th c. frescoes and a 16th c. canvas of Madonna and child. Across the street is the 18th c. **Santuario Madonna del Patrocinio**, or Madonnina, with a 16th c. Madonna and child fresco.

🏠 Ospitale San Giacomo e delle Madonnina ◉ Pr K Br S 3/8, €Donation, Piazza Libertà 4, ospitale.nicorvo.francigena@gmail.com, tel 371 5174578.

The track makes a right turn at the Madonnina chapel and then remains on the SP6 highway for the next 1km before turning right on gravel and joining a series of farm roads. After a time the road turns to grass with occasional deep ruts, sometimes filled with mud. A vast horizon surrounds you now on all sides, with only utility towers, scattered trees and barns raising their profiles above the fields. The gravel track changes

Mortara's 14th c. brick Cathedral of San Lorenzo holds several prized works of art

to asphalt at a collection of homes, which is the start of **Madonna del Campo** (5.0km, water). The 12th c. Romanesque Church of Santa Maria del Campo houses frescoes by 15th c. artist Giovanni Battista Crespi. After a visit to the church with its benches and water fountain continue on the road through the village, soon spying the outline of **Mortara**, framed under the highway bridge ahead.

Continue on the asphalt road as it leads across the train tracks and under the highway bridge. Follow a series of narrow asphalt drives to enter the surprisingly large town, coming to the train tracks, which you cross along with an arterial road in a long tunnel. Turn right after the train station to find the main street, Corso Garibaldi, and the central Municipio at Piazza Della Libertà (3.0km).

8.0KM MORTARA (ELEV 108M, POP 15,325) 🍴 ⊕ 🏛 🅲 ◉ ◎ ⊕ ⊛ (801.2KM)
In Roman times the town was named Pulchra Silva, but legends say that after the bloody 773 battle between Charlemagne and the Lombard King Desiderius, the name was changed to Mortis Ara (tr: 'altar of the dead') and then Mortara. Charlemagne established a monastery at the Church of Sant'Eusebio (now called the **Abbazie di Sant'Albino** after its first abbot) and buried two of his favorite knights and many of his soldiers there. In the Renaissance era the town was fortified by walls in the shape of a star. In the First War of Independence in 1849 Mortara was seized by the Austrians, leading to the Battle of Novara where the Austrians were victorious over the Piedmontese forces.

From the 11th–19th c. Mortara was home to the Mortariensis Ecclesia monastic movement, which once held vast lands and 14 monasteries throughout the region. The 16th c. **Church of Santa Croce** is the last surviving testament of this influential order. A block behind Piazza della Libertà is the 14th c. brick **Cathedral of San Lorenzo** which houses several significant Renaissance paintings by Lanino, Procaccini and others, as well as a large altar by Cerano and a wooden nativity scene of 80 characters by Crespi. Modern Mortara is an agricultural and commercial center, and is famous for its goose and pork salami, called **Salame d'Oca**.

🏠 Abbazia Sant'Albino 🅳🅾 🆁 🅱🅵 🅳🅵 🆂 🆉 1/12, €20/-/-/-, Via Sant'Albino 782, www.abbaziasantalbino.it, abbazia.santalbino@gmail.com, tel 038 4298609, 348 4283403. Closed 10 Dec –31 Jan. Dinner incl. 2 courses and wine. On the trail 1.5km beyond city center.

🏠 Foresteria Re Artù 🅾 🅿🆃 🆁 🅱🅵 🅲🅵 🆂 🆉 5/8, €-/55/75/95, Via Contrada della Torre 11, foresteriareartu@libero.it, tel 335 6003750.

STAGE 18
Mortara to Garlasco

Start	Mortara, Piazza della Libertà
Finish	Garlasco, Piazza Repubblica
Distance	20.1km
Total ascent	46m
Total descent	63m
Difficulty	Easy
Duration	5hr
Percentage paved	44%
Hostels	Sant'Albino Monastery 1.5km, Tromello 14.8km, Garlasco 20.1km

The fields of rice begin to thin out and are replaced by fields of corn. A lack of signage near Garlasco can put you onto the busy SP206 highway, so read the map and directions carefully as you near town. The intermediary stops at Remondò and Tromello offer some refreshment.

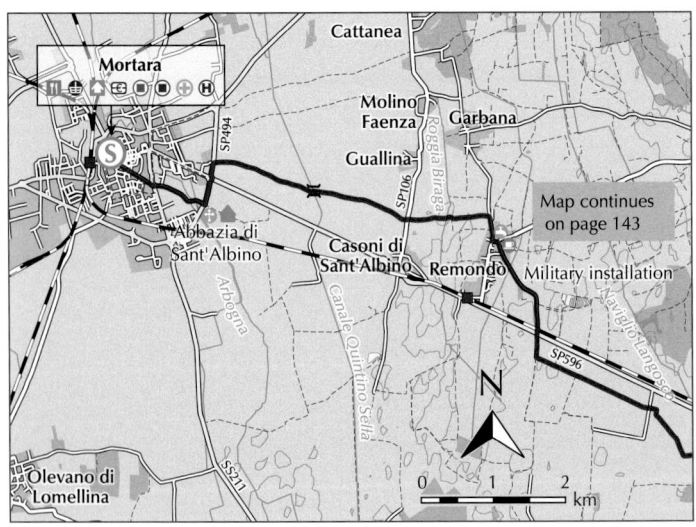

One of the area's many canals, this one after Mortara

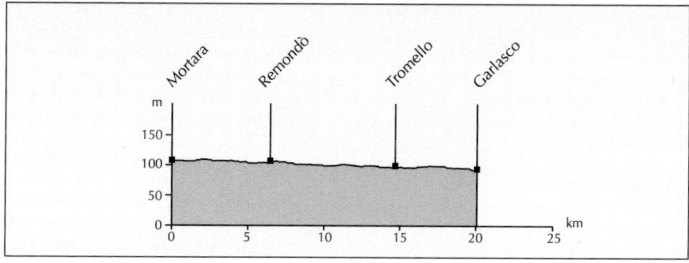

Continue along Corso Cavour, which becomes Viale Mario Parini that takes you all the way out of town. Pass a tall concrete water tower on the left and keep on straight through the roundabout. Continue to the **SP494** highway, which you can cross directly or by the river bridge 100m to the right. On the opposite side find the historic **Abbazia di Sant'Albino** building (**1.5km**) and its pilgrim hostel. Turn left after the highway and follow a driveway alongside the road, continuing straight on at the roundabout and then taking a right turn just afterward. A tree plantation transitions to cornfields on the left, with woods and a canal on the right. Though markings are lacking, follow a row of planted trees as it curves to the right along the canal until it dies out at a two-track grass road.

Cross a brick bridge (**2.1km**) over a canal, bearing right. Cross the **SP106** road at a farmhouse (**1.4km**) and continue on the dirt farm road, which ends at an asphalt road with a cemetery opposite, where you turn right to arrive in **Remondò** (**1.5km**, bar, water). Turn left in the direction of Gambolò and after the brick façade of Remondò's tall-towered parish church, turn right, passing a WWI memorial on the left.

Continue through a thin wood of deciduous trees and shrubs, passing a **military installation** and coming to the railroad tracks and **SP596** highway (**1.5km**). Cross them both and in a couple of hundred meters turn left on a quiet gravel road that parallels the SP596. After a series of left and right turns to avoid crossing canals, the road ends at the **SP77**. A left here brings you to the **SP183** highway (**5.6km**), which you cross to enter **Tromello**. Turn right on Via Cavour to the center of town (**1.1km**)

14.8 TROMELLO (ELEV 97M, POP 3561) 🏨 ⊕ 🛆 🅲 🅾 ⊕ (786.5KM)

This ancient, agricultural town is said to have had a castle in the Middle Ages, though the only trace of it seems to be the low **Torrione tower** in the center. Archbishop Sigeric recorded Tremel as his Stage XLII. In 1686 a nearby farmhouse called Donzellina, home to a beloved **painting of the Madonna**, was slated for demolition. Both Tromello and nearby Remondò claimed the painting, so to resolve the dispute the painting was loaded onto an oxcart and the oxen were set free to decide on their own which town should have the prize. The oxen walked toward Tromello, and the painting has been on display in the parish church here ever since. In May 2019 Gianmarco Negri was elected mayor, the first transgender mayor in Italy.

🛏 **B&B Casa Lucia** 🅿️ 🆁 🅺 🅱️ 🆆 🆂 🆉 1/2, €-/-/60/-, Via Delcroix 18, casalucia.tromello@libero.it, tel 338 7055302. Closed Jan–Mar. Reservations required.

🛏 **Hotel Duca di Tromello** 🅾 🅿️ 🆁 🅱️ 🆂 13/20, €-/65/80/110, Via Cesare Battisti 4, hotelducaditromello@gmail.com, tel 382 868089. Reservations required.

Turn left at the squat Torrione clock tower of the Pro Loco and then right onto Via Marconi, which becomes the main highway leading out of town. After crossing Torrente Terdoppio the route turns left, heading to the train tracks and then turning right to find itself back in the fields. Fork right after a farm and continue to a wide concrete-lined canal (**2.4km**) which you follow on the right side as it turns left. Avoid crossing to the left side of the canal which leads to an unsafe walk along the SP206 highway. Instead keep right to walk among fields.

Cross the railroad tracks (**2.0km**) and come to the first houses and businesses of **Garlasco**. Turn left at the roundabout and follow the street into the center of town, arriving at the main square, Piazza Repubblica, with

A war memorial to fallen soldiers in front of Garlasco's town hall on Piazza della Repubblica

the Municipio on one side and the yellow and brick Church of Santa Maria Assunta on the other (**0.9km**).

5.4KM GARLASCO (ELEV 91M, POP 9343) 🏨 ⊕ 🛆 🅒 ⊚ ⊙ ⊕ ⊕ (781.1KM)
Garlasco's name is believed to have been derived from the Celtic word *kerlescki*, 'village of cremation'; indeed the Roman historian Livy describes a Celtic village in this area where corpses were burned. Local legends say that **Hannibal** rested his elephants and army here in 218 BC. The town retains the **tower** of a 14th–15th c. castle, destroyed in a 1524 siege. The dome of the 18th c. **Church of Santa Maria Assunta** is tallest in the area at 33m.

🛏 **Casa del Pellegrino** 🇵🇷 🇩🇴 🇷 🇸 1/3, €10/-/-/-, Piazza San Rocco 2, bibliogarlasco@yahoo.it, tel 382 801009. Reserve at least 24hr prior.

🛏 **Casa del Pellegrino Fondazione Exodus** 🇴 🇵🇷 🇩🇴 🇷 🇰 🇧🇷 🇩🇷 🇼 🇸 🇿 2/12, €Donativo, Via Cascina Toledina 3, www.exodus.it/sedi-exodus/garlasco. html, garlasco@exodus.it, tel 038 2820002. Pilgrim housing inside teen rehab community. Breakfast and shared dinner with teens. No drugs or alcohol allowed.

🛏 **La Casa di Nonna** 🇴 🇵🇷 🇷 🇰 🇼 🇸 1/1, €-/35/-/-, Via Reale 21, fiorella.albini@me.com, tel 392 2819692.

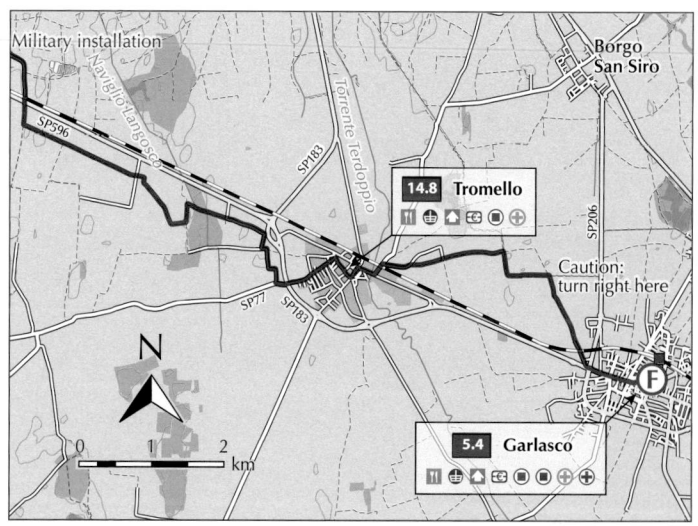

143

STAGE 19
Garlasco to Pavia

Start	Garlasco, Piazza Repubblica
Finish	Pavia, Corso Nuovo at Corso Garibaldi
Distance	24.3km
Total ascent	234m
Total descent	242m
Difficulty	Moderate
Duration	6½hr
Percentage paved	10% (48% via bike route option)
Hostels	Pavia 24.3km

A large portion of today's walk is a well-intentioned but difficult and perhaps unnecessary 9.5km ramble on isolated riverside nature trails along the Ticino River. The bike option provides an alternative, though at the expense of one treacherous automobile roundabout at the SP35. The goal is the medieval university town of Pavia, full of history, cafés packed with college students and architectural treasures.

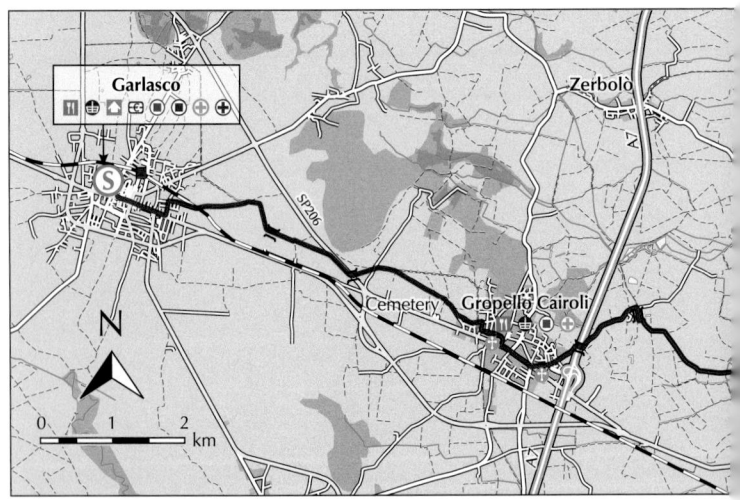

Continue on Corso Cavour out of town, the signs pointing you left onto Via Dante Alighieri and two blocks later right on Via Toledo, arriving before long back out in the fields. The asphalt road quickly turns to dirt just before the railroad tracks and you continue on through rice fields. Follow alongside a familiar concrete canal and turn right just before a bridge. At the canal locks, cross the bridge and continue to the **SP206** highway (**3.6km**), which you cross to find a two-track gravel road along the canal. Very soon, fork right to pass behind a **cemetery** and come to a wide gravel road leading toward town. Cross a canal on a narrow footbridge and follow the signs to Via della Libertà, main street of **Gropello Cairoli** (**3.0km,** food, groceries, bus, pharmacy).

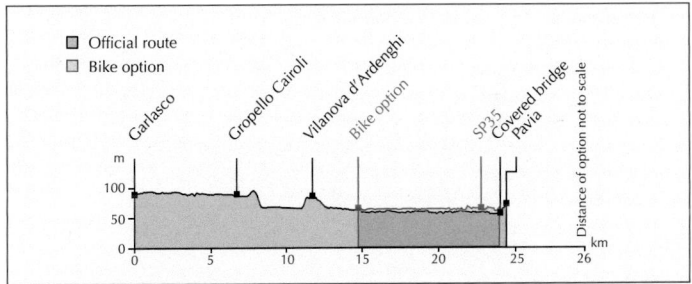

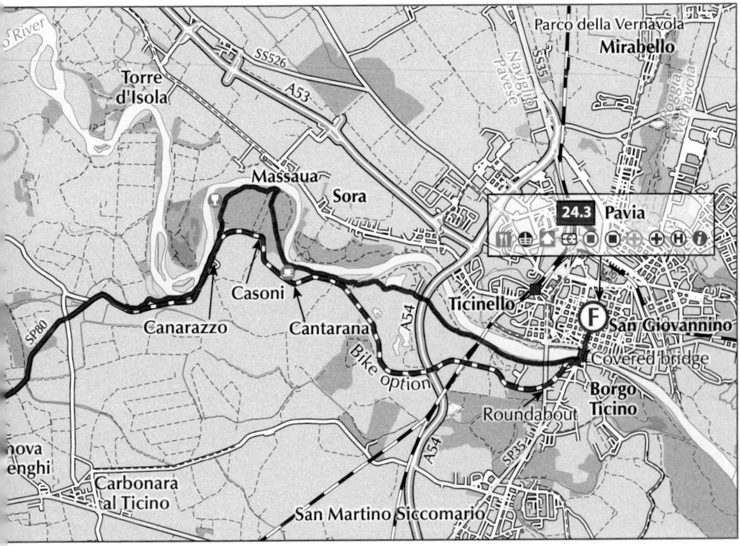

The town's ancient name derives from the Latin word *grupellum* (tr: 'high ground or riverbank'), likely referring to its location above the **Ticino River**. The name 'Cairoli' was added in 1888 to celebrate the life of Italian Unification patriot Benedetto Cairoli. Scholars hypothesize that Hannibal's battle against Scipio was fought in the vicinity. The modest Castello Gropello was built in the 14th–15th c. and today is a private residence. Built on medieval foundations, the early-20th c. façade of the Church of San Giorgio Martire features a dramatic equestrian statue of the saint, flanked by statues of St Peter and St Paul. The 17th c. Church of San Rocco and Santa Croce remembers a legendary visit by San Rocco who stopped in town on his return from Rome. (Consult online sources for tourist accommodation.)

Pass the grand San Giorgio Martire church with its bronze dragon-slayer and then the humble pink Church of San Rocco and Santa Croce set inside a traffic roundabout. Take the second left after the San Rocco and head behind town to a warehouse district before crossing over the **A7** Autostrada (**1.3km**). The pleasant, asphalt road on the other side leads through fields of corn and soy. Turn right and cross a canal (**1.2km**) at a farm, walking alongside the canal with corn fields on either side. After crossing back over the canal, the road turns to asphalt. Turn right and climb into the nondescript collection of houses called **Villanova d'Ardenghi** (**2.4km**, bar). After turning left and passing a soccer pitch continue on the very pleasant **SP80** Via Roma above the rice fields. The road leads atop a dyke, with the floodplain of the **Ticino River** to the left and the dyke protecting fertile farmland to the right.

Soon you come to an option. The official walking trail (marked E/1) forks down off the dyke road to the left, where it wanders on a poorly-maintained and isolated path through woods along the low riverside bluff. An easier and 800m shorter route follows the bike track, remaining atop this quiet dyke road. To take the bike track, follow the dyke road alongside **Canarazzo**, **Casoni** and **Cantarana**, cross under the **A54** and train tracks, and carefully make your way across the busy SP35 roundabout onto Via 25 Avrile, which you follow through Borgo Ticino to the **covered bridge**, Ponte Coperto, leading into Pavia.

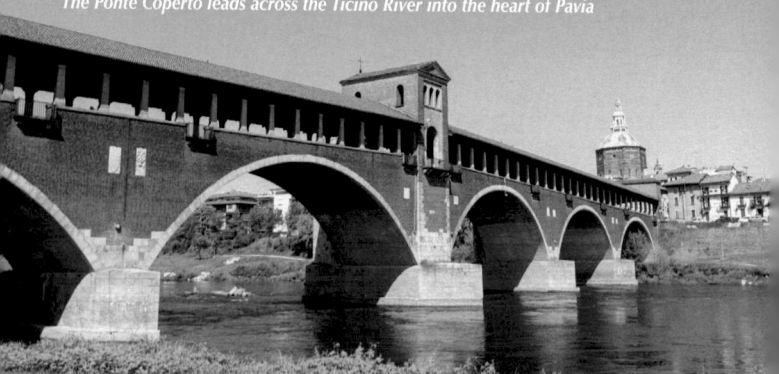

The Ponte Coperto leads across the Ticino River into the heart of Pavia

If you have stayed on the trail, you will find a narrow and often overgrown forest path, punctuated by a bar soon on the left and then about midway on the route a restaurant. Cross under the highway bridge and then the train bridge, after which you find yourself on a wide gravel path in a pleasant city park. Continue as you come to the steps leading up to the **covered bridge**, which you cross to enter **Pavia**. Go directly ahead onto Corso Nuovo, which leads you within two blocks of the cathedral.

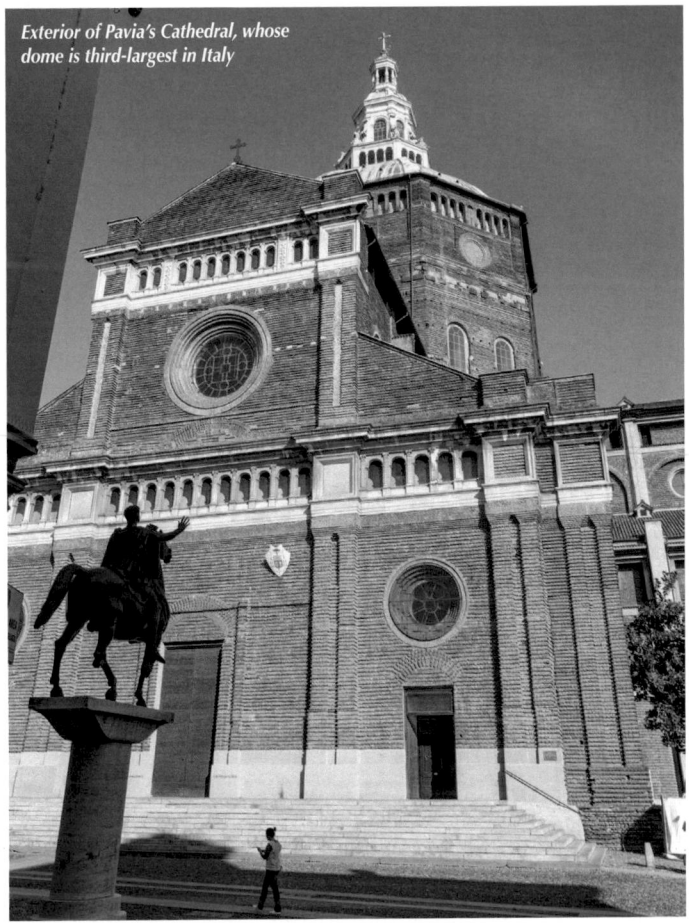

Exterior of Pavia's Cathedral, whose dome is third-largest in Italy

24.3KM PAVIA (ELEV 83M, POP 73,086) 🟦⊕◻️🄴◉◉⊕⊕🄷❶ (756.8KM)
One of the most historic cities on the Via Francigena, Pavia is the setting for many
key moments in Italian history and home to many artistic and cultural treasures.
Called Ticinum by the Romans – after the Ticino River – the town most likely
began as a Roman military outpost of Publius Cornelius Scipio in 218 BC in the
Second Punic War against Carthage. Six centuries later Pavia was site of the AD
476 killing of Flavius Orestes, which led his powerless son, **Romulus Augustulus**,
to become last Emperor of Rome. In the uprising that followed, Pavia was burned
to the ground. Theodoric, King of the Ostrogoths, invaded just 12 years later, and
he rebuilt the city to include Roman-style baths and an amphitheater.

The Ostrogoths of Pavia held out against the Byzantine armies in 535, but
Pavia fell to the Lombards in 572 after a three-year siege. Lombard King Liutprand
built the 8th c. **Church of San Pietro** in Ciel d'Oro and in about 720 the remains
of St Augustine of Hippo – one of Christianity's most important theologians –
were moved from Sardinia and interred there. Charlemagne and his Frankish
army defeated the Lombards here in 774, ending Lombard rule. In 961 King Otto
I of Germany invaded the area and was crowned King of Italy, a subject king-
dom of the German Holy Roman Empire. It was into this context that Archbishop
Sigeric stayed as his Stage XLI Pamphica. The **University of Pavia**, founded in
1343, is the world's 17th oldest university in continuous operation. The 1525
Battle of Pavia was the climactic battle of the Italian War in which the Habsburg
armies of King Charles V defeated the army of the French king Francis I, killing
over 13,000 French, Swiss and Spanish soldiers at the park outside the 14th c.
Castello Visconteo of Pavia.

There are several important buildings, including the 15th c. **Cathedral of
Pavia**, whose 19th c. dome is third largest in Italy. The cathedral's earthy, brick
exterior is a sharp contrast to its crisp, white interior. The adjacent tower fell in
1989. The Emperor Frederick Barbarossa was crowned at the 12th c. Lombard
Romanesque **Church of San Michele Maggiore** in 1155. On the opposite side
of the old city is **San Teodoro**, a 12th c. church that exemplifies the simplicity of
Romanesque style and includes a frescoed map of 16th c. Pavia. The large 14th–
15th c. **Church of Santa Maria del Carmine** is an important example of Lombard-
Gothic architecture, while the interior of the round 16th c. **Church of Santa Maria
di Canepanova** features frescoes depicting women of the Bible.

🛏 **Ostello Santa Maria in Betlem** 🅾🅳🅾🆁 6/21, €20/25/60/-, Via Pasino 7, www.
ostellosantamariainbetlem.com, info@ostellosantamariainbetlem.com, tel 331
3046459. Bed linens incl., towel rental €2.

🏠 **B&B Residenza i Mille** 🅿🆁🆁🅱🆆🆂🆉 2/4, €-/35/70/-, Via Dei Mille 117,
www.residenzaimille.it, info@residenzaimille.it, tel 334 8637017. Closed
Dec–Feb. Reservation required.

▲ **Camping Ticino** ⓟ ℝ 2/4, €-/30/40/-, Via Mascherpa, www.campingticino.
it, camping.ticino@libero.it, tel 382 527094 or 339 1166674. Campground
for tent €16, also 2 mobile homes with 2 beds each with 2 night minimum.
Swimming pool in season. 3km NW of city center.

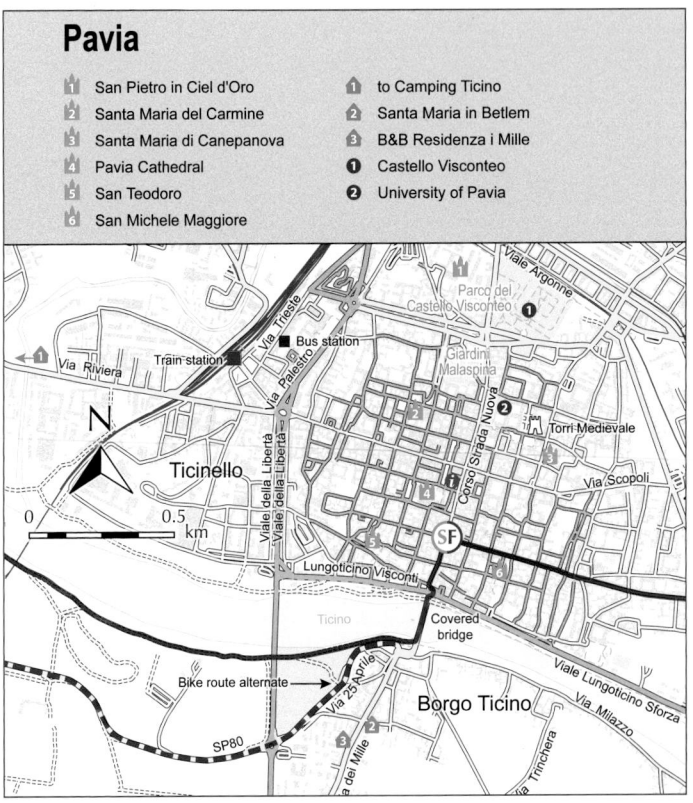

Pavia

🏛 San Pietro in Ciel d'Oro		🏠 to Camping Ticino
🏛 Santa Maria del Carmine		🏠 Santa Maria in Betlem
🏛 Santa Maria di Canepanova		🏠 B&B Residenza i Mille
🏛 Pavia Cathedral		① Castello Visconteo
🏛 San Teodoro		② University of Pavia
🏛 San Michele Maggiore		

STAGE 20

Pavia to Santa Cristina e Bissone

Start	Pavia, Corso Nuovo at Corso Garibaldi
Finish	Santa Christina e Bissone, Church of Santa Cristina
Distance	28.1km
Total ascent	305m
Total descent	317m
Difficulty	Moderate
Duration	7½hr
Percentage paved	73%
Hostels	Belgioioso 16.2km, Santa Cristina e Bissone 28.1km

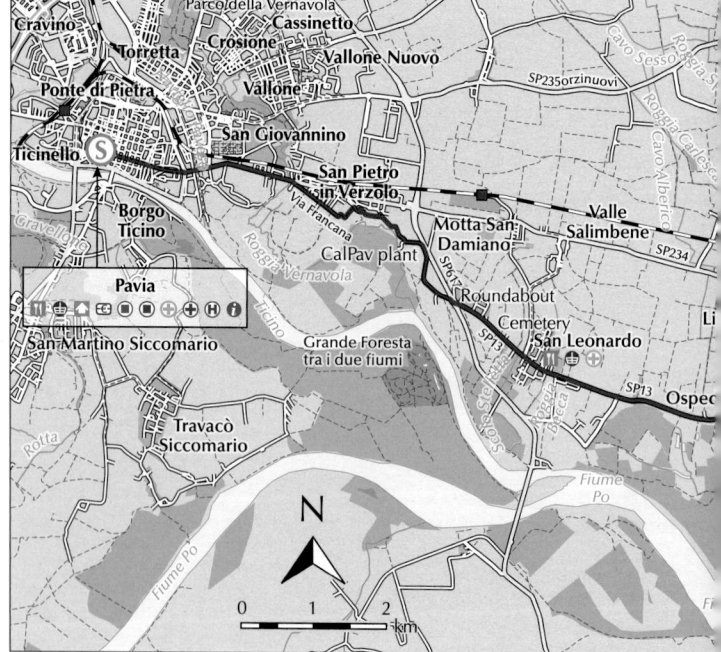

After a hectic exit from Pavia, the route finds quiet roads, mostly asphalt, to make its way among scattered villages to quiet Santa Cristina. A bleak sand quarry is the low-light of the day, but waterfowl make their home at a marsh in the bottom.

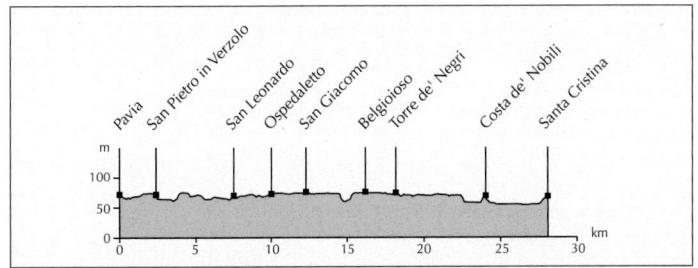

Head out of the old city on Corso Garibaldi, which hosts an off-and-on bike/pedestrian lane as it becomes a busy suburban arterial road. The route forks right at Via Francana (**2.6km**) in suburban **San Pietro in Verzolo**, where you enter fields temporarily before switchbacking up a hill to the back of town and finding a wide asphalt drive under maple trees in a park. Come to a large **CalPav** building material plant (**2.2km**) and turn left. Soon find yourself on a wide and quiet asphalt road though fields. Make your way carefully around a roundabout of the **SP617** to cross onto the narrow but quiet **SP13**. Pick up a brick sidewalk to the right, pass a **cemetery** and come to **San Leonardo** (**2.7km**, food, groceries, pharmacy).

Continue through town on the SP13 and soon you are back in the fields with corn on the left and rice on the right or vice versa. The fields are often separated by tall stands of trees or the symmetrical rows of tree plantations. Pass through **Ospedaletto** (**2.5km**, no services). The road turns right (**0.8km**) and before long you come to the hamlet of **San Giacomo dell Cerreta** (**1.5km**, pilgrim-friendly farm restaurant, www.ilgandulin.it open 10:00–15:00, 16:00–22:00, closed Tues) with its historic church, though it is now mostly a modern equestrian center and archery range.

> The **Church of San Giacomo** was a stop on the 'Queen's Way' leading to Santiago de Compostela. The 15th c. building is an excellent example of Lombard architecture in the High Middle Ages. It contains a cycle of frescoes by the Renaissance painter Giovanni da Caminata and a wooden statue of Saint James.

A long, winding asphalt road passes through the valley, ending at **Santa Margherita** (**2.4km**, no services) after which you turn left to climb a low hill to **Belgioioso** (**1.5km**). For services, instead of turning right onto Via Nenni prior to the commercial district, go straight ahead for two blocks to find the bars and cafés of this historic town.

16.2KM BELGIOIOSO (ELEV 74M, POP 6233) ▯ ⊕ △ ◉ ◉ ◉ ⊕ ⊕ (740.6KM)

From the 15th–19th c. the **Castle of Belgioioso** was used by wealthy Milanese nobility as a hunting lodge. Francis I, King of France, was held hostage in this castle after the Battle of Pavia in 1525. Today conventions and exhibits are hosted in the neo-classical palace and lawns behind its brick Renaissance walls (www.belgioioso.it).

⌂ Casa Maria Baldini ▯▯ ▯ 1/2, €Call, Via Mazzini 7, mara.garatti@gmail.com, tel 382 960204 or 338 1859701.

Coming back onto **Via Nenni**, continue until it ends, turning right onto a bike lane beside the **SP9** highway that leads to **Torre de' Negri** (**2.0km**, café), whose most notable features are an extravagantly decorated house and an unusually tall, white water tower. The SP9 turns right and, after some grain silos, the route leaves the SP9 by going straight onto a gravel road among farm buildings. In a few hundred meters cross the busy **SP199** highway (**2.1km**) and turn left onto a sandy road that partially circumnavigates the enormous, bleak, 20m-deep **sand quarry** of the Cargill company, where waterfowl have made a home in the lake-like puddles at the bottom. Follow signs around fields afterward until you cross **canal locks** (**2.3km**), after which the route makes its way on a flat, wide and well-graded gravel road. Turn left into tiny **Costa de' Nobili** (**1.3km**, groceries three blocks south of route).

A left turn after a modern cemetery leads to a zigzag of gravel roads alongside canals in the vast fields of rice and corn. Before long see the tall steeple of the Santa Cristina church on the far ridge. The road turns to grass and, after the **sewage treatment plant** at the foot of the ridge, becomes asphalt before it leads a few blocks up to the wide Via Vittorio Veneto at the heart of **Santa Cristina e Bissone** (**4.1km**).

11.9KM SANTA CRISTINA E BISSONE (ELEV 71M, POP 2021) 🏨 ⛪ 🏠 ◉ ◉ ⊕
(728.7KM)

An ancient **Benedictine monastery** was centered in Santa Cristina, but only a tall wall from its 18th c. remodeling is visible on Via Dante. Sigeric visited Santa Cristina as his Stage XL. The surprisingly grand 17th c. parish church sits on Via Veneto and its interior is flamboyantly decorated in the Baroque style. In 1863 the community of Santa Cristina was merged with the smaller community of Bissone, just to the south.

🏠 **Parrocchia S. Cristina** 🅳ₒ 🆁 🆆 🆂 4/20, €Donation, Via Vittorio Veneto 118, www.parrocchiasantacristinaebissone.it/pellegrini.html, scristinaparrocchia@ gmail.com, tel 0382 70106 or 333 3429685. Open Apr–Sept except Sundays and holidays.

The Church of Santa Cristina, whose parish hostel is just to the left

The interior of the Parish Church of Santa Cristina

STAGE 21
Santa Cristina e Bissone to Orio Litta

Start	Santa Cristina e Bissone, Church of Santa Cristina
Finish	Orio Litta, Piazza dei Benedettini
Distance	16.3km
Total ascent	155m
Total descent	168m
Difficulty	Easy
Duration	4¼hr
Percentage paved	58%
Hostels	Miradolo Terme 4.3km, Orio Litta 16.3km
Note	If you are planning to ride the Po River ferry, reserve your seat at least a day before by calling Danilo Parisi (0523 771607, cost €10)

The terrain changes slightly, now with a few low ridges. This is a short and easy stage, sprinkled with a few very small towns offering convenient services. If you plan to use the boat service across the Po in the next stage, you should call the boatman today (see next stage).

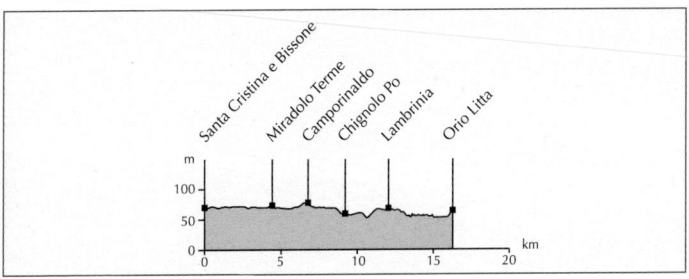

Follow the Via Veneto east, turning left onto a bicycle and pedestrian path for a short time before crossing the **SP234**. Soon cross the railroad tracks and turn right on a narrow bridge over a canal, following a grassy path separated from the tracks by a low ditch. Pass under the **SP412** bridge (**1.2km**) and then cross the canal to the right on a bridge, continuing on a gravel road. Soon the road crosses back over the canal and steers left, away from the tracks. The quiet farm lane wanders through the valley among corn and rice fields toward the far ridge and then crosses the **SP32** highway before rising into **Miradolo Terme** (**3.1km**).

4.3KM MIRADOLO TERME (ELEV 69M, POP 3738) 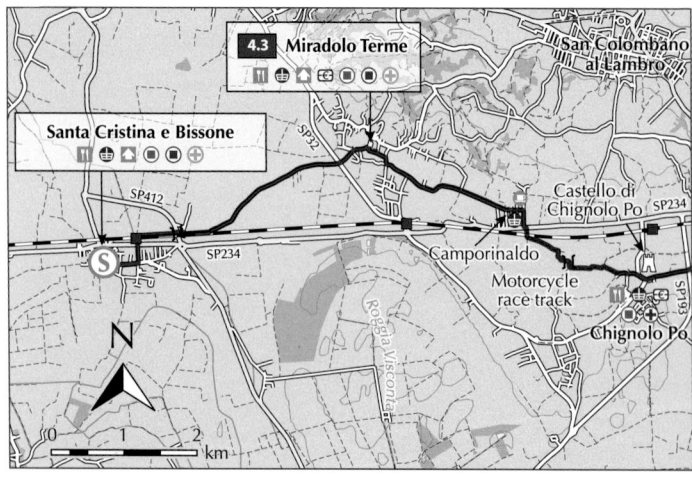 (724.4KM)

Archeological excavations show the town has been inhabited since the Bronze Age. The Castle of Miradoli was first mentioned in 1034, and the name 'Miradoli' likely refers to watch towers of the now-vanished castle that surveilled the surrounding ridges. **Thermal springs** were found here in the 18th c. and in 1911 a spa was built to take advantage of the waters' restorative properties (www.termedimiradolo.it). In 1938 the town was renamed Miradolo Terme.

🏠 Parrocchia San Michele Arcangelo ☑☑☑ 1/4, €Donation, Piazza IV Novembre 41, parrocchia.miradolo@gmail.com, tel 038 277116 or 340 2268426. Closed Oct–Apr.

🏠 Albergo Castello ☑☑☑☑☑ 16/32, €-/50/55/68, Viale Terme 19, www. albergoristorantecastello.it, prenotazioni@albergoristorantecastello.it, tel 0382 77139.

Leave town on the Via San Marco through residential areas as a bike-pedestrian path begins at a small grassy park. The road soon heads out into the fields with a line of windbreak trees to the left until it reaches **Camporinaldo** (2.4km, café, groceries). Turn right after the parish church and cross the SP234 to pick up a gravel road taking you back out into the fields. Cross railroad tracks and veer left onto another gravel road among the cornfields, hayfields and tree plantations with a **motorcycle race track** to

The Castello di Chignolo Po was once called 'the Versailles of Lombardy'

the right. Come to an unmarked intersection after the first stand of trees and turn right to cross a bridge over the adjacent canal (**1.2km**), keeping the fence of the motorcycle track to your right. A road of sand and gravel leads toward **Chignolo Po** (**1.3km**).

The tower of **Castello di Chignolo Po** was built in the 8th c., while the current castle/palace complex dates from the 17th c. In the early 18th c. the fortress was turned into a palace that hosted celebrities of the time, earning it the name 'The Versailles of Lombardy.' The buildings currently serve as a convention center and exhibition space (www.castellodichignolopo.it).

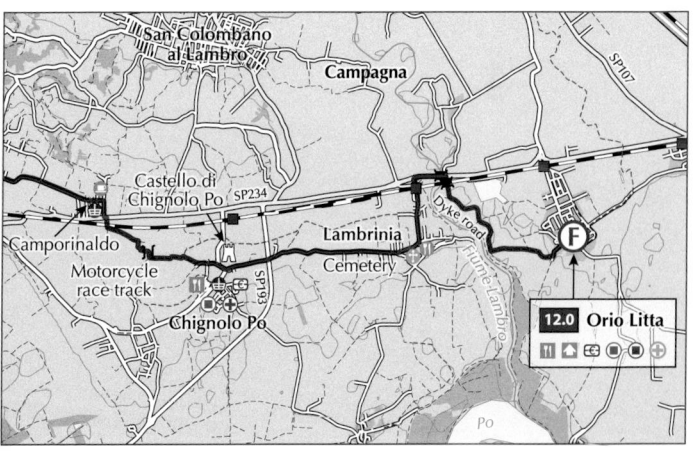

After the castle follow the road as it leads toward the **SP193** highway beyond. Cross the highway and continue as the road rises to climb the ridge to the left. Atop the ridge is a wide plain with crops of corn, hay and soy. The axis of the road now points straight to the front door of the large brick Church of Sant'Antonio da Padova in **Lambrinia** (**2.8km**, restaurant, pharmacy, bank) where you fork left. After a small, quiet retail area turn left to leave town on residential streets.

Cross railroad tracks and turn right, coming soon to the SP234 highway (**0.9km**). Turn right and cross the **Lambro River** on the highway bridge, then turn right again just after to walk under an opening in the adjacent three-arched brick railway bridge. On the other side come to a gravel road atop a dyke where you can see ahead the orange spire of the parish church of **Orio Litta**. Follow the dyke road then take a 90-degree turn left to walk through cornfields to the first streets of town. After the church the signs lead to the Piazza Della Benedettini, a quadrangle of buildings tucked behind the commercial district.

12.0KM ORIO LITTA (ELEV 58M, POP 1982) 🍴 ⌂ Ⓔ ⊙ ◉ ⊕ (712.4KM)

A fresco in the Vatican Museum shows the town with the name 'Orio,' likely referring to its role as a granary (Latin: *horreum*). In the 9th c. Orio was reclaimed from the surrounding marshy swamps by Benedictine monks. It was a fiefdom of various families throughout the Middle Ages and early modern period, ultimately being purchased by the Litta family. The family's imposing 17th–18th c. palace, the **Villa Litta Carini**, hosted notables including King Umberto I and Giacomo Puccini and is open for guided tours (www.villalitta.it). In 1765 a rabid wolf attacked the residents of town, biting 16 people, 14 of whom died. Wolves have long since vanished from the region.

⌂ Ostello Grangia Benedettina Ⓞ Do Ⓡ Ⓚ Ⓦ Ⓢ Ⓩ 2/16, €Donation, Piazza dei Benedettini, infograngia.oriolitta@gmail.com, tel 348 3637103 or 335 1720018.

The Villa Litta Carini palace at Orio Litta

STAGE 22
Orio Litta to Piacenza

Start	Orio Litta, Piazza dei Benedettini
Finish	Piacenza, Piazza Cavalli
Distance	25.9km walking option (or 19.0km walk plus 3.6km boat ride)
Total ascent	235m (174m boat option)
Total descent	233m (172m boat option)
Difficulty	Moderate (Easy for boat option)
Duration	6½hr (5½hr boat option)
Percentage paved	90% (86% boat option)
Hostels	Corte Sant'Andrea 4.1km (Calendasco 7.2km on boat option), Piacenza 25.9km (22.6km on boat option)
Note	To reserve your seat on the Po River ferry call Danilo Parisi at least a day before (052 377 1607, cost €10)

The important choice of the day is whether to follow in Sigeric's footsteps and take a boat across the Po River or walk the longer but still very pleasant route along the bike path directly into town. The boat ride offers a memorable and scenic 3.6km respite from constant walking, while the walking path offers a more pleasant entry into Piacenza that misses the industrial and commercial zones of the post-ferry walk. In crossing the Po, you leave the region of Lombardy and enter Emilia-Romagna.

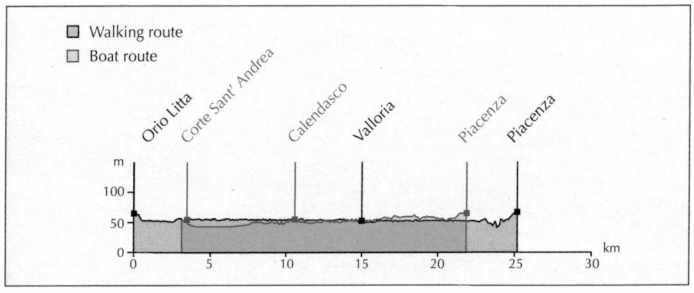

Follow signs to Villa Litta Carini, the 17th c. palace on the east side of town. Pass it on your right and continue down the hill on the SP206 then fork right onto a dirt road

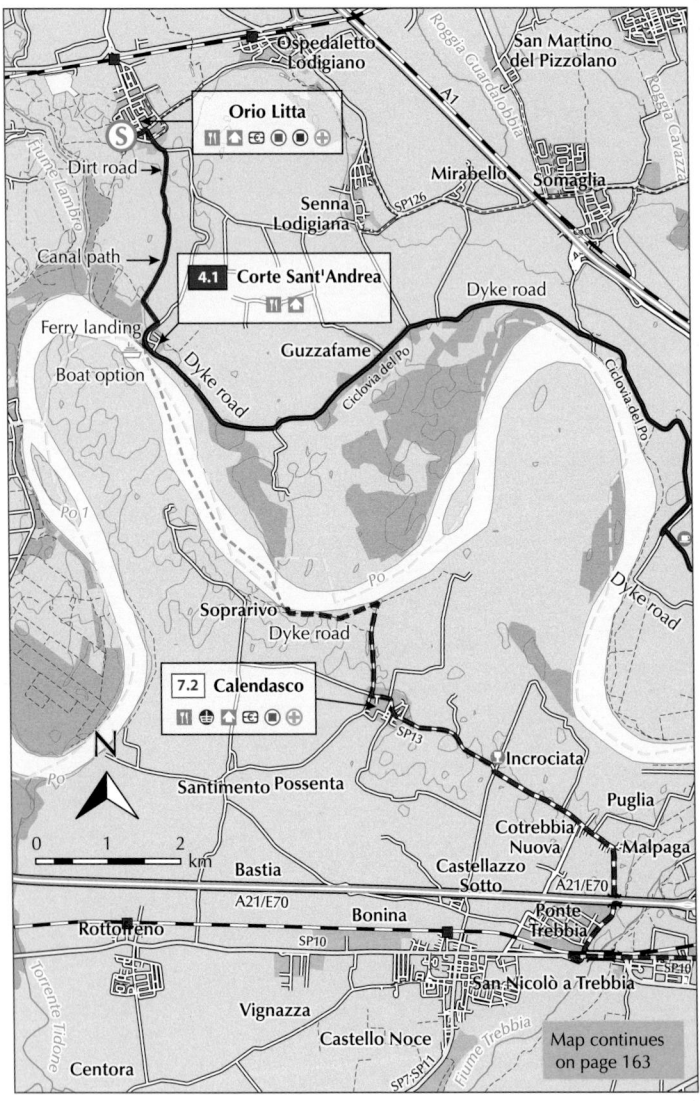

Map continues on page 163

160

Morning on the Po River

among fields of corn and soy. Soon fork left onto a **canal-side path** and left again to come back to the SP206, arriving soon at **Corte Sant'Andrea**.

4.1KM CORTE SANT'ANDREA (ELEV 58M, POP 22) 🍴 ⛺ (708.4KM)

Corte Sant'Andrea is a long row of shops and homes separated by a high bank from the Po River. Sigeric identified it as his Stage XXXIX.

🛏 Ostello ad Padum Ⓞ Ⅾⓞ Ⓡ Ⓚ Ⓦ Ⓢ Ⓩ 2/20, €Donation, Fraz. Corte Sant'Andrea, favarigiovanni@gmail.com, tel 339 1268946 or 037 7802155. Open May–Sept.

A right fork directs you back up on the dyke road, familiar from the last stage. Soon come to signs that point you right toward the ferry landing (**0.1km**) where the boat option awaits.

Boat option

Archbishop Sigeric's overnight at Corte Sant'Andrea suggests he crossed the Po on a ferry. In 2007 the village of Calendasco outfitted ferryman Danilo Parisi with a solid, aluminum boat to maintain the ferry service to pilgrims he began in 1998. People who have reserved their seat (tel 052 377 1607, cost €10) can descend to the floating dock and await Danilo, who generally arrives around 08:30 for his daily 3.6km trip across and down the river. After enjoying the scenic boat ride and after receiving his flamboyant credential stamp, climb up from the landing at Danilo's house and turn left to follow the dyke road. Continue and then turn right off the dyke just before a small brick building. Pass an *agriturismo* and continue on this quiet, asphalt farm road until you turn left to enter **Calendasco** (**3.5km** from ferry landing).

Santa Maria Assunta Church at Calendasco on the boat option

7.2KM CALENDASCO (ELEV 53M, POP 2412) 🚌 ⊕ 🏠 🅒 ⓜ ⊕ (697.8KM)
Founded in Roman times by the centurion Calendius, the town is located at a historic ford of the Po River. In the 10th c. the Bishop of Piacenza built the **Castello of Calendasco**, which ultimately became manor house of a fiefdom held by the bishop or one of several noble families over the centuries.

🏠 Ostello le Tre Corone Pr Do R Br W S Z 12/41, €20/35/60/75, Via Mazzini 59, info@trecorone.it, tel 340 6322837. Closed Nov–Mar.

Follow the **SP13** through town, lamenting the lack of sidewalks until you turn left onto a quieter road at a bar in **Incrociata** (**2.0km**, bar). Now the road aims you at the tall, slender steeple of the Church of San Pietro in **Cotrebbia Nuova** (**1.4km**, bar). Turn right onto a bike/pedestrian path in **Malpaga** and then cross under the **A21/E70** highway (**1.3km**) into the industrial suburb of **Ponte Trebbia**. Near this location the Romans were crushed by the Carthaginian forces under Hannibal in the 213BC Battle of the Trebia. The sides suffered a combined 30,000 casualties.

Soon pass under the double brick spans of the **SP10** highway bridges and turn right to curve up to a bike path on the far side of the second bridge (**1.3km**). Now begins a long walk on sidewalks of the SP10 among fast-food restaurants, car washes and car dealerships, continuing until a large roundabout where you turn left on Via XXI Aprile (**3.7km**). Turn right one long block later onto Via Campagna, which becomes Corso Garibaldi, which you take past Santa Maria di Campagna and the Church of San Sepolcro into the heart of **Piacenza**. At an intersection with Corso Vittorio Emanuele II turn left to find Piazza dei Cavalli at the center of town.

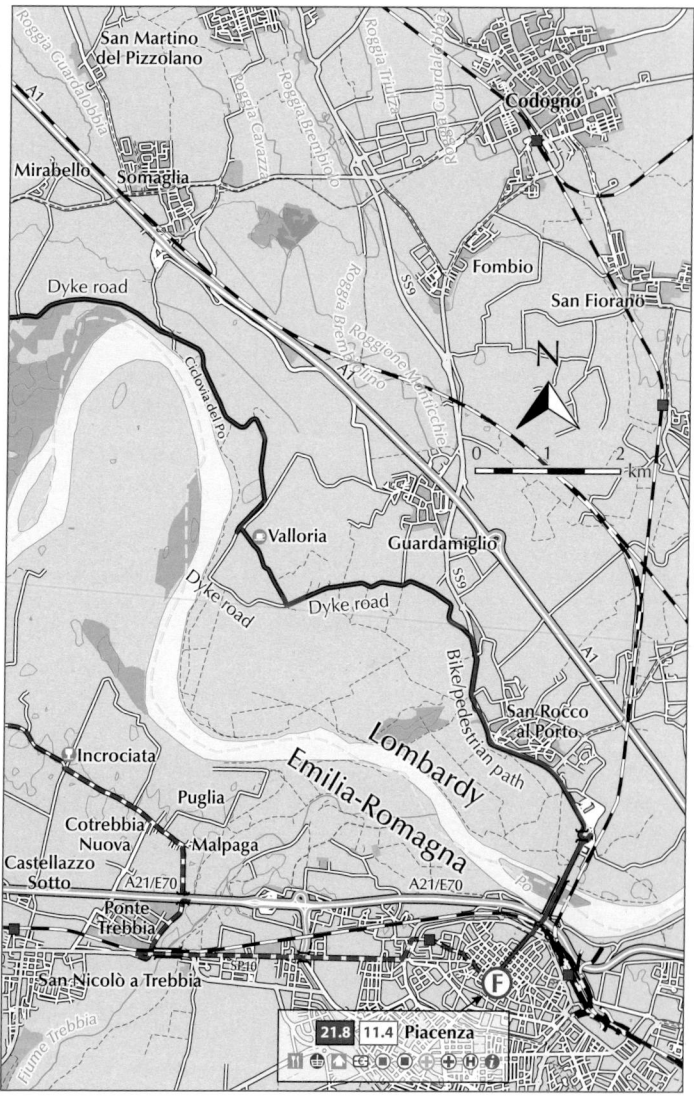

San Martino del Pizzolano

Codogno

Mirabello

Somaglia

Fombio

San Fiorano

Dyke road

Ciclovia del Po

Valloria

Guardamiglio

Dyke road

Dyke road

San Rocco al Porto

Bike/pedestrian path

Lombardy

Incrociata

Puglia

Emilia-Romagna

Cotrebbia Nuova

Malpaga

Castellazzo Sotto

A21/E70

A21/E70

Ponte Trebbia

Po

San Nicolò a Trebbia

SP10

fiume Trebbia

F

21.8 11.4 **Piacenza**

Walking option

Instead of heading down to the ferry dock at Corte Sant'Andrea, continue on the dyke road, where soon the gravel surface turns to asphalt. To the left and right are scattered trees and fields with the dyke-top road 5–8m above. Signs now announce that you are on the **Ciclovia del Po**, a bike/pedestrian trail that will take you more or less all the way into Piacenza. Pass a turn-off for the village of **Guzzafame** (**4.2km**) and after a time, signs point you left off the dyke down to **Valloria** (**7.3km**, café), clearly visible for its tall, modern church steeple.

Follow the main road back out into the fields and soon return to the dyke-top bike road, which here is wider than before. The road narrows and veers right as it approaches the **SS9** highway, gaining a wood railing on either side. Now see hints of the skyline of **Piacenza** ahead. The path veers to the left and crosses under the highway (**3.7km**) and continues on the other side. Now cross the floodplain of the Po on the road viaduct and then cross the river itself on a bridge, all the while remaining on the bike/pedestrian path. At the end of the bridge go straight ahead on Via Risorgimento, which soon becomes Corso Cavour. In less than a dozen blocks straight ahead you are in the heart of the historic city at Piazza dei Cavalli (**2.3km**).

21.8KM (11.4KM) PIACENZA (ELEV 63M, POP 100,413) ⊞ ⊕ ⊡ ⊡ ⊙ ⊚ ⊕ ⊕ ⊕ ⊕ ❶ (686.5KM)

Choosing the important junction of the Trebbia and Po Rivers for their city, the Romans who colonized Piacenza in 218 BC called it Placentia, meaning 'pleasant abode.' Here they built a fortress to protect their colonists, though in 200 BC it was sacked and burned and its residents carried into slavery. After they recaptured the colony they built a new road, the Via Aemilia, in 180 BC to better serve the area and increase its Roman population. Piacenza's first bishop, San Vittorio, was appointed in the 4th c. and the **Basilica di Sant'Antonino**, which houses his remains, was built in 324. Piacenza has long been a major stop on the Via Francigena, and Archbishop Sigeric stayed here on his return as Stage XXXVIII Placentia. The city was sacked by the Ostrogoths, recaptured by Rome, then conquered again by the Lombards. In 1095, at the Council of Piacenza, the First Crusade to the Holy Land was proclaimed.

Though captured and destroyed many times in its first centuries, Piacenza always recovered and its rich agricultural roots helped it become one of the most prosperous cities in Europe in the Middle Ages. In the 17th c. one-third of its residents died from famine and plague and in 1802 Napoleon annexed Piacenza and carried many of its artworks away to French museums. Piacenza was heavily bombed by the Allies in WWII to slow the German retreat. Rail lines, industrial areas and bridges were targets, but the center suffered collateral damage.

The center of town is the **Piazza Cavalli**, with two epic equestrian statues of father and son Alexander and Ranuccio Farnese, 16th c. dukes of Parma. The

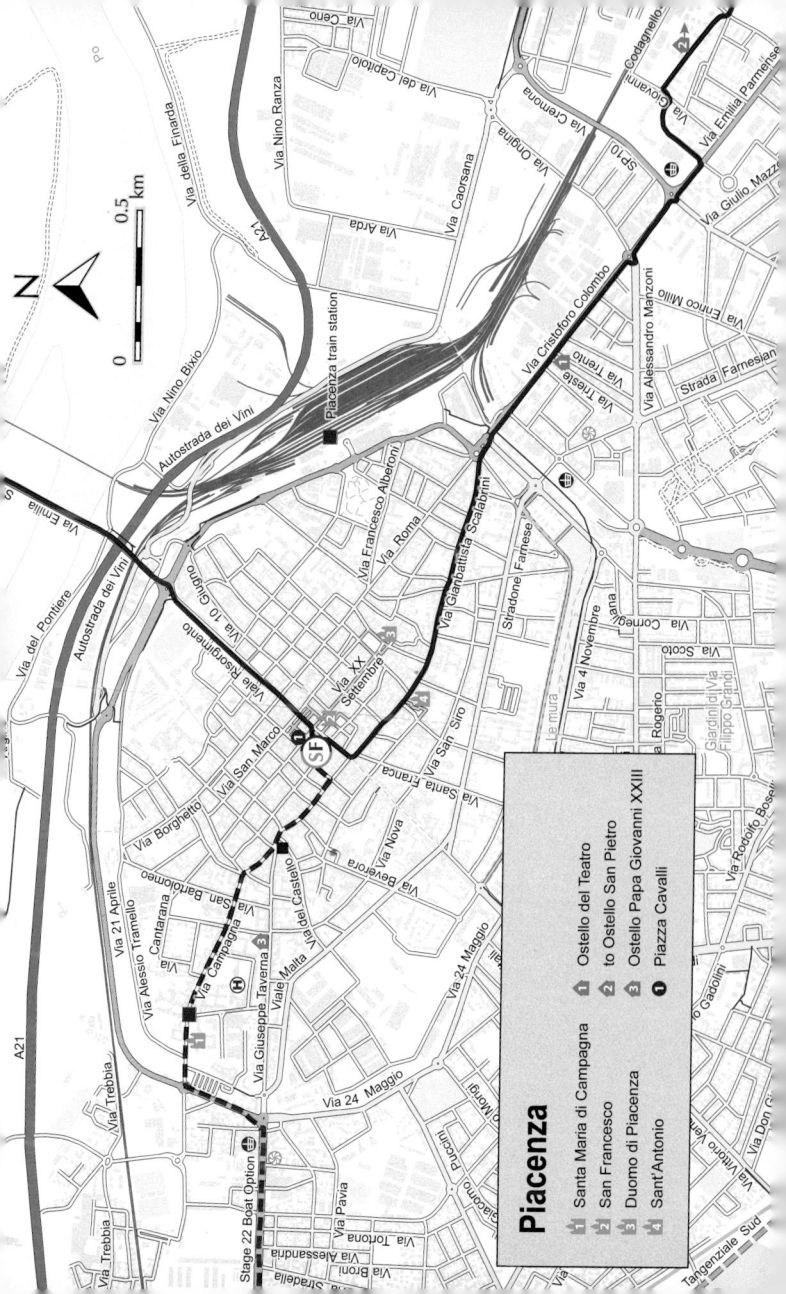

Piacenza

1	Santa Maria di Campagna	🏠 1	Ostello del Teatro
2	San Francesco	🏠 2	to Ostello San Pietro
3	Duomo di Piacenza	🏠 3	Ostello Papa Giovanni XXIII
4	Sant'Antonio	🔵	Piazza Cavalli

Stage 22 Boat Option

Piacenza train station

Turrets of the Church of San Francesco over Piacenza's rooftops

statues, by 17th c. sculptor Francesco Mochi, stand in front of the grand, arcaded 16th c. Palazzo Comunale. Just off Piazza Cavalli is the 12th c. **Romanesque Church of San Francesco** where civic events have been held over the centuries. The 12th–13th c. **Piacenza Cathedral** is a grand example of Romanesque architecture and its nave and dome are adorned with Mannerist-era frescoes. The cathedral crypt is a forest of 108 Romanesque columns and houses the relics of Saint Justine. The **Basilica of San Savino** was built from 903–1107 and retains an interior in Lombard-Gothic style with anthropomorphic figures on the capitals and a 12th c. wooden crucifix by an anonymous artist. **Via XX Settembre** is one of Piacenza's main shopping streets, where it is possible to buy clothes by the fashion designer Giorgio Armani, who was born here in 1934.

🛌 **Ostello del Teatro** ◘ Ⓡ Ⓚ Ⓖ Ⓦ Ⓢ Ⓩ 1/10, €18/-/-/-, Via Trento 29c, www. ostellodelteatro.it, info@ostellodelteatro.it, tel 0523 469599. Oct–Mar open only by appointment.

🛌 **B&B Lu.Lu** Ⓟ Ⓡ Ⓚ 2/4, €-/45/75/90, Via Giuseppe Mazzini 51, tel 375 6145158.

SECTION 5: EMILIA-ROMAGNA

Overlooking the Sporzana Valley after Fornovo di Taro (Stage 26)

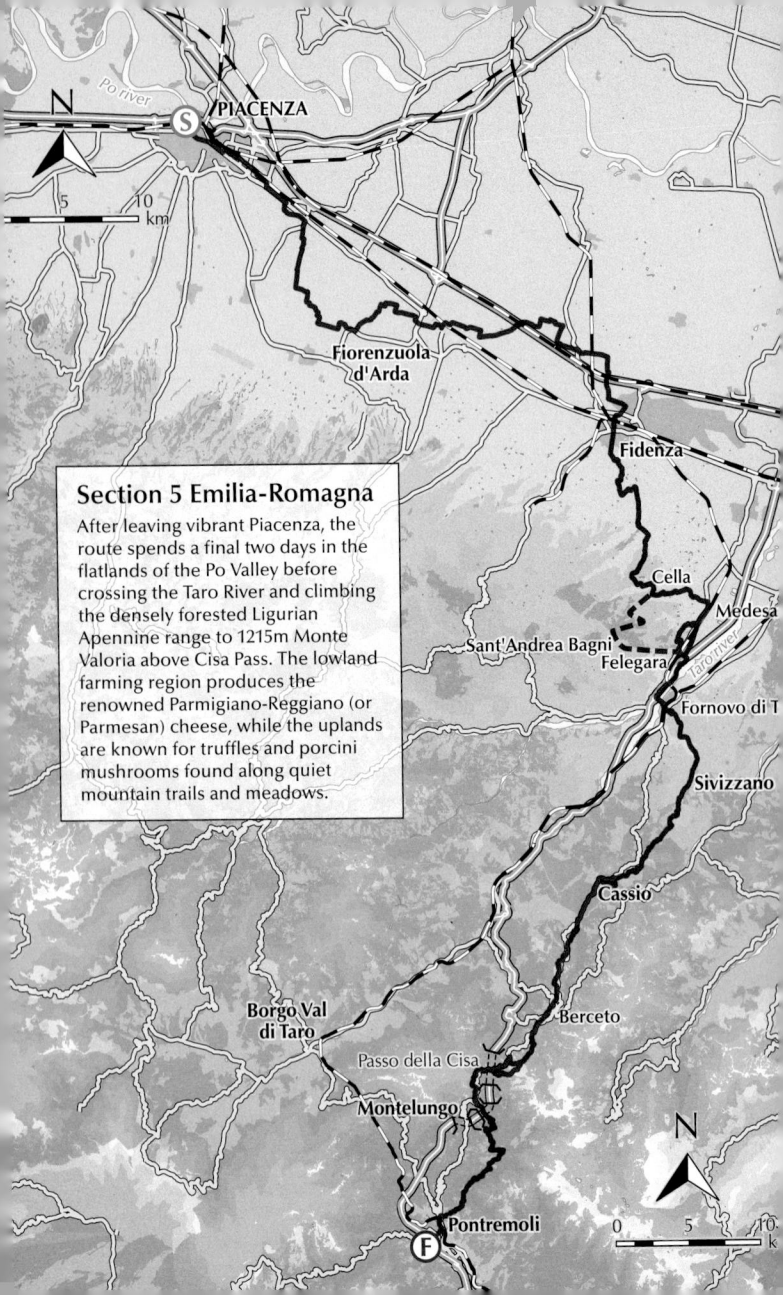

N

Po river

PIACENZA

S

5   10
km

**Fiorenzuola
d'Arda**

Fidenza

Cella

Medesa

Sant'Andrea Bagni

Felegara

Taro river

Fornovo di T

Sivizzano

Section 5 Emilia-Romagna

After leaving vibrant Piacenza, the
route spends a final two days in the
flatlands of the Po Valley before
crossing the Taro River and climbing
the densely forested Ligurian
Apennine range to 1215m Monte
Valoria above Cisa Pass. The lowland
farming region produces the
renowned Parmigiano-Reggiano (or
Parmesan) cheese, while the uplands
are known for truffles and porcini
mushrooms found along quiet
mountain trails and meadows.

Cassio

**Borgo Val
di Taro**

Berceto

Passo della Cisa

Montelungo

N

0   5   10
k

Pontremoli

F

STAGE 23

Piacenza to Fiorenzuola d'Arda

Start	Piacenza, Piazza Cavalli
Finish	Fiorenzuola d'Arda, Piazza Molinari
Distance	32.1km
Total ascent	347m
Total descent	325m
Difficulty	Moderately hard
Duration	8½hr
Percentage paved	89%
Hostels	Fiorenzuola d'Arda 32.1km

With the crossing of the Po the familiar corn/rice/soy combination changes to corn, tomatoes and other crops that require less irrigation. Over the flat terrain on a clear day you can begin to see the low hills of the Central Apennines. This stage includes several kilometers at the edge of sometimes-busy roads, along with long stretches of asphalt and gravel farm roads. The crossing of a small river adds a splash in the shallow and cool water, though it must be avoided in the rainy season. Pack plenty of food and water for the long distances between major towns.

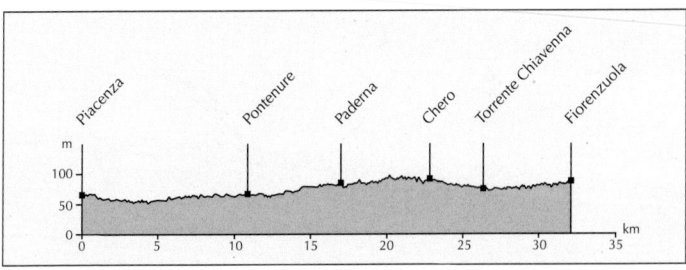

Looking the equestrian statues of Piazza Cavalli in the eye, head to the left side of the Palazzo Gotico and turn left at the next busy street, the Corso Garibaldi/Via Scalabrini, originally part of the Roman Via Aemilia that ran from here across the Italian peninsula to Rimini. At the roundabout outside the old city, veer right onto a sidewalk of the **SP10** highway (**1.3km**). After passing a large **Conad supermarket** (**1.2km**), turn left and continue a few blocks to find the Via Barbieri that leads to the right through the warehouse and industrial district onto a bike/pedestrian path. Cross the Strada Anselma

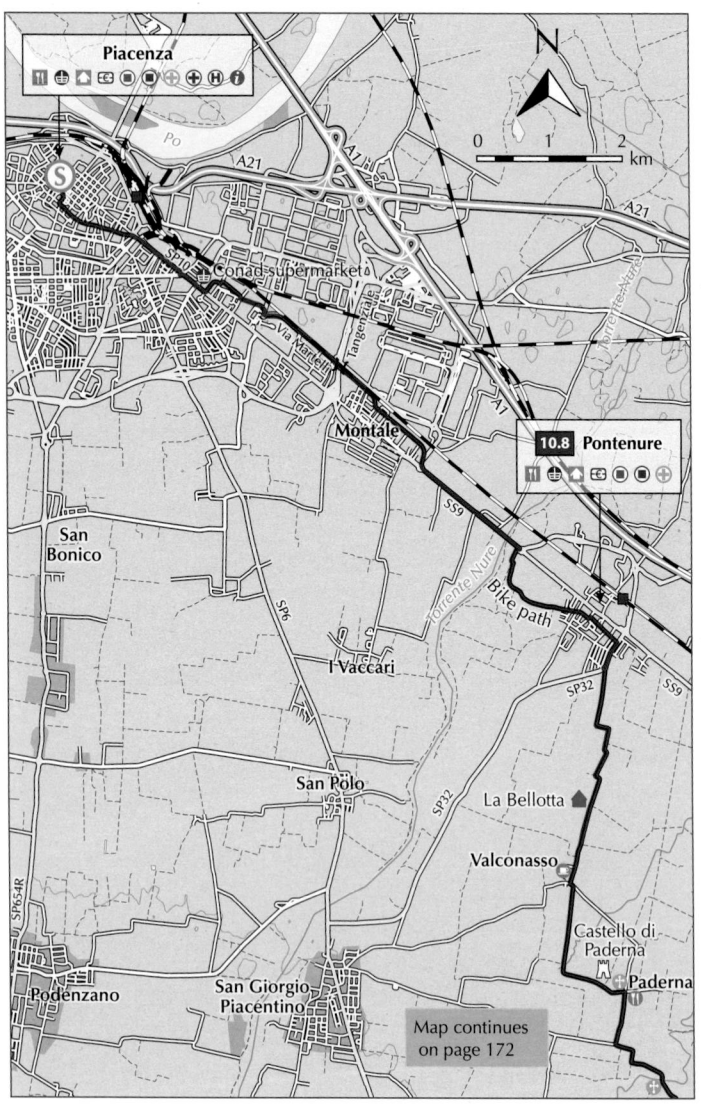

Map continues
on page 172

Hay fields before Fiorenzuola d'Arda with the Apennines in the distance

and continue on the **Via Martelli** alongside the railroad tracks. Pass under the **Strada Tangenziale** overpass (**2.6km**), head through a warehouse district, and after a time come to a roundabout where the route follows on the narrow shoulder of the **SS9** Via Emilia Parmense (**2.0km**), today's take on the historic Roman road.

After crossing the **Torrente Nure** (**1.6km**), say goodbye to the highway and turn right before a roundabout to take a narrow asphalt road and then a bike path among fields of hay and corn. The mountains you will soon cross are visible to the right on a clear day, and after a bit you come into the town of **Pontenure** proper. Head straight, jogging left one block before coming to a retail district of bars (**2.0km**), a block from a large church and the town's main street.

10.8KM PONTENURE (ELEV 65M, POP 6540) 🍴 ⊕ 🛏 € ⊚ ⊙ ⊕ (675.8KM)

A **fortified settlement** has existed here for centuries, and some scholars believe this town on the Nure is referenced in Livy's description of the Second Punic War in the 3rd c. BC. A 12th c. bell tower stands adjacent to the Church of San Pietro Apostolo. Pontenure suffered 600 deaths in the plague of 1630, and the survivors buried the remains near the riverbank. See online resources for tourist accommodation.

🛖 **La Bellotta Diocesan Hotel** 🅿🆖🅳 38/98, €-/35/55/-, Strada per Valconasso 10, www.bellotta.net, labellotta@virgilio.it, tel 0523 510896 or 370 3406124. Price incl bkfst, half and full board avail. Located 2.7km outside town on the route.

As the town comes to an end, make a right turn on the **SP32**, passing through an area of warehouses, then turn left off the highway onto a small country road with a convenient asphalt bike/pedestrian path on the right. The fields get wider and surrounding countryside quieter as you pass **La Bellotta** diocesan accommodation (see above) and come to **Valconasso** (**4.1km**, cafés). Afterward you are once again on a narrow asphalt road, this time with broad fields on either side and scattered farm houses ahead. Come then to the castle and church of **Paderna** (**2.2km**, pizzeria).

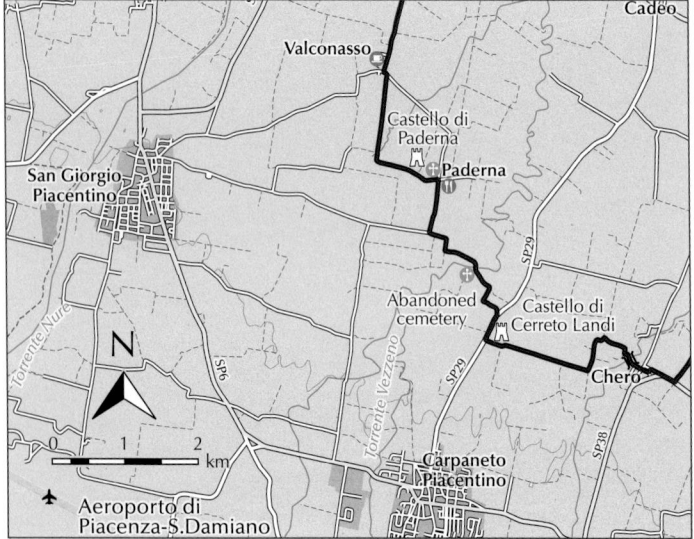

Documents attest to the existence of a **castle** belonging to San Savino Monastery in Piacenza at this location in 1028. The trapezoidal fortifications are surrounded by a large moat. Oldest of the castle buildings is the Oratory of Santa Maria, dating from the early Middle Ages (tours €7, www.castellodipaderna.it).

Afterward follow a zigzag pattern of narrow asphalt roads running at right angles along the edges of fields. Pass an abandoned **cemetery** and turn right at the **SP29** highway (**2.6km**), which you follow briefly before turning left at a settlement with tall grain silos, passing the **Castello di Cerreto Landi** (**0.6km**).

Earliest information about this castle is from 1385. It is surrounded by moats and its central tower is fortified as a last defense against attackers. Inside is the **Oratory of San Gaetano**, open to the public (tel 333 8499559).

The road heads straight through fields, goes left around a large field after which you cross a bridge over the **Torrente Chero** to enter **Chero** (**2.5km**, café, pizzeria). After town you are briefly on the **SP38** highway before turning left among wide fields of tomatoes and other crops. Before long, turn right onto a narrow gravel drive leading downhill to ford the **Torrente Chiavenna** (**3.5km**) on boulders. **Caution:** in the rainy season this stream can be flooded and dangerous to cross. If it appears fast-moving and dangerous, detour north to cross in Fontana Fredda.

A pilgrim's bicycle rests on a wall near the entrance to Fiorenzuola d'Arda's parish hostel

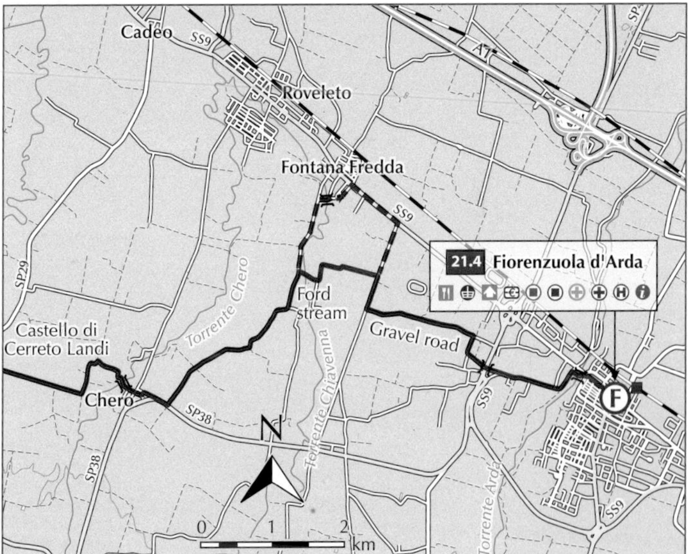

A three-arched bridge carries automobiles over the Arda River before Fiorenzuola

Head back up past a derelict farm and then zigzag among fields before turning right on an asphalt road. Soon make a left turn onto another gravel road, this time aiming at the **SS9** highway underpass (**3.9km**). Continue straight as the road veers left into **Fiorenzuola d'Arda** and then take a right to cross the **Arda River** on a pedestrian bridge. Cross a parking lot and turn right onto Via Europa then right again onto Via della Liberazione to find Piazza Molinari (**1.9km**).

21.4KM FIORENZUOLA D'ARDA (ELEV 85M, POP 15,313) 🍴 ⊕ 🛏 🅲 ⊚ ⊙ ⊕ ⊕ 🅗 ❶ (654.4KM)

The circular foundations of three **Neolithic-era huts** were found nearby, attesting to the long inhabitation of the area. Called Florentia by the Romans, the town was an important stop on the Via Emilia. The San Fiorenzo abbey is documented here in 830, and became the center of activity and commerce. The Battle of Fiorenzuola was fought here in July 923 between the forces of Rudolph II of Burgundy and Berengar I of Italy. That same century Sigeric stopped here as his Stage XXXVII Floricum. One tower remains of the medieval castle, which was augmented in the 19th c. to serve as a **clock tower**. It stands in Piazza Molinari at the center of town, adjacent to the 13th–15th c. **Collegiate Church of San Fiorenzo**.

🛏 **Parrocchia di San Fiorenzo** 🅞 🅿ⁱ 🆁 🆆 🆂 3/10, €15/-/-/-, Piazza Molinari 15, ufficiparrocchiasanfiorenzo@gmail.com, tel 0523 982247. Reservation required.

🛏 **Hotel Mathis** 🅿ⁱ 🆁 🅱ʳ 🅶ⁱ 🆆 🆂 🆉 22/38, €-/79/94/-, Viale G. Matteotti 68, info@mathis.it, tel 0523 943800. Closed annually for mid-August holiday.

🛏 🛏 **Bastimento Vintage B&B** 🅿ⁱ 🅱ʳ 🅶ⁱ 15/30, €-/40/70/-, Via XX Settembre 54, www.hotelbastimento.com, info@hotelbastimento.com, tel 0523 982827. Check-in at Hotel Mathis.

STAGE 24

Fiorenzuola d'Arda to Fidenza

Start	Fiorenzuola d'Arda, Piazza Molinari
Finish	Fidenza, Piazza Garibaldi
Distance	21.9km
Total ascent	268m
Total descent	271m
Difficulty	Moderate
Duration	5¾hr
Percentage paved	92%
Hostels	Chiaravalle 5.9km, Fidenza 21.9km (33.4km to Costamezzana on next stage)

A stage spent mostly on asphalt bounded by farmlands, where the Via Francigena stewards add distance in order to avoid the historic but busy SS9 Via Emilia. The Abbazia di Chiaravalle della Colomba (closed 12:00-14:30) is a highlight and Fidenza's cathedral is a must-see for its Romanesque sculpture. Some pilgrims extend the stage to Costamezzana to shorten the following day's distance.

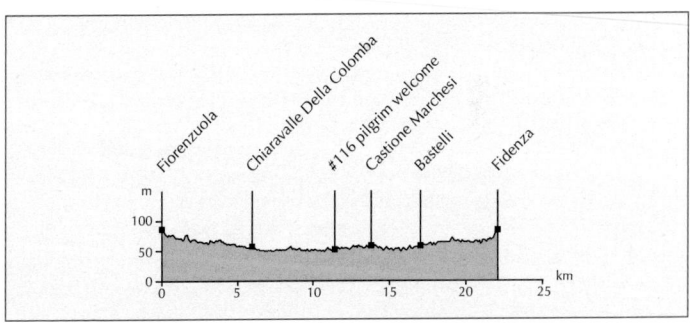

Find Corso Garibaldi and head out of town, crossing under the railroad tracks before turning right onto a pedestrian path on the opposite side. Follow it through parks and among scattered buildings as it curves around, leading to fields of corn, tomatoes, alfalfa and sunflowers. Come to the **Abbey of Chiaravalle della Colomba** a tall brick church and cloister of buildings in the midst of the countryside (**5.9km**).

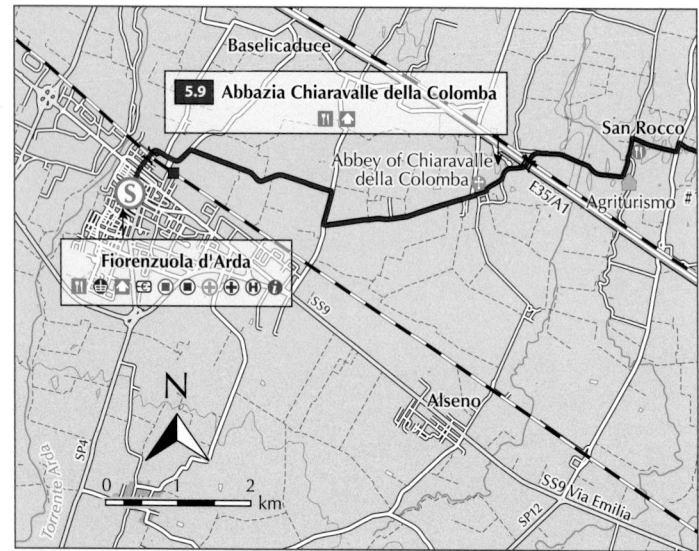

5.9KM ABBAZIA DI CHIARAVALLE DELLA COLOMBA (ELEV 58M, POP 50) 🍴 🏠 (648.5KM)

The abbey was founded in 1136 by the bishop of Piacenza. The name 'Chiaravalle' links it to the Cistercian Abbey of Clairvaux, earlier on the Francigena in France, and the name 'colomba' (tr: 'dove') likely refers to the symbolic dove that accompanied Mary at the Annunciation. The monastery was sacked and burned in 1248 and then suppressed by the Duke of Parma in 1769, only to be suppressed once again in 1805 under Napoleonic rule. While the buildings are primarily from the 15th c., the 13th c. **cloister** survives. Cistercian monks still live here and each year at the Festival of Corpus Domini the aisle of the church is covered in flowers. (Open daily 08:30–12:00; 14:30–18:30, www.chiaravalledellacolomba.it.)

🏠 Abbazia Chiaravalle della Colomba 🅿️ 🅳🅾 🆁 🅺 🆂 1/3, €Donation, Loc. Chiaravalle della Colomba, www.chiaravalledellacolomba.it, abbazia. chiaravalle@gmail.com, tel 0523 940132. Closed winters, reservation required.

After your visit, follow the outer walls left of the property to cross a bridge over the **E35/A1** Autostrada (**0.8km**). Now begins a long series of roads that detour far to the north to keep pilgrims off the busy SS9 Via Emilia. Turn left at the **Agriturismo all'Antica**

The church at the Abbey of Chiaravalle della Colomba

Ruggine and come to San Rocco (**1.9km**, restaurant). Turn right after the pizzeria onto a very narrow asphalt road in farms and cornfields. After a couple of turns the road becomes gravel and continues among fields, coming at one point to a quiet, shaded drive next to a dry canal where at #116 Frazione San Rocco a pilgrim welcome stop can be found. Leave a message in the mailbox for the friendly owners.

The quiet road ends with a left turn onto asphalt, with the train tracks and autostrada just ahead. Turn left and come soon to **Castione Marchesi** (**5.0km**, café, pizzeria, pharmacy).

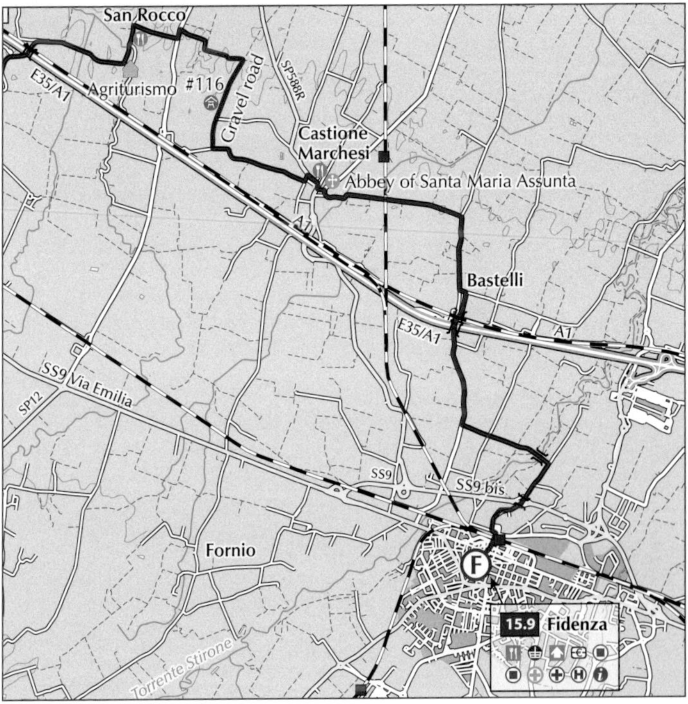

The large **Abbey of Santa Maria Assunta** is inside a courtyard on the fringe of the village. The abbey was founded in 1033 and served as a monastery until it was ceded to the Diocese of Parma in the 18th c. when it took on the role of parish church. Workers discovered the remnants of a 12th c. mosaic floor during renovation in 1954–1958.

Continue on a wide asphalt road, now among hayfields, crossing the train tracks and soon making a right turn toward **Bastelli** (**3.2km**). A right turn once in Bastelli takes you to a bridge back over the E35/A1 Autostrada and high-speed train line (**0.7km**). From the bridge you can see the tallest buildings of Fidenza ahead of you and the mountains rising behind. Pass among alfalfa fields and then turn left to cross a bridge over the **Stirone River** (**2.4km**), following the road as it curves to the right before heading into town. Cross under the **SS9bis** roadway and pass the cemetery's shaded parking lot. Turn right to cross under the train tracks and head up the steps to find yourself at Piazza Garibaldi in the center of **Fidenza** (**1.9km**) or follow signs right to find the must-see Duomo with its elaborate exterior sculptures.

15.9KM FIDENZA (ELEV 82M, POP 27,041) 🏨 🌐 🛖 🏦 ⊙ ⊛ ⊕ ⊕ 🅗 ⓘ
(632.5KM)

The town was founded by the Romans as a military outpost under its original Latin name of Fidenza, but was known from at least 923 as Borgo San Donnino, carrying the name of the saint who was beheaded here in the 3rd c. In 1927 the name was returned to the original. The Stirone River once passed through the heart of town, near the cathedral, but flooding moved its course out of town to the west. From Roman times Fidenza was an important waypoint on the Via Emilia, and in the Middle Ages the Via Francigena played a central role in the city's economic livelihood. Archbishop Sigeric stayed here as his Stage XXXVI San Domnine.

The Romanesque **Duomo of Fidenza** is one of the Via Francigena's artistic treasures, with exterior bas-reliefs by Benedetto Antelami and his school from the 12th–13th c. Episodes from the Old and New Testaments are depicted along the side walls. In a sculpture between the left and center portal the apostle Simon holds a parchment showing Via Francigena pilgrims the way to Rome. The scroll reads 'Simon Apostolus eundi Romam Sanctus demonstrate hanc viam' – 'The apostle St Simon indicates that this is the way to go to Rome.' Another scene, above a griffin and a capricorn, shows an angel leading a rich family of pilgrims while across from it a centaur hits a deer under a family of poor pilgrims. On the right tower a bas-relief seems to show pilgrims on the road to Rome, an image that has become iconic for the Via Francigena, though scholars generally interpret it as depicting Charlemagne returning to France. The nearby 14th c. **Porta di San Donnino** is the only surviving portion of the medieval fortifications. Fidenza's

Palazzo Comunale dates from the 13th–14th c. and bears striking similarities to the town hall in Piacenza.

🔺 Ospitale San Donnino 🄿🅁🄺🅆🅂🅉 3/10, €20.50/person, Via Giovanni Rossi 4, www.emc2onlus.it, sandonnino@emc2onlus.it, tel 331 1367510. One each double, triple, quad rooms. Open Apr–Oct. Reserv req, towel €2.50. Pilgrim and youth hostel.

🔺 Affittacamere Il Duomo 🄾🄿🅁🄺🅆🅂 6/11, €-/30/40/-, Via Arnaldo da Brescia 2, www.affittacamerealduomo.it, affittacamerealduomo@hotmail.com, tel 34 75819065. Laundry service incl. in price. Kitchen use allowed, but no utensils.

Intricate Romanesque sculptures grace the Duomo of San Donnino in Fidenza

STAGE 25
Fidenza to Fornovo di Taro

Start	Fidenza, Piazza Garibaldi
Finish	Fornovo di Taro, Church of Santa Maria Assunta
Distance	33.8km
Total ascent	789m
Total descent	720m
Difficulty	Moderately hard
Duration	9½hr
Percentage paved	63%
Hostels	Costamezzana 11.5km, Cella 16.5km, Medesano 22.3km, Fornovo di Taro 33.8km

This long stage over rolling hills of grainfields and vineyards makes for a challenging day as it leads to the foothills of the Apennines. An option to Sant'Andrea Bagni allows a visit to a pleasant resort town. On the main route a road walk before Felegara can shorten the day.

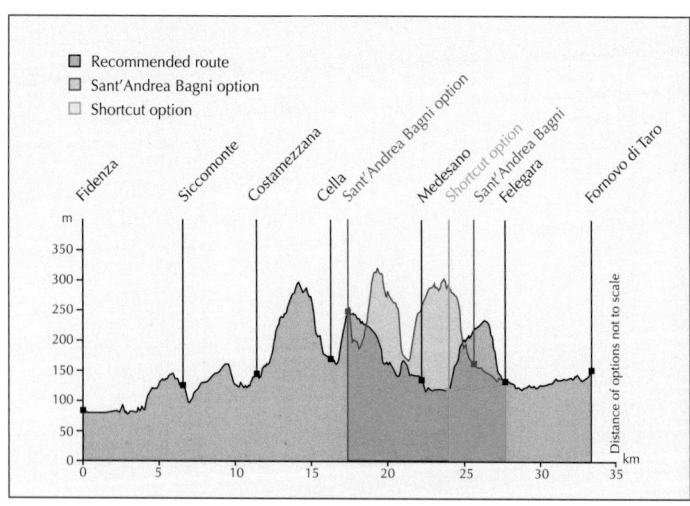

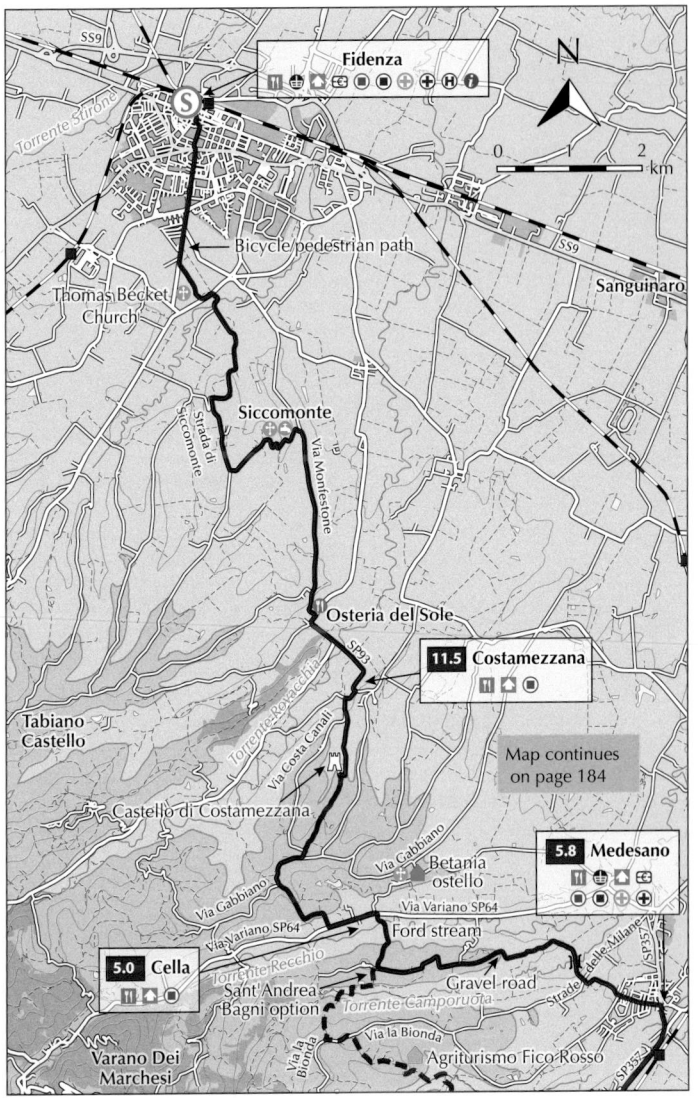

Fidenza

N

0   1   2
━━━━━━━━━━━━━ km

Torrente Stirone

SS9

S

Bicycle/pedestrian path

Thomas Becket
Church

Strada di Siccomonte

Siccomonte

Via Montestone

Sanguinaro

SS9

Osteria del Sole

SP93

11.5 Costamezzana

Tabiano
Castello

Torrente Rovacchia

Via Costa Canali

Map continues
on page 184

Castello di Costamezzana

Via Gabbiano

Betania
ostello

5.8 Medesano

Via Gabbiano

Via Variano SP64

Ford stream

5.0 Cella

Via Variano SP64

Torrente Recchio

Sant'Andrea
Bagni option

Torrente Camporuota

Gravel road

Strade delle Milane

SP357

Varano Dei
Marchesi

Via la Bionda

Via la Bionda

Agriturismo Fico Rosso

SP357

Head toward the clock on the Palazzo Communale in Fidenza's Piazza Garibaldi, veering left of the building and turning left at its end. Walk through Parco Matteotti and turn right to find yourself on a bicycle/pedestrian path heading out of town. The path becomes a wide pedestrian street and you fork left (**1.9km**) onto a shaded and grassy road with fields on either side beyond the trees. Instead of heading right to the highway the path veers to the right up a hill and comes to the handsome brick tower of the **Church of St Thomas Becket** (**0.8km**). The 12th–15th c. church was originally the chapel of a manor belonging to the Knights Templar. It features a series of frescoes, including one of the Trinity as three figures sitting down to eat. Turn left and walk down the driveway 100m to the busy Via Ponte Nuovo where you turn left and walk alongside on a pedestrian path before crossing at a crosswalk.

Now join an asphalt road on the opposite side that turns to gravel and heads straight across fields. After a short climb up the gravel road, which is now called the Percorso Natura Siccomonte-Cogolonchia, come to a hill with good views back to Fidenza. The gravel road ends at a hairpin turn of the **Strada di Siccomonte** asphalt road (**2.2km**). Turn left here and see to the right a series of ridges with fields, farms and trees interspersed, reminding you that the flat days of endless fields are now past.

Begin a long stretch on this narrow road that climbs gently among sparse gatherings of homes and farms. At a summit, turn left onto a gravel road and see that the route is aiming toward the steeple of the church at **Siccomonte** (**1.8km**, water fountain). Head downhill after the church and cross the stream at the valley floor, then head back uphill on the other side to turn right on the asphalt **Via Monfestone** (**0.8km**) The road climbs slowly in a fairly straight line. At another asphalt road continue straight and descend to **Osteria del Sole** (**2.6km**, restaurant closed Wed). Turn right and then immediately left onto the SP93 which leads you downhill to the outskirts of **Costamezzana** (**1.4km**, continue downhill on SP93 to enter the village).

11.5KM COSTAMEZZANA (ELEV 145M, POP 193) 🍴 🏠 ⊛ (621.0KM)

Salt was a key product of this region, situated near the Salsomaggiore Terme, a nearby hot spring with strongly saline water. Costamezzana (meaning 'halfway up the valley') and its rich agricultural environs were violently disputed by noble families from Parma in the 11th–15th c. The imposing 19th c. **Church of San Pietro Apostolo** houses mid-20th c. frescoes by Piero Furlotti.

🏠 Ostello comunale ⓞ 🅿️ 🅳🅾️ 🆁 🆂 🆉 4/17, €15/-/-/-, Via all'Isola 1, urp. informa@comune.noceto.pr.it, tel 0521 622130, 0521 629149. Reservation required.

Turn right before town and follow signs leading you left on **Via Costa Canali**. Fork left soon, toward a wood, going uphill on asphalt.

Obscured by trees on the right is the 11th–14th c. **Castello di Costamezzana** which today includes a castle keep and round tower along with the Osteria la Torre restaurant and 13th c. Church of San Pietro.

Continue on a two-track gravel road, which climbs to **Via Gabbiano** (2.7km). Follow this right before forking left onto a gravel road which then begins a very steep descent (a left on Via Gabbiano shortcuts to the Bettania hostel above Cella). Partway down the hill turn left to zigzag your way to **Via Varano** on the valley floor, turning left to come to **Cella** (2.2km).

5.0KM CELLA DI NOCETTO (ELEV 169M, POP <50) 🍴 🛏 ◉ (616.1KM)
A town is recorded here since 1230, while the **Church of Santa Maria Assunta** dates from the 17th c. (Trattoria Squeri closed Mon and Tues).

🛏 Comunità di Betania 🅞 🄿🅕 🄳🅞 🅡 🄱🅕 🄳🅕 🅂 5/15, €Donation, Via San Pio da Pietrelcina 3, www.ffbetania.net, cella.noceto@ffbetania.net, tel 0521 624052. Communal dinner onsite. Located 400m from village.

Continue through Cella and, just after the last house, turn right onto a gravel road heading to the **Torrente Recchio** at the valley floor, which you ford before climbing steeply up the opposite side of the valley. At the summit, turn left onto a very narrow asphalt road following the ridgeline to walk the main route through Medesano. Alternatively, turn right here (**1.1km**) to pick up an option to Felegara via Sant'Andrea Bagni.

Sant'Andrea Bagni option
This strenuous but picturesque option climbs two low ridges of 442m Monte Genesio on its way to the pleasant spa town of **Sant'Andrea Bagni**. 🛏 B&B San Nicola Mianq (tel 347 134 2889) kindly hosts Francigena pilgrims.

9.5KM SANT'ANDREA BAGNI (ELEV 164M, POP 934) 🍴 🛏 🄲 ◉ (606.7KM)
Saline waters were rediscovered in the late 19th c. and hotels sprang up to serve tourists using the spa facilities (www.santandreabagni.it). The **Palazzina** bath building is a treasure of Art Nouveau architecture, and a 1.3km nature walk to the water sources adds a pleasant diversion.

On the main route, at the end of the ridge the asphalt road turns left but instead go straight ahead onto a gravel road, continuing along the ridge. The road soon becomes a grassy track through fields. Pass a farmhouse and paddock with a vineyard. The road works its way to the valley floor and crosses the Torrente Camporuota before climbing the opposite side. Near the summit cross the **Strada delle Milane** asphalt road (**3.6km**) and descend toward the tall, narrow tower of **Medesano's San Pantaleone church**. The route heads to the church steeple (**1.1km**), missing the services of the main piazza, which are two blocks left.

5.8KM MEDESANO (ELEV 134M, POP 10,860) 🍴 ⛪ 🏠 🏧 ⊙ ⊙ ⊕ ⊕ (610.2KM)
Medesano sits above the Taro River, in a strategic position favored by the Romans, who founded the fortress of Castrum Medexani. Scholars believe Archbishop

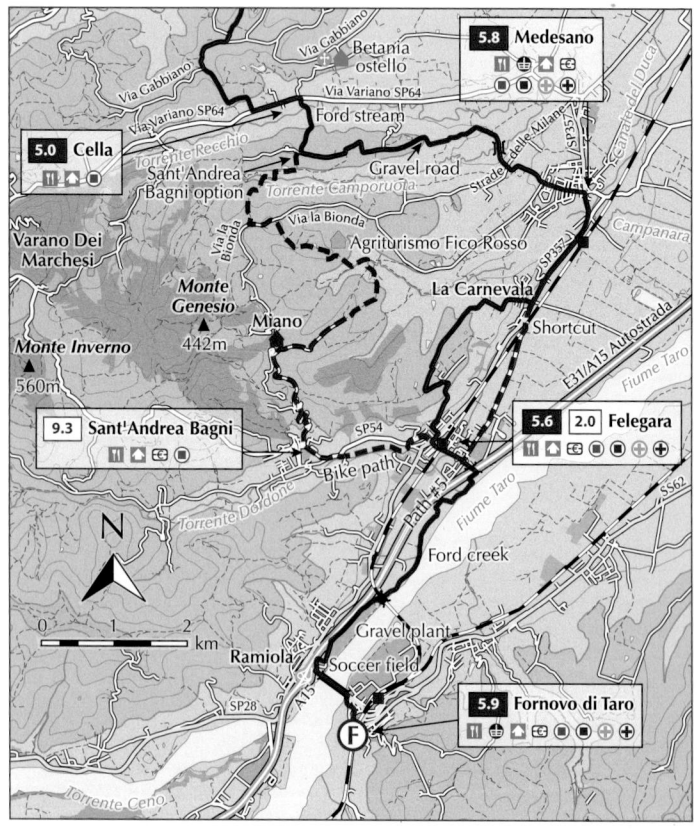

Local growers pick Lambrusco grapes in a vineyard near Medesano

Sigeric may have overnighted here as his Stage XXXV Metane. After the 1495 Battle of Fornovo, King Charles VIII of France stayed overnight and buried his brother here.

⌂ **Oratorio Don Bosco** Ⓞ Pr Do Ⓡ Ⓚ Br Dr Gr Ⓦ Ⓢ Ⓩ 1/4, €15/-/-/-, Via Conciliazione 2, www.parrocchiadimedesano.com, dontorri@libero.it, tel 0525 422136. The parish kindly accommodates pilgrims: 4 beds with bathroom. No kitchen access. Donation only.

After the church turn right onto the busy **SP357**. Follow this road for several kilometers on the sidewalk to the right and then, at the turn-off to Medesano train station, cross to follow it on the left. Come to the village of **La Carnevala** (**1.8km**).

For an optional shortcut, branch onto a bike trail after the railroad tracks alongside the Via Marchi to continue straight on for a 1.8km shorter and much flatter route to Felegara. For the main route turn right to climb the steep hill behind town and enjoy a respite from the highway, followed by a long stretch on asphalt atop the ridge with wide views of mountains. Continue with a descent to **Felegara** (**3.7km**) and turn right on the SP357 to the center (if you have taken the shortcut, turn right on Via Picelli and walk six blocks to find the commercial district).

5.6KM FELEGARA (ELEV 132M, POP 2702) 🍴 ⌂ Ⓒ Ⓟ ⊕ (604.7KM)
First mentioned in 924, Felegara stands at the confluence of the Taro River and the Dordone stream. The Sant'Andrea Bagni option rejoins here.

⌂ **La Casa Dei Nonni** Pr Ⓡ Br 1/3, €-/54/62/72, Via Damiano Chiesa 7, www. facebook.com/casadeinonnifelegara, casparius@yahoo.it, tel 347 840 3493.

Walk downhill on Via Picelli toward the river and cross the **E31/A15** Autostrada in a tunnel. Turn right on the Path #5 trail through sparse woods in the Parco Fluviale. Cross under the railway (**3.4km**), keeping right afterward, and continue past the

Grigolin **gravel plant** and then a **soccer field** before turning up onto the long Via Solferino Bridge (**1.6km**) that crosses the **Taro River** into **Fornovo di Taro**. Look for the tiny, bronze pilgrim at the end of the bridge railing, modeled after the now-headless pilgrim sculpture at the Fornovo church. Take the stairway down to the wide parking area below the bridge and veer left after the grocery store and right in one block to find the Via Cesare Battisti leading up to the Romanesque Church of Santa Maria Assunta (**0.9km**) and nearby pilgrim hostel. Turn left after the church and continue to the upper town square to find bars, shops, banks and pharmacies.

The figure of a pilgrim on the Taro River bridge

5.9KM FORNOVO DI TARO (ELEV 152M, POP 6007) ⬛ ⊕ 🏠 🅒 ⊙ ◉ ⊕ ⊕ (698.7KM)

This may have been an overnight of Archbishop Sigeric who identifies a town named Philemangenur as his Stage XXXIV. A signal event in Italian history occurred in 1495 as King Charles VIII of France was returning home after a successful conquest of Italian strongholds as far as Naples. An army of the Holy League (Venice, Milan, the Pope, Spain, England and the Holy Roman Empire) surprised the French at the Battle of Fornovo, just north of town. The French army was decimated and a humbled Charles VIII was forced to return to France.

In 1905 the Italian Oil Company (SPI) was established here and Fornovo led Italy in oil refinement from its nearby Valezza oil wells, accounting for 80% of the country's needs. The Allies heavily bombed the area in WWII and fought the Germans in the 1945 Battle of Collechio-Fornovo. After four days the 15,000 men of the Nazi army surrendered to the Allied General Mascarenhas de Moraes of Brazil. **Pieve di Santa Maria Assunta** is a jewel of Romanesque architecture, with sculptures on its façade dating from the 11th–12th c. The altar includes a 13th c. sculpture of the martyrdom of Santa Margherita. (Bus: route 2520 to Sivizzano, Cassio and Berceto www.tep.pr.it. It is possible to skip ahead to Pontremoli by train via Borgo di Taro www.trenitalia.com.)

🏠 **Ostello Parrocchia Santa Maria Assunta** ⓞ 🄿 🅁 🅂 2/4, €15pp in double rooms, Via Cesare Battisti 9, mario.mazza@libero.it, tel 0525 2218 or 333 2194636. Closed winters. Reservation required.

STAGE 26
Fornovo di Taro to Berceto

Start	Fornovo di Taro, Church of Santa Maria Assunta
Finish	Berceto, Duomo of San Mederanno
Distance	31.5km
Total ascent	1658m
Total descent	1000m
Difficulty	Hard
Duration	10hr
Percentage paved	58%
Hostels	Sivizzano 7.8km, Cassio 21.0km, Berceto 31.5km

Now begins the transit of the Passo della Cisa, the link that crosses the forested mountains to connect the Po Valley with the Luni coastal region, now spanned by the fairly quiet SS62 highway on the original Via Francigena route. This is certainly one of the hardest stages on the entire pilgrimage, with relentless, sometimes slippery climbs and descents. Lack of food along the way adds to the challenges, though a couple of intermediate lodgings allow the possibility of shortening the day's duration. Several slippery footholds call for hiking shoes or boots with good traction. **A more relaxed, three-night alternate staging between Fornovo and Pontremoli would replace one overnight at Berceto with one at both Cassio and Ostello della Cisa.**

Pass the 12th c. Pieve di Santa Maria Assunta on its right side, go two blocks and cross the street into Fornovo's modest upper piazza with its banks and bars. Cross the **SS62**, passing alongside the bakery, and take this road up and over the hill behind town in a series of switchbacks that ease the steep grade as the road rises among apartment blocks, many with views of the valley, river and mountains beyond. Once atop the ridge continue on the asphalt road that now goes straight, soon arriving at **Caselle** (2.5km, water). After the village come to a triple fork. Take the middle fork downhill on asphalt, enjoying views of the mountains ahead and the valley in the distance far below. At a green, Nissen hut building the descent into the **Val Sporzana** becomes steep. Tall Monte Prinzera looms ahead as you come to the first houses of **Respiccio** (0.8km). Turn left at the **SP39** highway near the valley floor and prepare yourself to walk the next half-dozen kilometers on this highway, which follows the course of the Sporzana River among farms. Pass the villages and occasional roadside lodgings of **La Capanne** (0.8km), **Roncolongo** (2.2km) and **Case Rosa** (0.7km) and before long see the yellow and gold cemetery walls of **Sivizzano** (0.7km). Enter on the back street where you can find the church and bar.

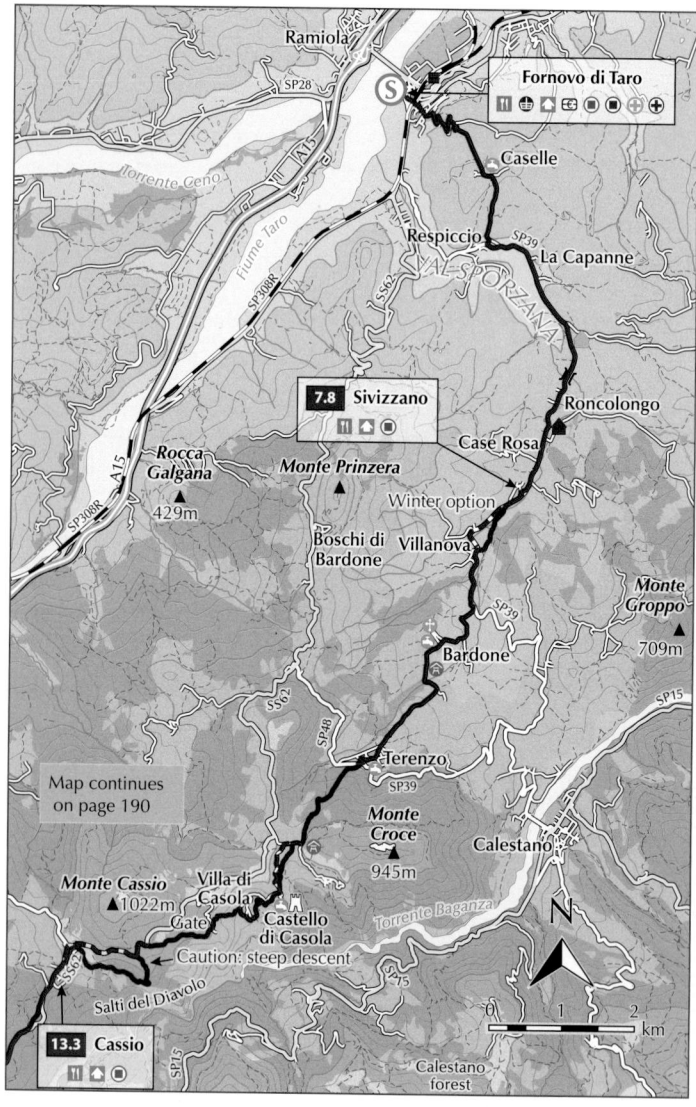

Ramiola

SP28

Fornovo di Taro

Torrente Ceno

Fiume Taro

SP308R

A15

Caselle

Respiccio

SP39

La Capanne

VAL SPORZANA

SP62

SSS2

7.8 Sivizzano

Roncolongo

Case Rosa

Rocca Galgana
▲ 429m

Monte Prinzera ▲

Winter option

Boschi di Bardone

Villanova

SP29

Monte Groppo ▲ 709m

SP308R

A15

✝

Bardone

SP15

SSS2

SP48

Map continues on page 190

Terenzo

SP39

Monte Croce ▲ 945m

Calestano

Monte Cassio ▲ 1022m

Villa di Casola

Gate

Castello di Casola

Caution: steep descent

Torrente Baganza

SP75

N

Salti del Diavolo

SSS2

13.3 Cassio

0   1   2 km

SP15

Calestano forest

188

7.8KM SIVIZZANO (ELEV 250M, POP 80) 🍴 ⛺ ◉ **(591.0KM)**
In 1098 Cistercian monks built a pilgrim hospital here with an attached chapel. The hospital was used until 1492 while the chapel became the parish church of town, reworked in the 17th c.

🛏 **Ostello Parrocchia Santa Margherita** ◉ Do R K S 1/6, €10/-/-/-, loc. Sivizzano, iatfornovo@gmail.com, tel 0525 56085 or 0525 56258. Use of kitchen €13. Closed May. Reservations required.

After Sivizzano, continue on the highway in the rainy season, or in summer fork left onto a more verdant but sometimes-overgrown trail that twice fords the flood-prone Sporzana. The two routes merge at **Villanova (1.2km)** where you continue until you fork right off the SP39 (**0.7km**) to climb to **Bardone (1.0km**, water). After town find a pilgrim rest area with benches and tables then begin the ascent on asphalt to **Terenzo (2.2km)**. In Terenzo fork left on flagstones, passing a crystal clear water fountain on the left, and then head up the hill behind town on switchbacks, passing the Municipio on the way. At the top of the road come to the **SP48** asphalt road where you turn left, looking for a gravel road in 30m that takes off steeply to the right. Follow this path on a relentless 250m climb up the hillside on jagged gravel until you pass a rest area (**2.0km**) with tables and benches and then come to an asphalt road

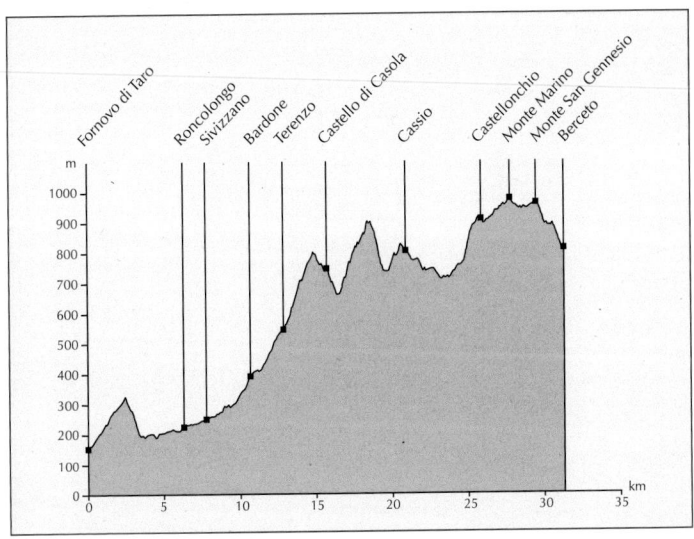

The village of Bardone, with the Sporzana Valley beyond

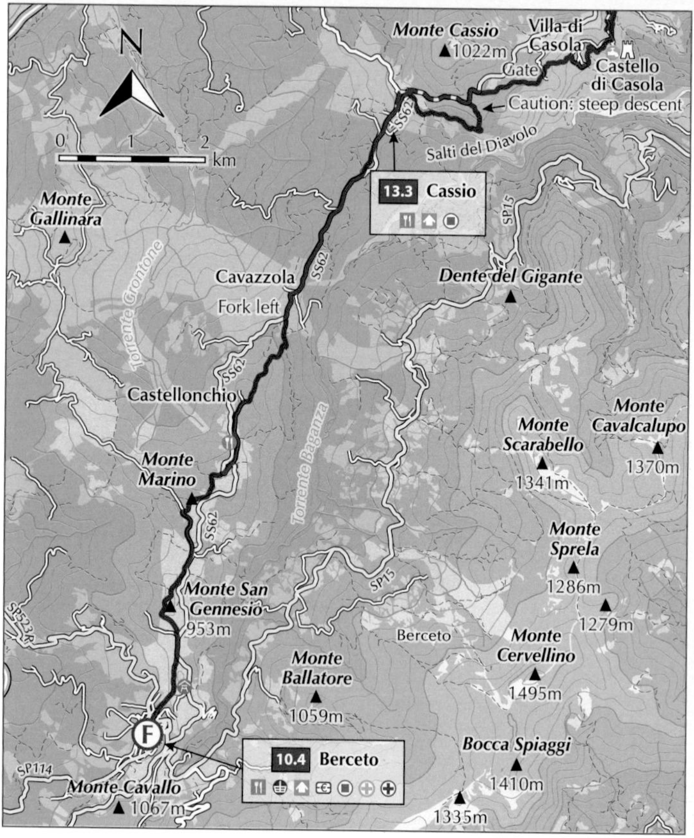

Monte Cassio
▲1022m

Villa di
Casola

Castello
di Casola

Gate

← Caution: steep descent

SS62

Salti del Diavolo

SP15

13.3 Cassio

Monte
Gallinara

Torrente Grontone

Cavazzola
Fork left

SS62

Dente del Gigante
▲

Castellonchio

Monte
Marino

Torrente Baganza

Monte
Scarabello
▲
1341m

Monte
Cavalcalupo
▲
1370m

Monte
Sprela
▲
1286m

SS62

SP15

1279m

Monte San
Gennesio
953m

Berceto

Monte
Cervellino
▲
1495m

Monte
Ballatore
▲
1059m

Bocca Spiaggi
▲
1410m

F

10.4 Berceto

P.114

Monte Cavallo
▲1067m

1335m

that spans the top of the ridge between two mountains. Looking on the opposite side of the ridge you can see an extraordinary view to Castello di Casola.

Turn right on the asphalt road and either fork left on the path that leads steeply downhill to arrive at **Castello di Casola** or simply continue on the road to reach the village (**0.8km**, water). At the start of town is a fountain and to its right a path, which you follow steeply downhill. After a while the path begins a gentle traverse of the mountainside, becoming steep again before reaching **Villa di Casola**. Here the gravel path turns to an asphalt drive as you walk behind houses and begin to climb again. After a modern **gate** with security cameras, continue uphill alongside a green, chain-link fence, with spectacular peekaboo views of the upcoming valley to the left.

The path soon becomes a pleasant woodland trail on pine needles, often gently undulating as it traverses the mountainside. Soon come to the asphalt SS62 highway (**2.1km**), which you follow around a curve. If you are concerned about the upcoming steep descent you can follow this road into Cassio, otherwise, follow the signs left off the highway and come to the Salti del Diavolo gorge, a geological formation with a very steep and treacherous descent, followed by a steep climb up into **Cassio** (**2.4km**). The Salti del Diavolo are unusual rock formations along the Baganza gorge, said in legends to have been left from 'jumps of the Devil' when he was run off by a local hermit. The path enters the old section of town on the Via Roma, one block off the SS62 highway.

13.3KM CASSIO (ELEV 801M, POP 130) 🏨 ⛺ ◉ (577.7KM)
Some remains from the Roman era can be found in the old part of town, including a milestone for the road to Parma. All traces of a medieval castle built here by the Counts of Cassio have now disappeared. The 12th c. **Church of the Assumption** was rebuilt in the 17th c. but suffered heavily in bombings during WWII. A wall of the presbytery holds a 15th c. fresco of St John the Baptist and St Benedict.

🛏 Ostello di Cassio 🄾 🄿🄻 🄳🄾 🅁 🄺 🄱🄵 🄳🄵 🄶🄵 🅆 🅂 🅉 4/13, €16/22/-/-, Strada della Cisa 100, ostello@asp-terenzo.org, tel 052 51700885, 351 6111362 or 347 9069545.

Head down the SS62 highway and after a time fork right onto a single-track gravel path that briefly ascends above the highway. Return to the highway and continue along the ridge line, coming to **Cavazzola** (**3.0km**, tourist lodgings avail). Continue along the highway, starting to climb, and then fork left (**0.5km**) onto an asphalt road, continuing to climb as the road turns to gravel and you enter a deep forest of deciduous trees on the mountainside. The road settles into a gentle undulation, and just after a wide clearing, look for a gravel road that climbs steeply to the right among sparse trees. After a time, fork left onto a single-track dirt path under trees, rejoining the gravel road before coming to the first houses of **Castellonchio** (**1.5km**, restaurant) a hamlet of older, well-cared-for homes, sprinkled with poetic placards and flowers.

After a restaurant to the left just outside the village fork left onto an asphalt road that gradually climbs out of town. The road ends at the SS62 highway – turn right to follow it a few hundred meters before turning left. Here two roads take off, with a directional sign ambiguously placed in the middle. Take the left of the two and climb gradually, after a time forking left onto a single-track path. As the highway joins alongside, fork right to cross a ridge in the midst of a hayfield. Pass an old water pump building on your right and very soon arrive at the summit of 989m **Monte Marino**, high point of the stage, which offers far-reaching views on a clear day.

Continue among hayfields and pastures as the narrow, grassy path descends to a road. Turn left and descend gradually, coming to a scattering of houses just before the SS62 highway. Turn right here to find a gravel road ascending, with a brown gate barring the way and signs warning of late season snow. Walk around the gate and climb among small oak trees to the summit of **Monte San Gennesio** (953m).

Begin descending on the single-track dirt path, sometimes steeply, climbing over a pair of barbed wire fences to continue. Come to the SS62 highway (**4.2km**), which you follow for a brief time before turning right after a guard rail onto a well-marked path. Climb steeply to an overlook, then start downhill, passing a shrine with picnic tables and after that a wooden cross. Descend now on asphalt, soon coming to the first houses of **Berceto** and then the ruins of the medieval walls before arriving at the piazza just before the Cathedral of San Moderanno (**1.2km**).

The streets of Berceto, shrouded in mist

A Romanesque-era relief over the portal of Berceto's Duomo of San Moderanno

10.4KM BERCETO (ELEV 810M, POP 1982) 🍴 ⊕ ⛺ 🅒 ⊚ ⊕ ⊕ (567.3KM)
This town of medieval stone buildings has long served pilgrims on the Via
Francigena. In the 8th c., Modanno, Bishop of Rennes, France, made pilgrimage
to Rome. Arriving in Reims, he received the relics of Saint Remigio to take to
the Pope. While taking a break on the Cisa Pass, Modanno hung the relics on a
tree, but forgot them when he left. Upon his quick return he could not reach the
relics because the tree where they were hung had grown so prodigiously. Later,
Lombard King Liutprando founded a monastery at the site and named Modanno
its prior. Saint Modanno became patron saint of Berceto, and when Archbishop
Sigeric traveled through here in 990 he stayed at the church of Sce Moderanne
as his Stage XXXIII overnight. In the 12th c. the **Duomo of San Moderanno** was
rebuilt in Romanesque style. The **Castello di Berceto** was built in 1221 by the
Municipality of Parma and was the site of battles between rival city states in the
15th c., after which it served as a manor house. By the 19th c. the castle had
fallen into disrepair and villagers used the stones as a quarry for building projects,
though much still remains of the medieval structures.

🛏 **Seminario di Berceto** ⊙ ⊡ 🅚 4/25, €Donation, Via Evasio Colli 15,
 amministrazione@seminariovescovile.parma.it, tel 0521 282951.

🛏 **La Casa dei Nonni** ⓟ 🆁 🅱 🆖 🆆 🆂 5/10, €-/40/70/90, Via Pier Maria Rossi
 8, www.lacasadeinonniberceto.it, info@lacasadeinonniberceto.it, tel 0525
 629103 or 333 2942210. Closed Dec–Mar. Baggage service available.

STAGE 27
Berceto to Pontremoli

Start	Berceto, Duomo of San Mederanno
Finish	Pontremoli, Piazza Duomo
Distance	28.2km
Total ascent	1270m
Total descent	1833m
Difficulty	Hard
Duration	8½hr
Percentage paved	19%
Hostels	Ostello della Cisa 7.0km, Previdè 18.1km, Toplecca di Sopra 21.7km, Pontremoli 28.2km

A challenging and beautiful stage of climbs and descents on mountain trails, but in clear weather it includes some of the very best scenery on the Via Francigena. Wild horses populate this region, and you may spy a shy herd across one of the many valleys. Here also you cross from the Region of Emilia-Romagna into the coastal Lunigiana region of Tuscany. The trails will test your footwear and your physical and mental stamina, but in clear weather they offer a sublime encounter with nature. The stage's only reliable food is at Passo della Cisa, so plan plenty of nourishment for the long day.

Pass the façade of the cathedral on your left and make your way out of the town center on Via Seminario. Pass the **Santuario della Madonna delle Grazie convent**, continue across the **SP114 (1.1km)** and pick up a gravel path at a white gate. Climb here through forest, sometimes steeply, but often with gentle undulations in the direction of **Cantoniera Tugo (1.6km)**. Pass a former **mineral water plant** and circle around to the **SS62** highway. Cross the highway and climb an asphalt road in the direction of **Felgara**, where the road varies between gravel and asphalt depending on steepness. The road forks to the right **(1.1km)** before town and climbs more steeply through forest after it passes a gate on the right. Come to a gate across the road (be certain to close it behind you) and soon arrive at an option **(1.7km)**.

Optional route to Cisa hostel
Fork right here and walk down a rutted dirt road to the SS62 highway, where you turn right to find the Cisa hostel (**1.5km ⌂ Ostello della Cisa** 🅳🅾 🆁 🆆 🆂 8/24, €20/-/-/-, SS62 km100, turismoberceto@gmail.com, tel 0525 64153 or 328 2114870. Closed

A mile marker overlooks the view atop 1238m Monte Valoria

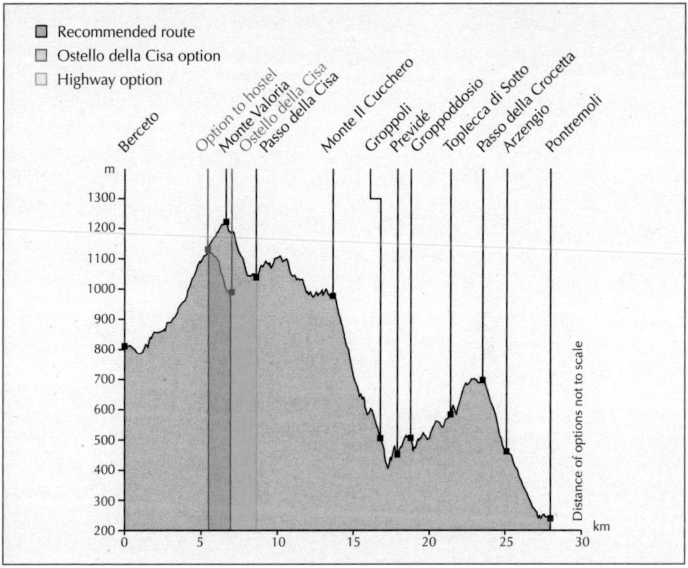

Recommended route
Ostello della Cisa option
Highway option

Berceto
Option to hostel
Monte Valoria
Ostello della Cisa
Passo della Cisa
Monte Il Cucchero
Groppoli
Previdé
Groppoddosio
Toplecca di Sotto
Passo della Crocetta
Arzengo
Pontremoli

m

1300
1200
1100
1000
900
800
700
600
500
400
300
200

0   5   10   15   20   25   30   km

Distance of options not to scale

Nov–mid Apr. Dinner €15, breakfast €3, self-serve laundry €5. Call 24hr prior with any dietary restrictions, no nearby restaurants.) After your overnight, either continue back up the path to the option (**1.5km**) to climb Monte Valoria or walk the SS62 highway to Passo della Cisa (**2.2km**).

For the main route, fork left and continue to climb the forest path toward **Monte Valoria** 1238m (**1.2km**). The peak is a high, bald mountain with a spectacular 360° view and on a clear day very likely will be a highlight of your entire walk. Continue along the ridge, which may inspire a bit of acrophobia though it is perfectly safe, and head sometimes steeply down to the SS62 and **Passo della Cisa** (**2.0km**, café).

8.7KM PASSO DELLA CISA (ELEV 1041M, POP 25) 🍴 ◉
NO ACCOMMODATION (558.6KM)
An ancient pilgrim hospice dedicated to Santa Maria was located on the north side of the pass. The **Sanctuary of the Madonna della Guardia**, just south of the pass, was built of ashlar stones in the early 20th c. and houses a bronze statue of the Madonna. The top of the pass marks the border between the regions of Emilia-Romagna and Tuscany. (Bus to Pontremoli L04, www.catspa.it.)

Turn left on the SS62 and cross the highway, climbing up the steps to the **Sanctuary of the Madonna della Guardia** and beyond onto a pleasant path well above the roadway in a forest of mature deciduous trees. Begin to descend after a well-marked fork, finding a rest area with picnic tables near a seasonal stream. Now begins a long descent through the woods, meeting the SS62 and soon crossing it (**3.5km**). Continuing on the SS62 you would arrive at the nearby town of Montelungo, where Archbishop Sigeric recorded his Stage XXXII as Sce Benedicte, named for the church in town. Continue down a narrow path through the woods. Begin soon to climb, enjoying occasional views to the left. As you near the highway, turn left, go through a gate and begin to climb on a gravel road, now with views to the right. Head toward a summit with lofty cellphone towers near its peak, and soon see the tall mountain-top meadow and obelisk of 994m **Il Cucchero**

Tall peaks of the Apennines stand out behind 994m Il Cucchero

Berceto

🍴 ⛪ 🏠 🛏 🏧 📮 ⊞

S23R
S
SS62

Madonna
delle Grazie

SP114

Mineral
water plant

Cantoniera
Tugo

Felgara

Fork-right

A15

SS62

8.7 Passo della Cisa

🍴 ◉

Ostello
della Cisa

Madonna della Guardia

Monte Valoria
1230m

*Monte
Zucchello*

1197m

A15

Emilia-Romagna

Tuscany

Terrente Baganza

Il Cucchero
994m

Steep
descent

Montelungo

A15

SS62

Cavezzana
d'Antena

Groppoli

Terrente Civasola

Fiume Magra

Suspension bridge

Previdè

Groppodalosio

SP42

Bridge

Cemetery

Casalina

Toplecca
di Sopra

SP42

Passo della
Crocetta

SP39

S62

Fiume Magra

Arzengio
Cemetery

N

0   1   2
km

F

19.6 Pontremoli

🍴 ⛪ 🏠 🛏 🏧 📮 ⊞ ➕ 👫 ℹ

SS62

A15

A suspension bridge crosses Torrente Civasola after Groppoli

(**1.5km**) where in good weather you can enjoy a majestic view across many peaks and wide valleys. Go across the ridge line to begin a very steep and for 30m somewhat slippery descent. The gradient improves as you come within sight of **Cavezzana d'Antena** (**2.3km**), which has the high motorway viaduct as its backdrop.

After another long downhill pass through **Groppoli** (**0.9km**) and continue to descend, heading down the cobblestone path as it turns to dirt and comes to a road. Cross the road to pick up the path on the other side, descending sometimes very steeply to cross **Torrente Civasola** on a **suspension bridge** before re-ascending on the opposite side of the valley and arriving in **Previdè**. Turn left on the asphalt road and then fork left at the end of town just after a shrine.

Now begins a fairly continual climb up the hill on a two-track gravel road, at first with terraces on the left and right. Tucked onto the mountainside opposite is Casalina with its tall church steeple which you will soon see up close. As you begin to traverse the mountainside see straight ahead the first signs of **Groppodalosio** (**0.9km**, ⌂ Temperance ᴮʳ ᴰʳ 3/13 €Donation, Loc. Groppodalosio Inferiore 8, temperance1617@ gmail.com, tel 375 7825734). Follow the cobblestone lane directly through town, switching back on a stairway to head directly downhill. Come to a spectacular stone bridge of fairytale proportions, the Ponte di Groppodalosio, built in 1574 and standing tall and proud over the for-now-tiny **Magra River** below. Soon after the bridge begin a steep climb, arriving at the SP42 where you turn right. Just before town fork left onto a grassy path atop a wall that leads to a back street in **Casalina** (**0.7km**). Continue through the back of the old and somewhat abandoned looking hamlet, following this route that cuts through its middle. Find yourself then on the road that climbs up behind the hamlet.

After crossing a stream, the gravel path levels out, gradually descending among trees. It joins an asphalt road and, just after a **cemetery**, becomes a steep, stone path, which ends at a gravel road under power lines. Turn left, and then at a bend in the gravel road, go straight ahead between two marked trees to descend on a dirt path. This comfortable road rises and descends occasionally until it becomes an asphalt driveway in **Toplecca di Sopra** (**2.0km**). Turn left here and in about 60m turn left again after a metal storage shed, and climb up to cross an asphalt road. Take the path opposite and immediately begin to climb for a very long distance. Come to a church-like building on the left with a cross and benches to find yourself at **Passo della Crocetta** (**2.1km**).

Turn right here and descend on a path marked with bronze plaques attached to yellow stone crosses signifying the Stations of the Cross. The Roman numerals give a countdown as you head down this rough and wide stone pathway finally ending at picturesque **Arzengio** (**1.6km**), with Pontremoli far below and to the right. The route leads around Arzengio and alongside the **cemetery** before heading steeply downhill, ultimately onto a road of large stones. After a series of switchbacks, reach the valley floor and turn right to cross a stone bridge over the now-much-larger Magra River (**2.1km**). Head through a building's archway and turn left on the SS62. Cross to a road that forks off the highway and continue over the railroad bridge and through the Porta di Parma in the historic city walls of **Pontremoli**, noting the elevator leading to Piagnaro Castle high above. A few more blocks on Corso Garibaldi brings you to the Piazza Duomo (**0.7km**).

19.6KM PONTREMOLI (ELEV 245M, POP 7137) 🔢 ⊕ 🏠 🄲 ⊙ ⊕ ⊕ ⊞ ❶
(539.0KM)

Pontremoli stands at the foot of the Apennines, at the confluence of the Magra and Verde Rivers in the far northwest of the coastal region of Lunigiana. The Romans, who conquered the area in the 2nd c. BC, called the town Pons Tremulus (tr: 'shaking bridge'), perhaps due to a wooden span across the Magra that needed continual replacement. Sigeric stayed here as his Stage XXXI Puntremel and in the 12th c. the Icelandic monk Nikulás Bergsson also records stopping here on his journey to Rome and Jerusalem. From the 12th–13th c. it was an independent city, and afterwards was subject variously to Verona, Genoa and Milan. In 1495 Pontremoli was sacked by Charles VIII of France.

The dome of the 17th c. **Cathedral of Santa Maria Assunta** dominates Pontremoli's skyline and the church's interior is a festival of 17th c. Italian painting. St Francis himself founded the **Church of San Francesco** in 1219 and prominent Pontremolese of earlier centuries are buried here. The **Piagnaro Castle** above town was a key part of the city's medieval defenses and was rebuilt several times until in the 19th c. it became a home for poor families. The castle was fully restored in 1975 and houses a pilgrim hostel as well as the Museum of the Stele Statues of the Lunigiana, displaying pre-Roman archeological finds from the region (www.statuestele.org/en).

The skyline of Pontremoli

⚐ **Ostello Castello del Piagnaro** Ⓞ 𝗣𝗿 𝗗𝗼 𝗥 𝗖𝗿 𝗦 𝗭 6/21, €15/-/-/-, Porta di Parma, www.statuestele.org/foresteria-castello-delpiagnaro, info@statuesele. org, tel 0187 831439. Hostel in the scenic Castle of Piagnora.

⚐ **Convento Padri Cappuccini di Pontremoli** Ⓞ 𝗣𝗿 𝗗𝗼 𝗥 𝗞 𝗦 18/60, €16/-/-/-, Via ai Cappuccini 6, www.cappuccinipontremoli.it/convento, info@cappuccinipontremoli.it, tel 0187 830395. Linens €5. Recently renovated convent. Arrive 15:00–19:00.

⚐ **Seminario di Pontremoli** Ⓞ 𝗣𝗿 𝗥 𝗞 𝗪 𝗦 𝗭 15/23, €-/15/30/-, Piazza San Francesco 10, foresteriaseminario.pontremoli@gmail.com, tel 333 3321782. Linens €5. 18th c. cloister in heart of Pontremoli.

SECTION 6: LIGURIA AND TUSCANY

Looking toward the coast from Via Palatina (Stage 31)

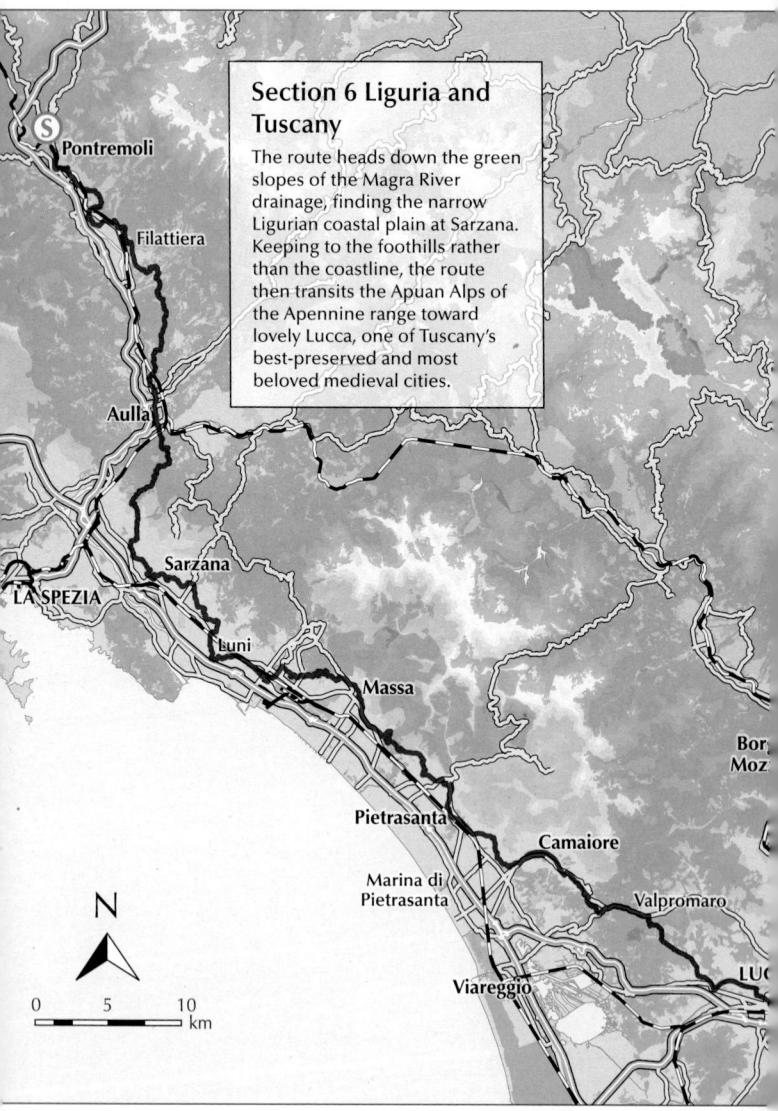

Section 6 Liguria and Tuscany

The route heads down the green slopes of the Magra River drainage, finding the narrow Ligurian coastal plain at Sarzana. Keeping to the foothills rather than the coastline, the route then transits the Apuan Alps of the Apennine range toward lovely Lucca, one of Tuscany's best-preserved and most beloved medieval cities.

Start	Pontremoli, Piazza Duomo
Finish	Aulla, Parrocchia di San Caprasio
Distance	32.1km
Total ascent	725m
Total descent	912m
Difficulty	Hard
Duration	9hr
Percentage paved	49%
Hostels	Migliarina 8.2km (rooms), Aulla 32.1km

In order to avoid the busy SS62 the official route zigzags across the Magra valley before skipping the valley altogether to traverse the forested eastern slope of Monte Alin. This wise diversion adds a bumpy and somewhat disjointed 10km to the highway's quick 22km to Aulla. A tough but beautiful day of trail walking results, with scattered historic villages and monuments connected by an assortment of paths, driveways and stairs. The 23-minute train ride and €3.60 fare to Aulla will seem an attractive option in bad weather. Intermediate services are available at Filattiera (11.0km) and Filetto (16.9km).

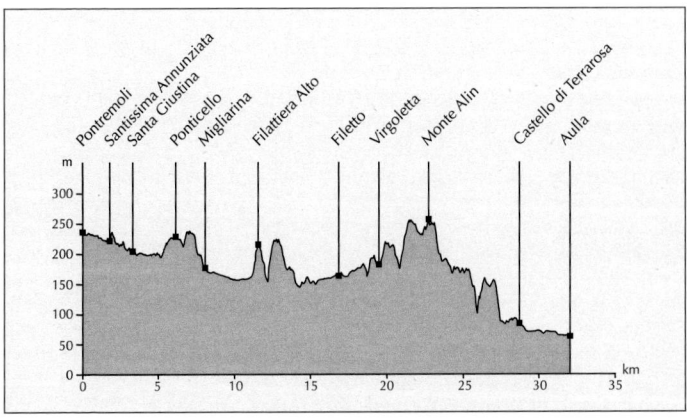

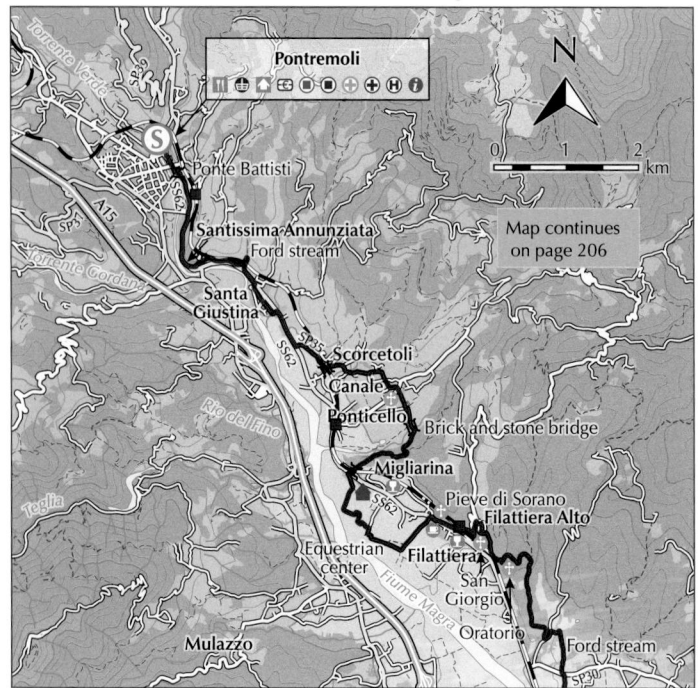

Map continues on page 206

Continue down Corso Garibaldi and take a left just before the road ends to cross the **Ponte Battisti** and turn right. As you leave the old city you merge onto the **SS62** highway and at a curve in the road fork left into the ancient suburb of **Santissima Annunziata**, (**1.8km**), a quaint neighborhood of colorful homes. The 15th c. Church of the Santissima Annunziata remembers a vision of the Virgin Mary. Before the church, turn left and pass under an archway leading to a sidewalk on the left where you catch a path that takes you alongside and above the SS62 highway. Soon veer left to cross under the railroad bridge and ford a stream, then return to the highway. Carefully walk 250m along the treacherous roadway before forking right to an asphalt road among warehouses at **Santa Giustina** (**1.6km**) before heading back to the highway again. After another 500m on the road cross left just before a furniture store and find the asphalt **SP35** that aims toward the left side of the valley. Now you are among vineyards and fields of corn, with the mountains on both sides of this broad basin. Turn left under the train tracks to reach **Scorcetoli-Monteluscio**. Cross a stone bridge and make a gentle climb to **Canale** (**0.7km**), and then cross the Via Ponticello and turn left toward the church with a small dome at **Borgo Ponticello** (**0.5km**). Ponticello-Filattiera is a partly-restored medieval village that includes a 10th–12th c. fortified tower-house.

Follow a straight asphalt lane to cross a small stream on a large **brick and stone bridge** of four arches. For a time, head up onto the hillside under trees, then head downhill somewhat steeply over loose stones. The road narrows to a one-track path through the woods, crossing under a train bridge. Look for a small passageway in the building ahead and find yourself on the highway in **Migliarina** (**2.0km**, bar on highway to left, ♠ Casa Sofia O Pr R K Br Dr Gr W S 1/3, €-/-/40/-, Via delle Cunelle 8, moni-acobelli@gmail.com, tel 392 7099959. Breakfast and dinner incl.). In order to keep you off the narrow SS62, the VF stewards now send you across the highway and onto a succession of roads among small gardens and horse pastures, the highlight of which is an **equestrian center** with paddocks, stables and a stand for spectators. The diversion leads back to the SS62 as you come to Pieve di Santo Stefano di Sorano of **Filattiera** (**2.0km**, bars, train).

This 12th c. **masterpiece of medieval architecture** is one of the most significant historic buildings in the region. The fully restored church, much of it constructed from river rocks and local sandstone, features three semi-circular apses. Housed in the building are five pre-Roman stele (flat, slab-like statues) that attest to the ancient roots of the area.

Exterior of the Pieve di Sorano at Filattiera, one of the best examples of Romanesque architecture in the region

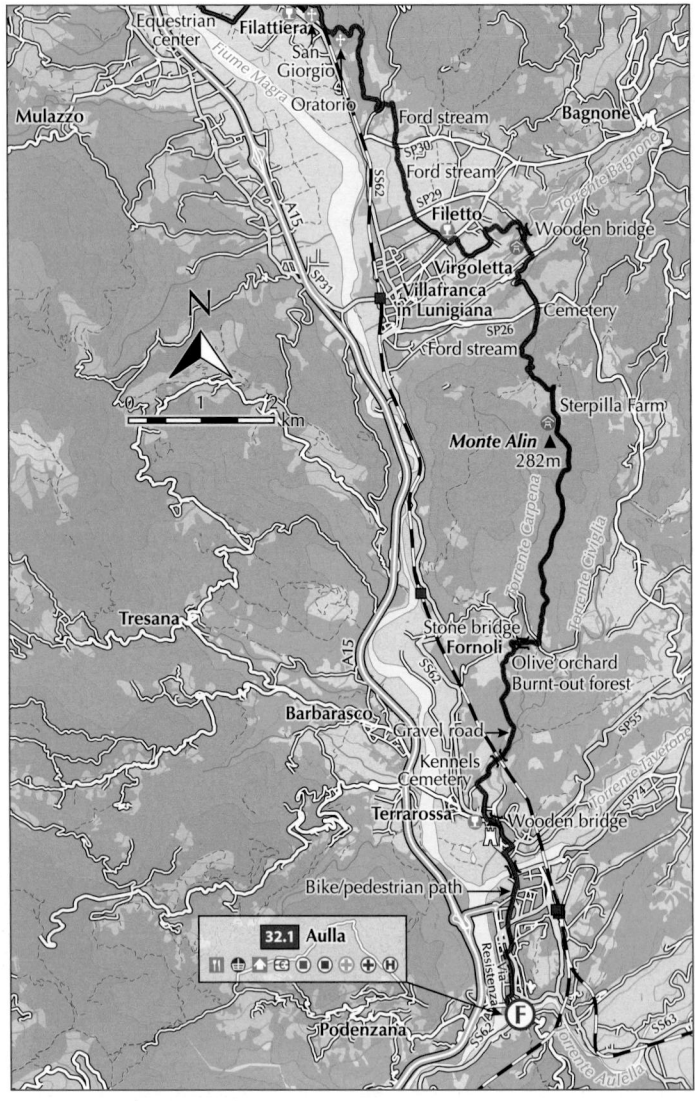

The back of buildings at Virgoletta shows their medieval roots

Pass the historic church and fork left after the roundabout, then after the post office turn left and cross under the railroad tracks, taking a switchback on an asphalt road and a stairway up to medieval **Filattiera Alto**. Filattiera Alto grew around the Castle of San Giorgio, established in the 6th c. to stem the tide of invaders from the north. The castle has vanished, leaving a picturesque stone village of narrow streets and the 12th c. Church of San Giorgio as a window to its past. Follow the quiet lane out of town, passing the foot of the **Church of San Giorgio**, and continue down the hill. Alongside the railroad tracks turn left to cross a stream over a low, concrete bridge. Come to a grass and stone path that climbs the hill steeply to the 15th–19th c. **Oratorio dell'Annunciazione**. Continue uphill on the cobblestone path, which levels out as you come to a barbed wire fence on the right, reaching a summit. After a time, a path joins from the left and the descent begins.

Just after crossing a stream on a concrete bridge turn left onto an asphalt road slowly climbing the hill. Take the first right onto a gravel road and cross a stream. Soon ford a small stream, cross the quiet **SP30**, and ford another stream, this time on stones. Very soon the gravel road turns to a narrow stone path under chestnut trees on flatter terrain. Cross the surprisingly busy **SP29** highway next to a park and continue into the lovely and well-preserved medieval village of **Filetto** (**5.3km**, bars). Turn left into the 16th c. Porta Sud and come to the 17th–18th c. Palazzo Ariberti connected to the Church of Saints Filippo and Giacomo by a photogenic two-level arcaded passageway. Just after crossing under a second gate, turn right onto an asphalt road and walk around the old town walls. Come to an asphalt road and turn left, following it for a time before turning right onto a gravel road making its way among gardens and small vineyards and orchards. Turn right onto a path between stone walls and after a right turn following a house, cross a large stream on a **wooden bridge** and then go uphill on an extremely steep path of loose dirt. Come to an asphalt road and go straight on a grassy track leading up the hill. At a stairway turn right onto an asphalt road. Circle left to find another stairway before the arch where you can climb to the upper piazza of **Virgoletta** (**2.6km**).

The **small passages** of this 12th c. town make it one of the area's most atmospheric villages. The 15th c. parish church contains relics of Saints Gervasio and Protasio, two early church martyrs celebrated each year on 2 May.

Turn left and descend to cross a stream on a stone bridge then climb up an asphalt road out of town as it makes a switchback up the hill. Come out onto a flat road among fields and scattered houses. Cross the **SP26** toward a **cemetery** where the road turns to gravel, heading toward the hillside where you will spend the next 90min crossing two summits on forested roads and trails. After a few hundred meters veer left onto a narrow stone path that descends through the woods, fording another stream and climbing uphill on the other side, sometimes over deep ruts. Finally come to a gravel

The tower of the Parish Church of Saints Gervasio and Protasio in picturesque Virgoletta

road at the end of a very long climb and turn left. The road starts to level out then makes a hairpin right turn onto another gravel road for a short climb, with a descent beginning alongside a fence toward the **Sterpilla Farm** (**2.7km**) with cypress trees along the fence line. Pass the front gate and come to a shaded and grassy rest area.

The route continues on a dirt road through the forest, remaining flat for a few hundred meters until a fairly steep climb begins. Reach a summit on **Monte Alin** 282m and then the descent begins fairly gradually on a stone and dirt path. After some time reach another summit and come to a road surface of crushed rock, showing signs of civilization – notice beehives on the left and the first house for quite a while. The gravel road turns to asphalt at the grey gate of a farm. Cross the asphalt road and take a concrete drive uphill next to a house. Just after the house turn right and find a path that descends quickly. At the bottom of this little valley cross the **Torrente Carpena** on a two-arched stone bridge.

Now climb very steeply, turning onto a steep and grassy path between two houses on the outskirts of **Fornoli** (**3.9km**). A series of driveways, roads and paths now lead to what appears to be a summit in an **olive orchard**.

Among pastures and orchards begin a descent, making your way through 50m of overgrown bushes to find a dirt path slowly climbing the hill in a **burnt-out forest** of sparse trees. Now begin the stage's final steep descent on yellow-brown earth. At a gravel road with horse pastures on the right, pass under a train bridge and alongside noisy **dog kennels** before spilling out onto an asphalt road just after a **cemetery**.

The signs now direct you downhill, past an infant/primary school and then onto Giuliano Street, leading to the sidewalk in Terrarossa on the busy SS62 (bar) where you continue straight. Turn left before the imposing 16th c. **Castello di Terrarossa** and go around behind it to cross the **Torrente Civiglia** on a wooden bridge. At the end of the bridge turn right onto a wide asphalt path, then cross the SS62 to find the pedestrian/cycle path leading alongside the busy highway. Cross the **Torrente Taverone** and continue on this path until it ends in **Aulla**, then follow signs three blocks to the right to reach Via Resistenza (**2.3km**). Follow this street downhill through commercial areas at Parrocchia di San Caprasio (**0.7km**).

32.1KM AULLA (ELEV 59M, POP 11,065) 🔢 ⊕ 🔲 🄲 ⊙ ◉ ⊕ ⊕ ⊕ (506.9KM)
Aulla sits at the confluence of the Aulella and Magra Rivers, along the ancient road that crosses the Cisa Pass. Its strategic importance is demonstrated by the presence of the hulking 16th c. **Brunella Fortress** on the hillside east of town, which today houses the Natural History Museum of Lunigiana. The town grew up around its abbey, established in 884 by Count Marquis Adalberto of Tuscany, and in the same year the chapel of the abbey, now the **Church of San Caprasio**, was built. Archbishop Sigeric recorded Aulla as his Stage XXX Aguilla, and likely stayed at the abbey which for centuries served pilgrims. The town lost many of its historic buildings in Allied bombing attacks in 1943 and battles during the Nazi retreat in 1945.

🏠 **Abbazia di San Caprasio** ◉ 🔠 🆁 🔠 🆂 4/25, €10/-/-/-, Piazza Abbazia 1, www.sancaprasio.it, sancaprasio.aulla@gmail.com, tel 0187 1780776.

STAGE 29
Aulla to Sarzana

Start	Aulla, Parrocchia di San Caprasio
Finish	Sarzana, Piazza Matteotti
Distance	17.1km
Total ascent	892m
Total descent	923m
Difficulty	Moderate
Duration	5½hr
Percentage paved	43%
Hostels	Bibola 3.1km (B&B), Sarzana 17.1km

Rather than following the busy SS62 through a narrow gorge in the Magra River valley (Sigeric's itinerary), the route traverses the far slope of Monte Grosso, covering the journey in about the same distance, but in quieter and more verdant surroundings. This is the last mountainous stage of the Via Francigena as now you emerge onto the Lunigian coastal plain in the region of Liguria. The stage is short but not easy, with some significant climbs and descents interspersed with fantastic views in clear weather and a few atmospheric mountain hamlets. Enjoy your first peek at the Mediterranean from above Sarzana. Footing can be tricky on the paths between Vecchietto and Ponzano Superiore. There are no services, so bring a lunch and plenty of water.

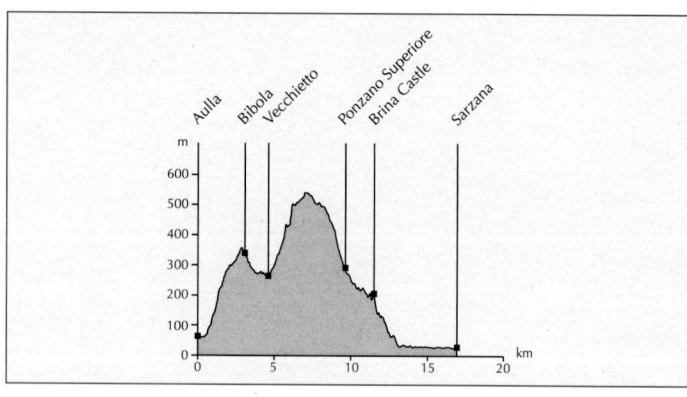

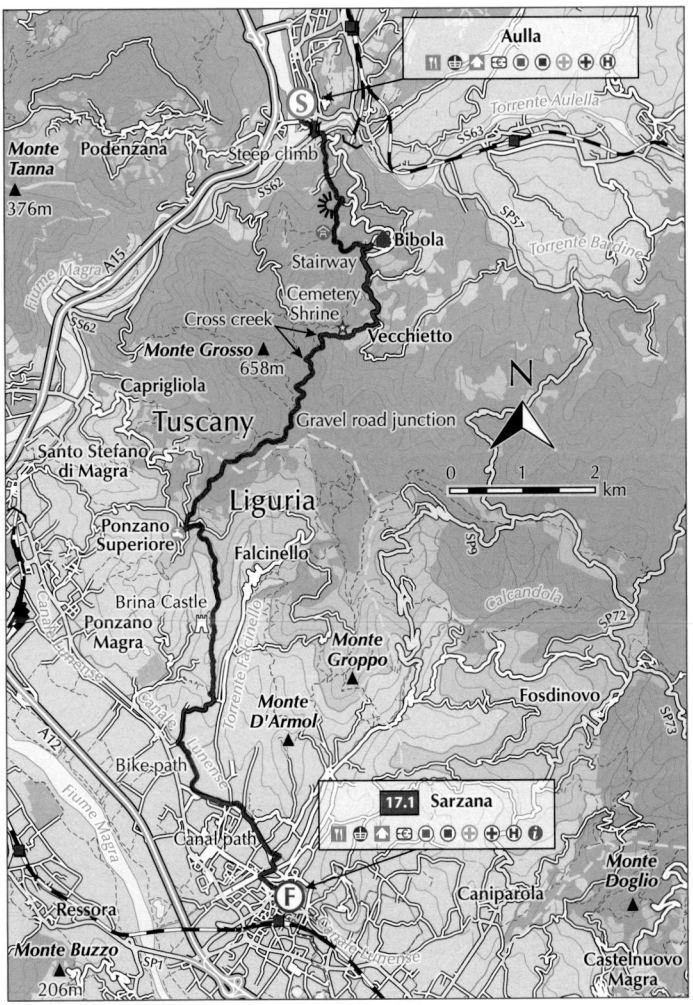

Turn left from the abbey and make your way onto Via Andrea for a block. Continue when it seems to end, finding on the other side of a garden space a wide asphalt road leading left toward the bridge. Cross the bridge over the **Aulella River**, carefully cross the **SS62**, and go left on an asphalt road leading up the hill. Curl around the face of the hill and on the opposite side find another asphalt road that climbs very steeply. Partway up fork left onto a single-track path leading into the woods. Soon the path begins to climb steeply – stairway steeply – on dirt and rock. Cross an asphalt drive between two houses and continue up the hill with some excellent views back to Aulla. The path is deeply rutted and difficult until it levels out and you meet a gravel road. Turn right and continue to climb.

Before long come to a viewpoint and then a rest area with picnic tables. Go straight at this intersection of three gravel roads and continue up the hill, circling to the left of the ridge. At a small shrine a **stairway** leads up to a shortcut on black gravel where after 200m you reunite with the gravel road, along the way finding a beautiful vista of successive Apennine ridges beyond. Soon come to **Bibola,** perched on a promontory with a ruined castle atop (**3.1km**, bus ⬆ Al Castello di Bibola 🅾 Pr R K Br W S ⓩ 2/6, €Variable, Via Luigi Pirandello 5, tamara.casciari@gmail.com, tel 370 3318871. Reservation required. Dinner on request €15). This isolated hilltop castle has stood here since at least the 7th c. when it was named on a list of fortified towns in the area.

Turn right and descend toward the town on the next ridge with the tall, white church steeple. The path becomes a deeply rutted gravel road heading somewhat steeply along the hillside. Soon come to a quiet asphalt road where you turn right to continue the descent among woods and then vineyards, gardens and a **cemetery** before the hamlet of **Vecchietto** (**1.6km**, bus). Make your way through narrow streets alongside snug homes squeezed together. On the far side of Vecchietto begin to ascend on a gravel path that seems to lead out among the ridges covered by deciduous trees. Pass a **shrine** and begin a moderate climb, still on gravel.

The climb becomes steeper as it comes to a small olive orchard, and in parts it is overgrown. Cross a seasonal rivulet and continue to climb. At a dirt road turn left. Continue uphill but now more gradually as the dirt road ends in just 100m and the route goes right, continuing to climb on a steep and treacherous path of stone and loose rock. Cross a seasonal creek which in season would be at the top of a low waterfall and begin to climb again very steeply until the dirt path levels out as it traverses the mountainside, often with views behind and to the left.

After a brief climb come to a **junction of gravel roads** (**2.5km**). Take the gravel road right ahead, slowly descending at first. A right fork in about 400m takes you onto a shortcut path that descends more quickly. Watch your footing on the shale and bedrock and when you come to the gravel road continue across it on the path. You've now crossed from Tuscany into Liguria. Finally, the path ends at another gravel road with spectacular views to the right of the Magra Valley and to the left of the Ligurian Sea, as the Mediterranean is here called. Soon arrive at **Ponzano Superiore** (**2.6km**, water), itself a picturesque site.

Archbishop Sigeric stayed just downhill in Santo Stefano di Magra as his Stage XXIX and Ponzano's castle dates from about the same period as his visit – the year 1000. Five-hundred years later, in 1495, **King Charles VIII of France**

The village of Ponzano Superiore stands on a bluff overlooking the Magra Valley

gathered his troops here as part of his campaign to control Italy. Ponzano Superiore made history once more when it became a center for Italian partisans in WWII fighting Nazi rule. The town was liberated by US soldiers on April 23, 1945.

Either spend some time exploring the narrow streets of this small town that time has forgotten or turn left between two buildings in Piazza Aia di Croce and descend on a gravel drive leading downhill among orchards. Turn right on another asphalt road and continue to descend on this road that sometimes is only as wide as a single path. Come to a wide, flat junction of roads just below a mountain-top with a path leading up the hill on loose rock, aiming at a protruding peak. Follow this track until you come to a second peak jutting from the mountainside that holds the ruins of **Brina Castle** (**1.9km**).

Modern archeological studies have documented settlement at this site, with its commanding view of the **Magra River Valley** out to the coast, from the 5th–4th c. BC. Fortified by the Romans and then repopulated and refortified in the Middle Ages, the castle was intentionally destroyed in the 1306 Peace of Castelnuovo. Informative kiosks through the site describe both the history and the recent archeology (www.castellodellabrina.it).

After visiting the ruins, head downhill on a very steep dirt path. Below the steepest part, enter the woods and descend more gradually and comfortably through the forest. Come to the camp of a recluse who has set up somewhat alarming warning signs, and veer left onto the path marked as 'dangerous bend.' Continue downhill on a succession of roads and driveways and at the bottom of the hill turn right at a sign that announces the new (2018) route into Sarzana. This new direction follows an asphalt road that makes its way downhill among large homes. At a stop sign turn left to climb onto an undulating path through the woods. Go straight at a fork and come to a tall concrete bulkhead. Just to the left is an entrance to the bike path (**2.2km**) which, though

The Fortezza Firmafede of Sarzana

prepared for walkers and bikers, here feels remote and disused. Following the signs continue as it comes alongside a **canal** among orchards and gardens, passing a bakery advertising pizza and then a cemetery. Canalside walks like this will be common in the next two stages. The path spills out into the parking lot of a soccer field. Turn right, off the canal path (**2.5km**), and follow signs onto city streets before crossing over a bridge and turning right into a riverside park. At the end of the park turn left and cross under the Porta Parma into the historic center of **Sarzana**, with the central Piazza Matteotti just a few blocks ahead.

17.1KM SARZANA (ELEV 28M, POP 22,104) 🔢⊕🔯🅒◉◉⊕⊕🅗🛈 (489.8KM)

It is easy to fall in love with Sarzana, whose city center combines a distinctive medieval character with the relaxed vibe of the seaside Lunigiana region. Sarzana's strategic importance at the entrance to the Magra River valley caused it to change hands several times in the Middle Ages, and it was variously ruled by Pisa, Florence and Genoa. The Pisans built the **Fortezza Firmafede**, which was demolished and rebuilt by Lorenzo de'Medici, an impressive construction that stands today just north of the Porta Romana (€5, www.fortezzafirmafede.it). The 13th–15th c. **Sarzana Cathedral** holds the 1138 Cross of Maestro Guglielmo, as well as relics of Saint Andrew and the Blood of Christ. Sarzana is the perfect place to enjoy two foods synonymous with Italian cuisine that originated in kitchens of this region – hearty focaccia bread and tasty pesto sauce, made from basil grown in this ideal seaside climate of Liguria.

🏠 **Parrocchia del Carmine** 🔟🅡🅢🆉 1/14, €15/-/-/-, Via Paganino 80, www.parrocchie.it/sarzana/carmine, gilbertcarcere@alice.it, tel 0187 620260 or 348 7294423. Closed winters. Arrive after 15:00.

STAGE 30
Sarzana to Massa

Start	Sarzana, Piazza Matteotti
Finish	Massa, Piazza Aranci
Distance	29.0km
Total ascent	635m
Total descent	600m
Difficulty	Moderately hard
Duration	8hr
Percentage paved	80%
Hostels	Caniparola 4.9km, Provasco 10.9km (B&B), Avenza 17.3km, Massa 29.0km

This stage is bookended by two climbs – one to the castle above Sarzana and the other to the mountain above Massa – as you bounce back and forth across the border between Liguria and Tuscany. Highlights are the Roman city of Luni, the medieval center of Avenza, and the world-famous marble industry of Carrara. A harrowing walk down the busy, modern version of the ancient Via Aurelia would shave a third off the day, but the patient pilgrim can find treasures in the full itinerary, including spectacular views of the sea from above Massa.

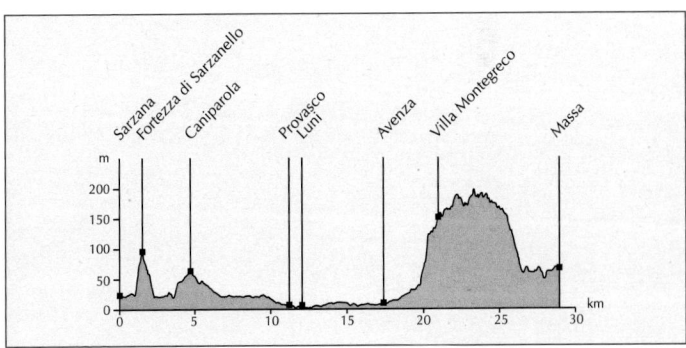

Continue along the Via Mazzini in Sarzana to the piazza just before the Porta Romana. Follow the signs to the left that lead you up the steps to the right of the Oratoria della

Misericordia to the plaza below the impressive **Fortezza Firmafede**. Now zigzag your way up to the Via San Francesco, where you turn right. Signs soon point you up the hill, first on asphalt and then onto a sometimes steep trail of grass, gravel or cobblestones. Come to the hill just below the massive **Fortezza di Sarzanello (1.5km)**. Built as early as the 11th c. the fortress was seat of the bishops of Luni who controlled the region in the Middle Ages (€4, www.fortezzadisarzanello.com).

After the fortress fork right on the descending asphalt drive, Via Luparello. After a salmon-colored house the road becomes a path that gradually descends under trees, ending at an asphalt road. Follow the signs that lead you to a familiar canal-side path (**0.8km**), which you follow for about 0.5km. A left turn at the end of the canal path (**0.5km**) takes you onto the **Via Canalburo** that follows the bottom of the ridge as it meets the valley floor. The road turns left to climb the low ridge ahead then ends. Turn

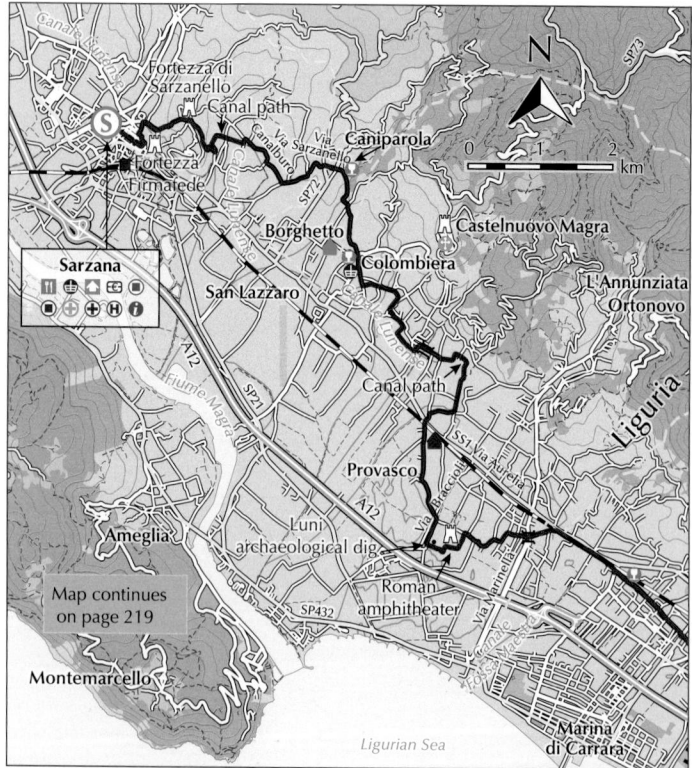

216

left onto **Via Sarzanello**, which is joined by a succession of busier roads until you come to a former town wall at **Caniparola** (**2.0km**, bar, ♠ Ospitalità Sant'Antonio Ⓞ Ⓓⓞ Ⓡ Ⓚ Ⓑⓕ 3/15, €Donation, Via Borghetto 111, https://ospitalita-sant-antonio.webnode.it, tel 339 638 0331 or 0187 673530, reservation req, located one km downhill on Via Malaspina). The route continues on a narrow asphalt lane that descends through woods and among fields with views uphill to Castelnuovo di Magra. Arrive in **Colombiera** (**1.4km**, bar, groceries) and then walk downhill through town on an asphalt road with no sidewalks before turning left onto the path alongside the **Canale Lunense** (**0.4km**).

Follow this for the next 45 minutes, only leaving it for a few blocks after Colombiera to cross a bridge over a drainage channel. When the canal path ends (**3.2km**) prepare to cross the busy **SS1 Via Aurelia** – location of the original Roman road through this area – following brown signs downhill toward Luni. After crossing the highway (note the cafés and bars to the right), carefully go through the one-lane tunnel under the railroad tracks and follow the road downhill through the sparse suburb of **Provasco** (**1.0km**) (♠ Affittacamere Ca' Thomas Ⓞ Ⓟⓕ Ⓡ Ⓑⓕ Ⓖⓕ Ⓢ Ⓩ 6/8, €-/45/70/90, Via Della Stazione 8/B, info@cathomas.it, tel 0187 670555 or 328 2706534. High season prices €-/55/90/110.) Cross the **Via Braccioli** to the gates of the archeological dig at **Luni** (**1.9km**, café).

For over a thousand years, **Luni** was the major city in this region. Settled first by the Ligurians and Etruscans, Luna, as it was called at first, served as seaport for the area. The Romans established a colony here and in the 2nd c. AD built the Via Aurelia to connect Luna to Rome. It flourished for centuries, in part due to its access to the marble quarries in the nearby mountains, and 'Luna marble' was considered the best in the Empire. After the fall of Rome, Luna was attacked by the Goths, recaptured by the Byzantines, and then taken by the Lombards. Vikings, who mistook it for Rome, sacked it and martyred the bishop, canonized as Saint Ceccardo.

By the time of Archbishop Sigeric's visit as his Stage XXVIII, it was no more than a village with dim memories of its past glories. A brief return to prominence came in the 10th c. with investment by Emperor Otto I, but in 1015 the Andalusian leader Mujahid waged battle with Pisan and Genoese forces, destroying the city for one final time. As the harbor silted up, even the location was forgotten within a few hundred years. It was in 1442 that the location of Luni was reidentified, and Pope Pius II, at the urging of the local cardinal, forbade any further pillaging of its ruins. Nevertheless, the Palazzo del Commune of Sarzana was constructed in 1471 using dressed stone from the site. Excavations began in the 1970s revealing a large theater, amphitheater and forum, attesting to the prominence of this once-proud city (€4, closed Mondays, www.luni.beniculturali.it).

After the museum and dig, follow the wide, white gravel path toward the **A12 motorway** which you can now see ahead. As you turn left to circumnavigate the dig, you come within 1.5km of the Ligurian (Mediterranean) Sea – as close as you will get on the official Via Francigena walking route. (A bike option takes you along the shoreline, which here is fairly urban. Instead, consider walking or taking the bus from Pietrasanta on Stage 31 to enjoy the sandy beaches farther south). At the end of the gravel road, turn right on an asphalt road that in 200m will pass the **Roman amphitheater**, said in its heyday to have seated 7000 people.

Now the route wends its way among the back streets of scattered villages interspersed with vineyards. Turn right onto a narrow, asphalt lane, cross the **Via Marinella** and then a ramp and bridge over the **Torrente Parmignola**. Continue along the bulkhead of the canal, followed by a bulkhead below the railroad tracks (**2.7km**), here decorated with colorful murals. You have crossed the border now back into Tuscany. Leave the tracks and join the Strada Provinciale Avenza-Sarzana (**1.1km**, bar) at a roundabout as it begins to veer away from the railroad tracks, taking this commercial arterial road directly to the center of **Avenza** (**1.8km**), which you reach after a bridge across the Aventia River.

Cross under the archway adjacent to the historic **Castracani Tower** at the heart of Avenza and follow the signs to a street a block off the river that curls up and out of

---

17.3KM AVENZA (ELEV 7M, POP 13,728) 🅿 ⊕ 🏠 Ⓒ ⊙ ⊕ ⊕ (472.4KM)

The earliest mention of Avenza is AD 950, but archeological remains in the parish church are from the 6th–7th c. when the town prospered due to its position between the seaport and the marble quarries of nearby Carrara. The fortress in the town center – of which just the **Torre di Castruccio Castracani** remains – dates from the 15th–17th c. when it defended the area for the Malaspina family. It was sold to private individuals in the 19th c. and used as a stone quarry for local building projects until preservationists saved it from further destruction. The 16th c. **Church of San Pietro** has a 15th c. triptych by Maestro di Sant'Ivo, purchased by the congregation in 2019 after it disappeared from the church some 500 years earlier.

🛏 **Ostello Antonio Mazzi** Ⓞ Do R Br Z 3/13, €Donation, Piazza Finelli 11, tel 338 8333413 or 0585 857203. Run by the Parish of San Pietro. Seaport is 30min walk away.

🛏 **B&B New Life** Ⓞ Pr Do R K Br W S Z 3/10, €20/-/-/-, Via Provinciale Avenza-Sarzana 48, newlifecarrara@gmail.com, tel 373 7482862. Reservation required.

---

the center of town. Cross left over the train tracks at grade and then walk among the marble factories and outlets, often with large trucks transporting sparkling white hunks of Carrara marble to destinations worldwide.

Carrara marble, once called 'Luna marble' for the name of the region, has been quarried here since ancient times. Prized for its often uniform, stark white color the marble has been used on prominent buildings around the world, including the Pantheon and Trajan's column in Rome, the Marble Arch in London, the Duomo of Siena, and statues like the David of Michelangelo and many others.

The Torre di Castruccio Castracani in Avenza

Follow the long, straight Via Provinciale Carrara-Avenza as it soon crosses the SS1 Via Aurelia and heads up toward the carved mountains that source the world-famous stone. Come to a roundabout (**1.9km**) and cross right to the asphalt Via Forma Bassa that leads up into the hills, where you'll

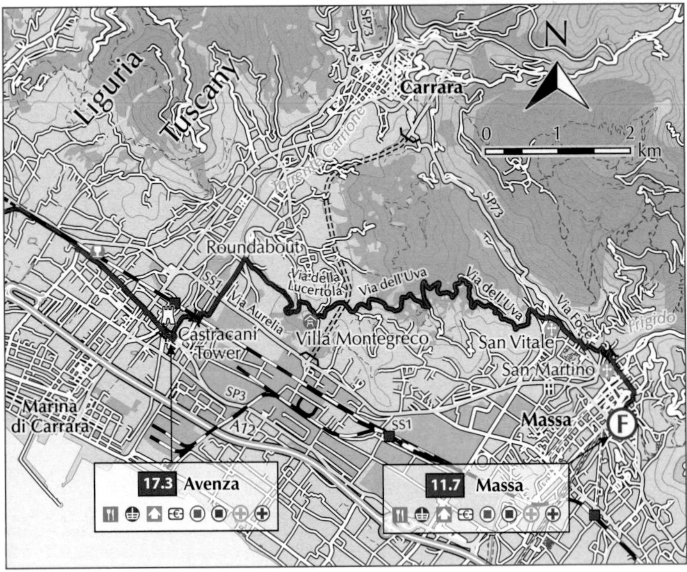

Views toward Massa from the Via della Lucertola

remain for the next two hours or so. In about 500m the asphalt road becomes steep as it climbs among suburban homes, many with sweeping views of Avenza and the sea. After a switchback, the asphalt ends and a two-track grassy road begins. As it ascends it steepens and becomes a dirt path. Just before a small house turn right and find the **Via della Lucertola** that climbs, turns to white gravel, then back to asphalt, continuing to climb steeply.

Come to signs for a pilgrim rest area (200m off the track) at **Villa Montegreco (1.8km)**. Just afterward there are spectacular views above Massa out to the mountains on the left and the sea. The road on broken gravel soon crosses a ridge, offering views to the left, including the Carrara peaks, and then enters a wooded area. Soon you are in an area of terraced vineyards that begin to the left and cascade down the slope nearly to the valley floor. The aptly named **Via dell'Uva** (Way of the Grapes) snakes along as a pleasant, descending traverse of the line of mountains behind Massa. Finally, the road ends and a succession of roads leads you through the first houses above Massa, past the **Church of San Vitale (6.0km)**, and then briefly onto **Via Foce**, an auto road leading directly to the heart of town. Instead the route turns left, aiming for the historic Ponte Vescuovo

The Arco del Salvatore leads into central Massa

220

through the old villa of Borgo del Ponte and onto a gravel path along a stream. Cross a somewhat creaky metal bridge over the Frigido stream and climb the stairs. At the top is a glass display case at the 16th c. Church of San Martino, once site of a pilgrim hospital, with a mannequin of the bishop and plaque with the history of Ponte Vescovo (The Bishop's Bridge). Turn left to go through the gate. Head straight down the Via Palestro to the Via San Francesco, where you go one block right to the steps of the Basilica Cathedral of Santi Pietro e Francesco, crafted from the region's pure, white marble. Turn right and in one block arrive in Piazza Aranci, the main square of **Massa** (**2.0km**).

11.7KM MASSA (ELEV 63M, POP 68,946) 🔢 ⊕ 🛆 ⓒ ◎ ⊕ ⊕ (460.8KM)

There are two sides to central Massa. On the downhill side of Piazza Aranci is a bustling, modern shopping district. Uphill are the narrow streets of old Massa, with its faded stucco buildings and sidewalk cafés. Mentioned first in the 9th c., Massa was a possession of the bishops of Luni, becoming property of the powerful Malaspina family in 1421. They rebuilt the medieval castle and renamed it **Castello di Malaspina** in the 15th–17th c. to serve both as a fortress and residence. Though it fell into disuse and was used as a prison until the 20th c., the renovated residence contains a beautiful courtyard and fine frescoes decorate the interior (€5.50, open afternoons, www.museimassacarrara.it/castello-malaspina).

The **Cathedral of Santi Pietro e Francesco** was originally the church of the Franciscan convent, tracing its origin to 1389. In the 16th c. its expansion as a cathedral was begun and its ornate marble façade was finally completed in 1936. At the center of town is **Piazza Aranci**, expanded during the rule of Grand Duchess Elisa Baciocchi, Napoleon Bonaparte's sister, in 1809. The red, Renaissance-era **Palazzo Ducale**, also known as the Palazzo Rosso, dominates one side of the square. Behind is the **Piazza Mercurio**, built in the 16th c. as the town's commercial hub. In the midst of the piazza is statue of the god Mercury, protector of commerce.

🏠 Ostello Palazzo Nizza ◎ 🄿 🄳 🅁 🄺 🄶 🆆 🆂 🆉 14/25, €20/-/-/-, Piazza Mercurio, 12/14, ostellopalazzonizza@gmail.com, tel 0585 1886345. Reservation required.

STAGE 31

Massa to Camaiore

Start	Massa, Piazza Aranci
Finish	Camaiore, Piazza Bernardino da Siena
Distance	25.7km
Total ascent	651m
Total descent	681m
Difficulty	Moderately hard
Duration	7¼hr
Percentage paved	82%
Hostels	Pietrasanta 16.8km, Camaiore 25.7km

Here you turn away from the sea and head through the Apuan Alps toward the rolling hills of Tuscany. This is a stage spent mostly walking on asphalt, with views from the hills above Massa one highlight and the center of medieval Pietrasanta another. There are ample services along the way since much of the territory is urban. A few spare hours and a 4km bus ride can allow you to dip your toes in the waters of the Ligurian (Mediterranean) Sea at Marina di Pietrasanta.

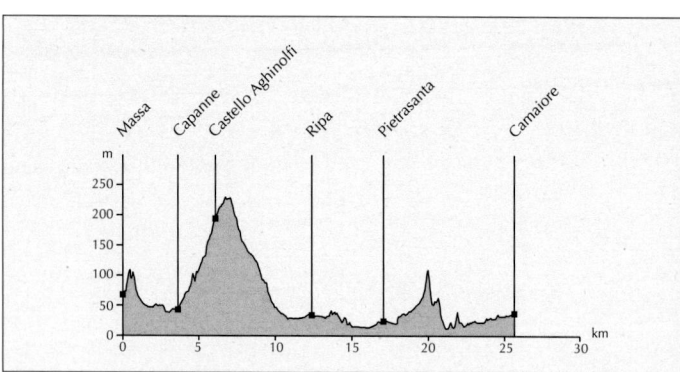

In Piazza Aranci, go to the left side of the large, red Palazzo Ducale and continue straight. Walk among the shops of this pleasant part of town to Piazza Mercurio, clustered around a statue of the ancient Roman god Mercury perched atop a tall obelisk.

Ruins of Castello Aghinolfi from Via Palatina

Turn left here, climbing steps to the right and at the top walking under the archway of the **Santa Chiara** church. Work your way back down the hill alongside the foundations of the **Castello di Malaspina** and right on the Via del Bargello toward the busy **SS1 Via Aurelia** (**1.2km**), where you turn left and walk on sometimes sketchy and other times non-existent sidewalks. Finally fork left onto the quieter **Via Sforza** (**1.7km**) at a large **winery** and follow it up before turning left on the **SP1** that heads through the lively and busy center of **Capanne di Montignoso** (**0.8km**, cafés, bakery, bank, ⌂ Ostello Parroquial Il Pane e La Rosa ☒ ☒ ☒ ☒ 4/8, €Donation, Via Santa Maria 43, ostellomontignoso@gmail.com, tel 353 4302467).

On the far side of town, walk through a parking lot, cross the SP1, then cross a bridge over the **Torrente Montignoso** and head up the hill on a quiet asphalt road, with the busy street now behind you. Just before a sculpture, turn right on another quiet asphalt road and switch back up a long but gradual climb to **Castello Aghinolfi** (**2.5km**)

An 8th c. document confirms existence of the castle here, and in the Middle Ages it was a part of the **defensive perimeter** for the city of Lucca. It was last used by a Nazi garrison as part of the 'Gothic Line' of German defenses. A panoramic terrace gives sweeping views of the coastline (€5, www.istitutoval-orizzazionecastelli.it/castelloaghinolfi).

Continue to climb on the asphalt road as it forks right at the castle gate. Pass a restaurant (closed Tues) and continue on this road, the **Via Palatina/Via Casone** that features amazing views of the coast, the sea and back to the castle. Begin a long descent, with olive trees at first and then in a forest of chestnut and pine. Gradually the houses begin to multiply, at first on large lots, often with vineyards and large gardens. Pass pilgrim rest areas with water fountains as the road descends. A right turn leads down to **Strettoia** (**3.5km**, bar, pizzeria, groceries) where you turn right onto a very narrow street and then left toward a church with a yellow, modern steeple. Follow alongside the olive orchard adjacent to the Parish of Saints Ippolito and Cassiano and after a time make a right turn on Via Risciolo, a left onto Via Romana which becomes **Via Gramsci** that leads onto the SP9 into **Ripa** (**2.8km**, bars).

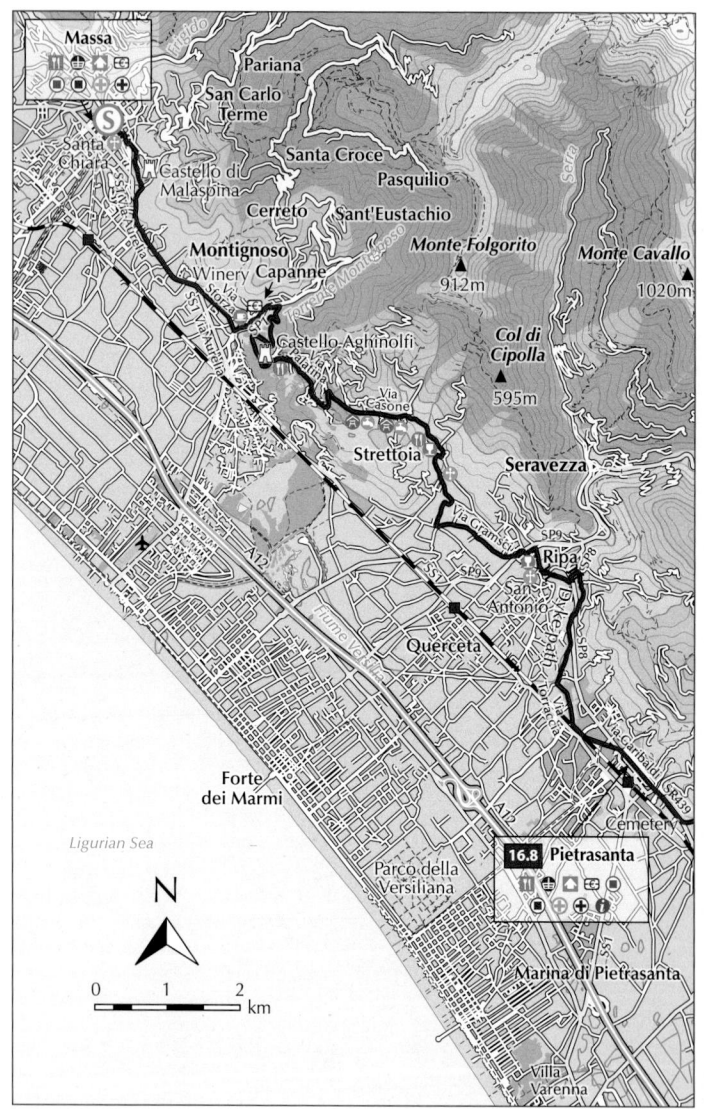

Pass the **San Antonio Abate** church with its modern mural above the front portal and turn right. The road here goes along the channel of the Versilia River with vast marble factories opposite and then turns left to cross the river on a long, sweeping bridge. Just after crossing, turn right onto a gravel path that descends along the top of the dyke. Follow along the dyke path with just one detour across the SP8 until you walk down the steps of the dyke path and turn left on the **Via Torraccia** (**2.9km**) just afterward. Go straight at the roundabout and follow this gradually descending road through a zone of marble factories and storage yards. Turn left to walk alongside the railroad tracks onto Via Fossetto that will take you to the heart of **Pietrasanta**. Come to a large parking lot at the Municipio and continue along the pedestrian shopping street, the **Via Garibaldi**, toward the church tower to find the lovely and large central square.

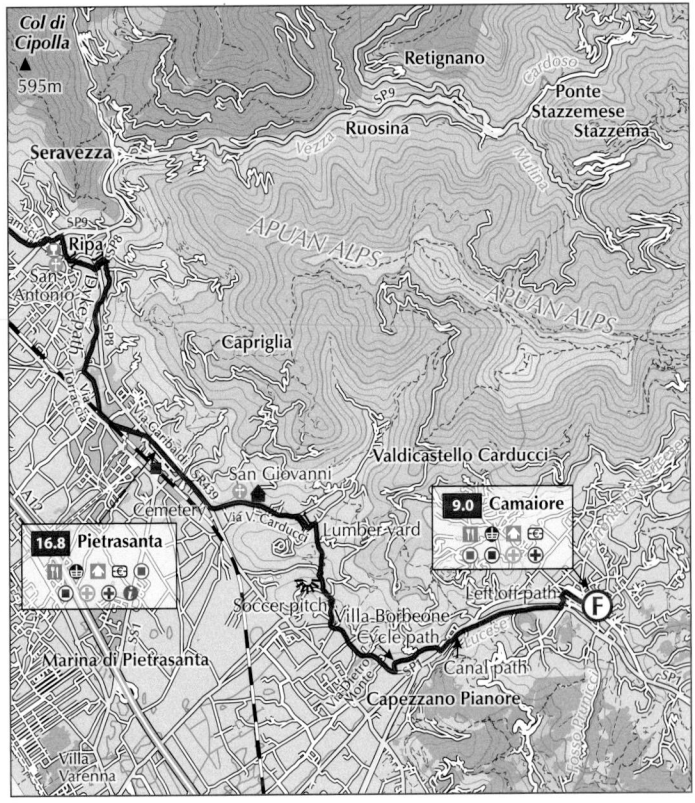

The streets of Via Garibaldi in Pietrasanta are decorated for a festival

16.8KM PIETRASANTA (ELEV 26M, POP 23,666) 🍴 ⊕ 🏠 ⑤ ◉ ◉ ⊕ ❶
(444.0KM)

Pietrasanta's cozy shopping district and grand café-filled central piazza make it a pilgrim favorite. Though a fortress stood at this location from Lombard times, the medieval village of Pietrasanta was founded by its namesake Luca Guiscardo da Pietrasanta in 1255. It is considered part of the Versilia region along the foothills of the Apuan Alps. In the Middle Ages Pietrasanta was variously under sway of Pisa, Genoa, Lucca and Florence. The interior of the white marble 13th–14th c. **Cathedral of San Martino** is adorned in 17th frescoes by Florentine artists, but most important is the Madonna del Sole, a beloved 15th c. painting that hangs in the right transept chapel. Adjacent to the church is a rough, brick tower, meant also to be clad in white marble to match the cathedral. (For those wanting to experience the Mediterranean, the E26 bus connects hourly from Pietrasanta bus station to Marina di Pietrasanta, an 11-min trip https://lucca.teseo.app/planner. Most beaches along this coast are private, costing €10–30 a day in exchange for a sunbed, umbrella and shower.)

🏠 **Casa Diocesana La Rocca** 🔟 🆁 🆂 1/6, €10/-/-/-, Via della Rocca 10, casarocca@tiscali.it, tel 0584 793094. Reservation required.

Continue on the Via Garibaldi as the road opens to automobiles and becomes the SR439 leading out of town. At the Pietrasanta **cemetery (1.0km)**, cross left to leave the highway and begin to climb the green hill now directly ahead which separates the seaside plain from the mountain valley where Camaiore is located. Pass the **Church of Santi Giovanni and Felicità** on the left and continue up the somewhat perilous, sidewalkless **Via Valdicastello Carducci** before turning right on a road that continues up toward the low ridge. Immediately afterward, cross a bridge by a small waterfall

(**1.6km**) on the left. Turn left and soon afterward turn right before a tall, terraced and green hillside on Via Orticeto to aim at the low saddle between the two hills ahead.

At a triple fork go straight, passing alongside a **lumberyard** and beginning to climb up the saddle. After climbing partway on the road, take a shady dirt path to the right. Climb and then descend under tall bushes and trees passing the occasional sheepfold, chicken coop and bamboo forest. Arrive at the concrete driveway of a farm and continue downhill. Follow signs to an overlook where you can see down to Santa Lucia and off in the distance to the seacoast as far as Viareggio. Continue to descend, passing another bamboo forest and a soccer pitch. The road turns to asphalt and passes **Villa Borbeone** (**2.0km**), where the last empress of Austria was born.

Continue to descend among trees until you veer left onto the **Via Dietro Monte**, and then connect to a narrow, asphalt bike path (**1.2km**) that points to a gap between the mountain to the right and the ridge to the left. This pleasant path leads all the way to Camaiore, first through the valley, then on the left side of the tree-lined **SP1** leading into town, and then after crossing the highway and the river, to the opposite side on a narrow, gravel path in the grass. Following the signs, turn left off the path (**2.7km**), cross a bridge and then the highway and veer left toward the Piazza XXIX Maggio. Halfway through the piazza turn right and walk several blocks among shops and restaurants on the pedestrian Via Vittorio Emanuele to come to Piazza San Bernardino di Siena, the heart of **Camaiore** (**0.5km**).

9.0KM CAMAIORE (ELEV 35M, POP 32,513) 🚉 ⊕ 🛏 🄲 ⊙ ⊕ ⊕ (435.1KM)

The Romans planted a settlement in this large valley at the foot of the Apuan Alps as a defensive outpost to protect the city of Lucca, calling it Campus Maior (tr: 'large field'). Archbishop Sigeric visited here as his Stage XXVII Campmaior. In medieval times it became property of the Sforza family, and in 1799 was plundered of its art treasures by Napoleon's army. Its most ancient building is the 13th c. **Collegiate Church of Santa Maria Assunta**, founded in 1260. The area's archeological museum resides in the **Palazzo Tori Massoni** and specializes in 'tactile' experiences, allowing visitors to touch reproductions of archeological finds. The church building of the **Abbey of San Pietro** dates from the 12th c., though the community's presence here dates at least to the 8th c. The abbey's 17th c. organ is heart of an annual international organ festival. Camaiore is connected to the coast by the SP1 Via Italica, just 7km away at **Lido di Camaiore**, a popular beach resort located just north of the famous beach town of Viareggio.

🏠 Ostello del Pellegrino 🄾 🄳ₒ 🅁 🄺 🅆 🅂 🅉 5/24, €24/-/-/-, Via Madonna della Pietà 1, www.ostellodicamaiore.it, info@ostellodicamaiore.it, tel 345 1168661. Linens €4. Closed Nov & Jan. At the Abbey of San Pietro.

🏠 Oratorio Il Colosseo 🄳ₒ 🅁 1/3, €Donation, Via Tabarrani 26, tel 335 8025290 or 339 1832857.

STAGE 32
Camaiore to Lucca

Start	Camaiore, Piazza Bernardino da Siena
Finish	Lucca, Piazza San Michele
Distance	24.6km
Total ascent	673m
Total descent	684m
Difficulty	Moderately hard
Duration	7hr
Percentage paved	70%
Hostels	Valpromaro 9.5km, Lucca 24.6km

Frayed nerves caused by a hazardous stretch along the narrow shoulder of the SP1 highway may be calmed by the green and pleasant walk through the Parco Fluviale. The lovely and historic walled city of Lucca awaits at the end of the stage. There are opportunities to refuel at Montemagno and Valpromaro, but the route is otherwise without services until the end of the stage.

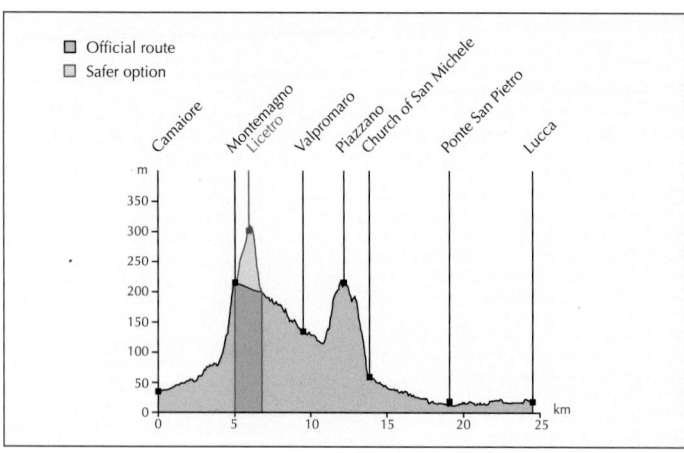

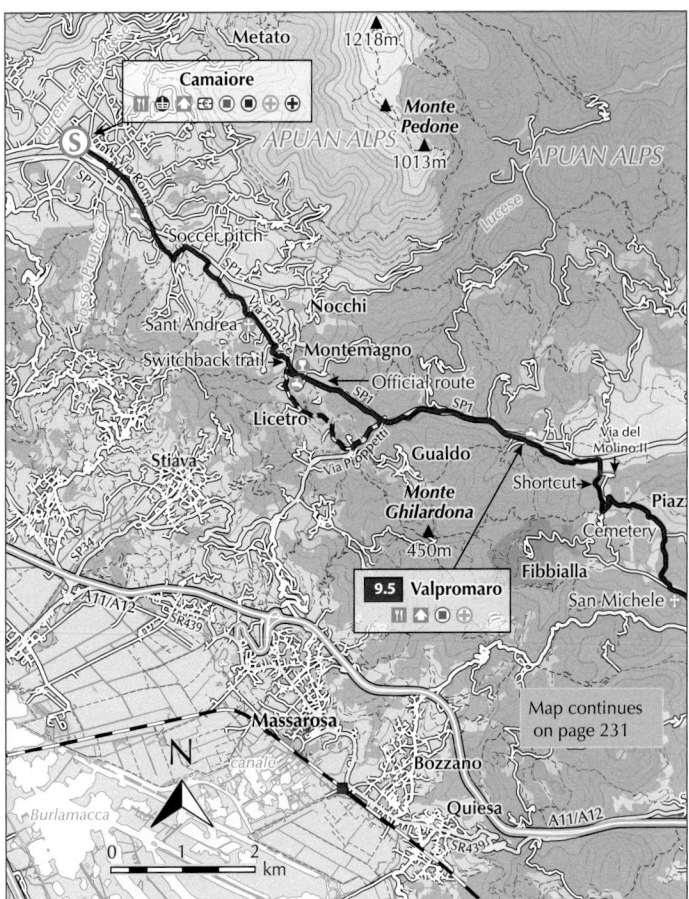

The pedestrian street Via Vittorio Emanuele becomes the **Via Roma** as you walk out of town. Walk along it, often without benefit of sidewalks, until the road comes to an end at the **SP1** highway. Cross the highway and cross the canal next to it before turning left onto the canal-side path. Pass a **soccer pitch** and after a few turns through a small suburb join a bike path alongside the canal once more. The route turns right onto a gravel road that leads into the woods alongside fields. Pass the **Church of Sant'Andrea** (**3.8km**) on its left side and turn right on the Via della Fornace, gradually climbing

A carved sign directs pilgrims near Valpromaro

toward the high green ridge ahead. Come to the SP1, which you briefly follow until a steep path that bypasses the long switchback of the SP1 takes you to a concrete stairway that climbs onto the SP1 once again, right at **Montemagno** (**1.2km**, bar). Looking back here, on a clear day, you can catch one last glimpse of the sea. The official route now follows the narrow and hazardous SP1 for most of the next 4km. The recommended alternate route on the hillside above the highway (see map) passes through **Licetro** (**0.8km**) before rejoining the SP1 (**1.6km**). Walk carefully against traffic on the highway, with a few brief diversions off the pavement, before forking right at **Valpromaro** (**2.1km**).

9.5KM VALPROMARO (ELEV 140M, POP 133) 🍴 🛏 ◉ ⊕ (425.6KM)
The 12th c. **Church of San Martino** cared for pilgrims and the poor in its annex.

🏠 Casa del Pellegrino ⓞ 🅓ⓞ 🅡 🅚 🅑🅻 🅓🅻 🅦 🆂 🆉 5/35, €Donation, Via Vecchia
   Provinciale 15, www.facebook.com/CasaDelPellegrinoValpromaro,
   valpromaro@gmail.com, tel 0584 956028 or 327 6948204. One of VF's most
   beloved hostels, run by volunteers.

After town, fork right onto an asphalt road separated from the highway by pastures until you come to the Via del Molino II (**1.4km**) where you turn right heading toward the ridge. At a curve in the road, turn right to walk a 10–15min shortcut path over the ridge ahead. Come to the original road, much higher up now, and turn left to continue the climb as you walk among woods with scattered farm houses to the first buildings of the hamlet of **Piazzano** (**1.4km**, no services). Pass the pale green church building on its right side. Take the asphalt road downhill and across the narrow valley, aiming at the **cemetery** (**0.8km**) across the gap. **Caution: after the cemetery, turn right and**

take extreme care as you descend a very steep bank on sandstone and gravel. Finally come to asphalt **Via delle Gavine** (**0.9km**) where you turn left. You will remain on this quiet road for nearly the next 4km, passing the one-time pilgrim hospital at the 12th c. **Church of San Michele Arcangelo**.

> Built here in 1175 by the donation of two private individuals, the **church and hospital** served pilgrims and the poor until it was closed in 1730. The small hospital building stood across the road from the church but was destroyed in WWII in the German retreat.

The valley widens as the ridges on either side diminish in height. Come to the outer fringe of **San Macario** (**3.7km**, bar along the SR439, 400m south). The signs take you through the back of town to a road below the tall dyke of a canal. Cross the **SP24** and continue as the canal veers toward the SR439. Climb up onto the sidewalk of the **San Pietro Bridge** (**1.5km**) across the **Serchio River**. After the bridge turn left and take the asphalt driveway down to the gravel **Via della Scogliera** that follows the top of the

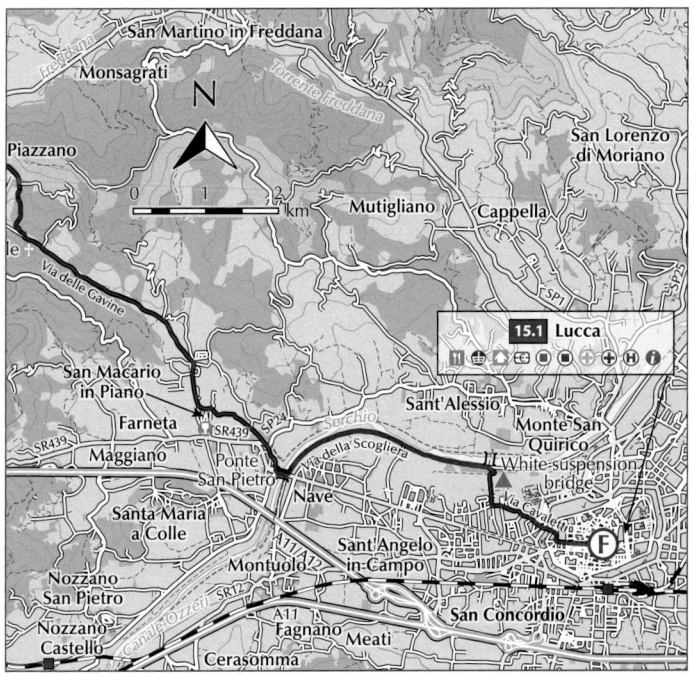

green and serene river dyke for 3km toward Lucca. Walk under the **white suspension bridge** (**3.4km**) at the end of the path and find the asphalt road that passes a **campground**. As you enter the outskirts of Lucca, turn left and follow the narrow patchwork sidewalk along the **Via Cavaletti** before picking up a bike path to the right. Cross the SS12 toward the famed city walls of **Lucca**. Once inside Porta San Donato, veer right one block to turn left onto Via S Paolino, the start of Lucca's main east/west pedestrian street. In a few blocks arrive at Piazza San Michele in Foro (**2.1km**) at the heart of town.

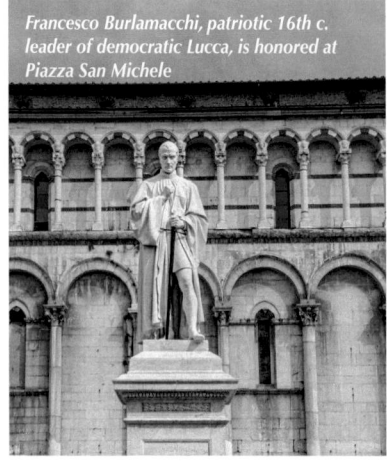

Francesco Burlamacchi, patriotic 16th c. leader of democratic Lucca, is honored at Piazza San Michele

15.1KM LUCCA (ELEV 24M, POP 88,397) 🟦 ⊕ 🛏 🅒 ⊛ ◉ ⊕ ⊕ 🅗 ❶ (**410.5KM**)

Lucca's well-preserved and atmospheric center makes it one of Italy's most beloved towns. Although best known for its intact, walkable and bike-able Renaissance-era walls, Lucca hosts one of Italy's most famous religious treasures, the Volto Santo (Holy Face), a carved wooden crucifix venerated at the **Cathedral of San Martino** since medieval times. Legend attributes the crucifix to Nicodemus, and for centuries it has been paraded through town on 13 September during Lucca's festival of Luminara di Santa Croce. The annual procession begins at the 12th c. **Church of San Frediano**, itself a prized monument that honors the Irishman Fridianus, 6th c. bishop of Lucca. The 13th c. mosaic on the façade sets San Frediano apart from Lucca's other 100 churches and its Trenta Chapel holds the tomb of an early Via Francigena pilgrim, Richard of Wessex, who died in 722 en route to Rome.

Pilgrims will also want to visit the 12th c. **Church of San Michele in Foro**, whose stunning 13th c. façade makes it the center of attention at the heart of town and whose name recalls the town's Roman roots (*foro* tr: 'forum'). These Roman roots are visible in the town's layout – a grid of streets culminating in gates at each of the cardinal directions – and in the shape of its most beloved piazza, the **Piazza Anfiteatro**. Buildings in this iconic albeit touristy square were built at the edges of the Roman amphitheater and the resulting layout preserves the original oval shape. A visit to Lucca is not complete without a 45m climb up the 14th c. **Guinigi Tower**, crowned with a garden that features seven small holm oak trees (Via San Andrea, €5, summer hours 09:30–19:30). Opera lovers will not want to miss the **Puccini Museum** that celebrates Lucca's most famous son (€9, Corte San Lorenzo 9, www.puccinimuseum.org). If you are leaving the Via Francigena at Lucca, it is most convenient to take a train to Pisa International Airport (www.trenitalia.com, 45 min, €9), which has direct flights to all major European hubs.

🏠 **Ospitale San Martino e Giacomo** 〚Pr〛〚Br〛〚Dr〛 4/16, €Donation, Via della Rosa 38, www.confraternitadisanjacopo.it, tel 333 4461186. Opened in 2022 by the Italian confraternity, adjacent to Lucca's Duomo.

🏠 **Pellegrinario San Davino** 〚O〛〚Do〛〚R〛〚S〛〚Z〛 1/10, €Donation, Via S Leonardo 12, www.luccatranoi.it, sandavino@luccatranoi.it, tel 0583 53576.

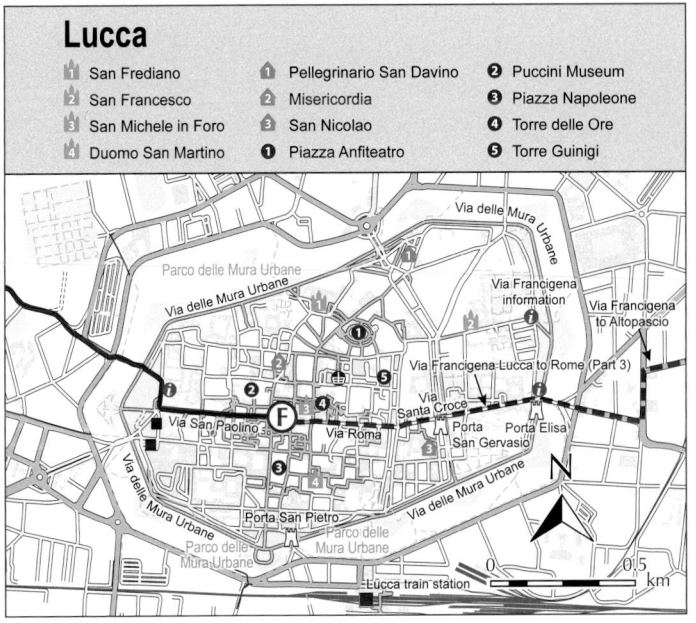

Lucca

- 🏛 San Frediano
- 🏛 San Francesco
- 🏛 San Michele in Foro
- 🏛 Duomo San Martino
- 🏠 Pellegrinario San Davino
- 🏠 Misericordia
- 🏠 San Nicolao
- ❶ Piazza Anfiteatro
- ❷ Puccini Museum
- ❸ Piazza Napoleone
- ❹ Torre delle Ore
- ❺ Torre Guinigi

An intricate pattern of columns and arches grace the facade of Lucca's San Michele in Foro
(photo: Rod Hoekstra)

APPENDIX A
Stage planning table

Book stage #	Location	Distance from start	Distance from previous point	Distance, book stages	My itinerary
1	Lausanne	0.0	0.0		
	Cully	9.0	9.0		
2	Vevey	21.2	12.2	21.2	
	Montreux	28.0	6.9		
	Villenueve ferry dock	33.4	5.4		
3	Aigle	46.0	12.6	24.9	
	Ollon	50.5	4.5		
4	Saint-Maurice	63.2	12.7	17.1	
	Evionnaz	68.9	5.8		
5	Martigny	79.9	11.0	16.7	
	Sembrancher	92.0	12.2		
6	Orsières	98.1	6.1	18.3	
	Liddes	106.4	8.3		
7	Bourg-Saint-Pierre	112.1	5.7	14.0	
8	Col du Grand St Bernard	124.5	12.4	12.4	
	Saint-Rhémy-Bourg	131.2	6.6		
	Saint-Oyen	135.9	4.7		
	Etroubles	137.6	1.7		
	Echevennoz Superior	139.6	2.0		
9	Aosta	153.3	13.7	28.8	
	Nus turn-off	167.8	14.4		
10	Châtillon	181.2	13.4	27.8	
	Saint-Vincent	186.3	5.1		
11	Verrès	199.5	13.2	18.3	
	Hône	209.7	10.2		
	Donnas	212.9	3.2		
12	Pont-Saint-Martin	215.5	2.6	16.0	

Book stage #	Location	Distance from start	Distance from previous point	Distance, book stages	My itinerary
	Settimo Vittone turn-off	223.4	7.9		
	San Germano	227.8	4.4		
	Borgofranco d'Ivrea	229.8	2.0		
13	Ivrea	238.6	8.8	23.1	
	Burolo	244.9	6.4		
	Piverone	253.8	8.9		
14	Viverone	258.8	5.0	20.2	
	Roppollo	260.0	1.2		
	Cavaglià	263.8	3.8		
15	Santhià	275.2	11.4	16.4	
	San Germano Vercellese	283.7	8.5		
16	Vercelli	302.7	19.0	27.5	
	Palestro	313.7	11.0		
17	Robbio	321.2	7.6	18.6	
	Nicorvo	327.7	6.5		
18	Mortara	335.7	8.0	14.5	
	Sant'Albino Monastery	337.2	1.5		
	Tromello	350.5	13.3		
19	Garlasco	355.8	5.4	20.1	
20	Pavia	380.2	24.3	24.3	
	Belgioioso	396.3	16.2		
21	Santa Cristina	408.2	11.9	28.1	
	Miradolo Terme	412.5	4.3		
22	Orio Litta	424.5	12.0	16.3	
	Corte Sant'Andrea	428.6	4.1		
23	Piacenza	450.4	21.8	25.9	
	Pontenure	461.1	10.8		
24	Fiorenzuola d'Arda	482.5	21.4	32.1	
	Chiaravalle della Colomba	488.5	5.9		
25	Fidenza	504.4	15.9	21.9	

Book stage #	Location	Distance from start	Distance from previous point	Distance, book stages	My itinerary
	Costamezzana	515.9	11.5		
	Cella	520.9	5.0		
	Medesano	526.7	5.8		
	Felegara	532.3	5.6		
26	Fornovo di Taro	538.2	5.9	33.8	
	Sivizzano	546.0	7.8		
	Cassio	559.2	13.3		
27	Berceto	569.7	10.4	31.5	
	Option to Ostello Cisa (add 1.4km to hostel itself)	575.1	5.5		
	Previdè	587.8	12.7		
	Toplecca di Sopra	591.4	3.6		
28	Pontremoli	597.9	6.6	28.2	
	Migliarina	606.1	8.2		
29	Aulla	630.0	24.0	32.1	
	Bibola	633.1	3.1		
30	Sarzana	647.2	14.0	17.1	
	Caniparola	652.0	4.9		
	Provasco	658.1	6.1		
	Avenza	664.5	6.4		
31	Massa	676.1	11.7	29.0	
	Pietrasanta	692.9	16.8		
32	Camaiore	701.9	9.0	25.7	
	Valpromaro	711.3	9.5		
	Lucca	726.4	15.1	24.6	
	Average distance/day			22.7	

APPENDIX B

Useful contacts

If you are dialing from an international phone, or with an international SIM card, always use the country code: +41 for Switzerland and +39 for Italy. From outside Switzerland – or from inside with a non-Swiss SIM card – it is necessary to add the prefix '0' after the country code.

Swiss emergency phone numbers

- 117 Police
- 118 Fire
- 144 Ambulance
- 1414 or 1415 Helicopter rescue

Italian emergency phone numbers

- 112 Carabinieri (national police)
- 113 Local police (also ambulance and fire)
- 115 Fire department
- 117 Finance police
- 118 Medical emergencies
- 1515 Forest fires

Baggage services

SloWays

Aosta to Lucca: At present, organized baggage transport service is only available for groups in the stages between Aosta and Lucca (€15/ea, info@sloways.eu, min 5 bags from Aosta to Pontremoli, min 4 bags from Pontremoli to Lucca).

After Lucca: €15 per stage per bag, priced per official stages.

More details at www.sloways.eu/luggage-transfer-via-francigena, or reserve at info@ sloways.eu.

BagsFree (€20, https://bags-free.com/francigena-luggage-transport. Daily pick-up is by 08:30 each day with delivery by 15:00. BagsFree also offers a baggage storage service near Rome's Termini train station (www.bags-free.com) and can deliver your bags to your hotel from storage.

Credential locations

Aigle: Tourist Office, rue Colomb 5

Saint-Maurice: Abbaye de Saint-Maurice -Porterie-, av. D'Agaune 15

Orsières: Au Pays du St-Bernard of Orsières, route de la Gare 34

Col du Grand-Saint-Bernard: Hospice du Grand-Saint-Bernard

Saint-Rhémy-en-Bosses: 'Enoteca Enoetica,' SS 27 km 30+500

Aosta: Tourist Office, Porta Praetoria, Piazza Porta Pretoria 3

Saint-Vincent: Tourist Office, Via Roma 62

Verrès: Hostel 'Il Casello', Via Stazione 79

Saint Martin: Ostello Saint Martin, Via Schigliatta

Pont-Saint-Martin: Tourist Office, Via Circonvallazione 30

Ivrea:
Associazione La Via Francigena di Sigerico, Corso Botta s/n

Tourist Office, Piazza Ottinetti

Roppolo: Casa del Movimento Lento, Via al Castello 8

Santhià: Associazione 'Amici della Via Francigena Città di Santhià' in Cavaglià, Via G. Gersen 6

Belgioioso: Farm hoydays 'Il Gandulin,' Via Frazione S.Giacomo 4

Piacenza:
Tourist Office, Piazza Cavalli 10 (angolo Via Calzolai)

Musei Civici di Palazzo Farnese, Piazza Cittadella 29

Ostello del Teatro of Piacenza, Via Trento 29C

Operational Headquarters of European Association of Via Francigena, Palazzo Farnese, Piazza Cittadella 29, tel 0523 492792, segreteria@viefrancigene.org, Opening by appointment only.

Fidenza:
Tourist Office, IAT R Casa Cremonini. Piazza Duomo 16

Decathlon Fidenza, Fidenza Shopping Park, Via F. Fellini

Latteria 55, Via Cavour 16

Fornovo di Taro: Tourist Office, Via dei Collegati 19

Pontremoli: Tourist Office, Piazza Duomo 22

Filattiera: Centro Didattico Pieve di Sorano – Info Point Via Francigena, near the parish church of St Stephan of Sorano, Via Ponte Nazionale

Aulla: Museo e Abbazia di San Caprasio, Piazza Abbazia

Pietrasanta: Tourist infopoint, Piazza Statuto 1

Marina di Pietrasanta: Tourist infopoint, Via Donizzetti 14

Camaiore:
Tourist infopoint, Viale Cristoforo Colombo 127/129

Infopoint of Municipality of Camaiore, Piazza San Bernardino

Ostello del Pellegrino of Camaiore, Via Madonna della Pietà 18

Lucca:
Via Francigena Entry Point of Lucca, Via dei Bacchettoni 8

Lucca Tourist Office, Vecchia Porta San Donato, Piazzale Verdi

Tourist Center of Lucca, Piazzale Ricasoli 203

Museo della Cattedrale of Lucca, Piazza Antelminelli 5

Tourist information offices

Switzerland (country code +41)

Lausanne
Avenue d'Ouchy 60, tel (0)21 613 26 26, info@region-du-leman.ch

Vevey
Grande Place 29, tel (0)848 868 484

Montreux
Grand' Rue 45, tel (0)848 868 484, info@montreuxriviera.com

Villeneuve
Place de la Gare 5, tel (0)21 962 84 81, info@montreuxriviera.com

Aigle
5 rue Colomb, tel (0)24 466 30 00, info@aigle-tourisme.ch

Saint-Maurice
Avenue des Terreaux 1, tel (0)24 485 40 40, info@saint-maurice.ch

Martigny
Avenue de la Gare 6, tel (0)27 720 49 49, info@martigny.com

Orsières
Route de la Gare 34, tel (0)27 775 23 81, info@saint-bernard.ch

Liddes
Route Grand-Saint-Bernard 18, tel (0)27 775 23 82, liddes@saint-bernard.ch

Italy (country code +39)

Etroubles
Rue du Mont Velan, tel 0165 78568

Aosta
Via Porta Pretoria, tel 0165 236627, aosta@turismo.vda.it

Saint-Vincent
Via Roma, tel, 0166 512239, saintvincent@turismo.vda.it

Pont-Saint-Martin
Via Circonvallazione, tel 0125 804843, pontsaintmartin@turismo.vda.it

Ivrea
Piazza Ottinetti, tel 0125 618131, info.ivrea@turismotorino.org

Vercelli
Corso Giuseppe Garibaldi, tel 163 564404, infovarallo@atlvalsesiavercelli.it

Piacenza
Via Calzolai, tel 0523 492001, iat@comune.piacenza.it

Fidenza
Piazza Duomo, tel 0524 83377, iat.fidenza@terrediverdi.it

Fornovo diTaro
Via dei Collegati, tel 0525 2599, iatfornovo@gmail.com

Pontremoli
Piazza del Duomo, tel 0187 832000, iat@comune.pontremoli.ms.it

Terrarossa
Via Nazionale Cisa, tel 331 8866241, info@sigeric.it

Marina di Massa
Viale Amerigo Vespucci, tel 0161 58002

Lucca
Vecchia Porta San Donato and Piazzale Verdi, tel 0583 583150, info@luccaitinera.it

APPENDIX C
Bibliography

Travelogues

Belloc, Hillare. *The Path to Rome.* New York: Wallachia, 1953.

Bucknall, Harry. *Like a Tramp, Like a Pilgrim: On Foot, Across Europe to Rome.* London: Bloomsbury Continuum, 2014.

Egan, Timothy. *A Pilgrimage to Eternity: From Canterbury to Rome in Search of a Faith.* New York: Viking, 2019.

Mooney, Brian. *A Long Way for a Pizza: On Foot to Rome.* London: THO, 2012.

Muirhead, Robert. *The Long Walk: A Pilgrimage from Canterbury to Rome.* CreateSpace, 2015.

Warrender, Alice. *An Accidental Jubilee: A Pilgrimage on foot from Canterbury to Rome.* York: Stone Trough Books, 2011.

Historical – Via Francigena

Caselli, Giovanni. *Via Romea, Cammino di Dio.* Florence: Giunti Gruppo Editoriale, 1990.

Champ, J. *The English Pilgrimage to Rome.* Herfordshire, England: Gracewing, 2000.

Magoun, F.P. 'The Rome of Two Northern Pilgrims: Archbishop Sigeric of Canterbury and Abbot Nikolas of Munkathvera.' *The Harvard Theological Review*, 33(4), 267–289.

Ortenberg, Veronica. 'Archbishop Sigeric's Journey to Rome in 990.' In M. Lapidge, M. Godden, & S. Keyes (eds.) *Anglo-Saxon England* Vol 19. (pp.19–26) Cambridge, UK: Cambridge University Press, 1990. Ortenberg studies the meaning of the 23 churches visited by Sigeric in Rome.

Historical – Italy, pilgrimage and general

Birch, Debra J. *Pilgrimage to Rome in the Middle Ages.* Woodbridge, Suffolk: Boydell Press, 1998.

Gilmour, David. *The Pursuit of Italy: A History of a Land, its Regions, and their Peoples.* New York: Farrah, Strauss and Giroux, 2011.

Webb, Diana. *Pilgrims and Pilgrimage in the Medieval West.* London: I.B. Tauris, 2001.

APPENDIX D

Sigeric's journey: then and now

Stage no. from English Channel to Rome	Sigeric's stage no. from Rome to English Channel	Sigeric's place name	Modern place name	Guidebook stage no.
Via Francigena Part 1: Canterbury to Lausanne				
1	LXXX	Sumeran	Sombre (Wissant)	
2	LXXIX	Unlisted by Sigeric		
3	LXXVIII	Gisne	Guînes	
4	LXXVII	Teranburh	Thérouanne	
5	LXXVI	Bruwaei	Bruay-la-Buissière	
6	LXXV	Atherats	Arras	
7	LXXIV	Duin	Doingt	
8	LXXIII	Martinwaeth	Séraucourt-le-Grand	
9	LXXII	Mundlothuin	Laon	
10	LXXI	Corbunei	Corbeny	
11	LXX	Rems	Reims	
12	LXIX	Chateluns	Châlons-sur-Marne	
13	LXVIII	Funtaine	Fontaine-sur-Coole	
14	LXVII	Domaniant	Donnement	
15	LXVI	Breone	Brienne-la-Vieille	
16	LXV	Bar	Bar-sur-Aube	
17	LXIV	Blaecuile	Blessonville	
18	LXIII	Oisma	Humes-Jorquenay	
19	LXII	Grenant	Grenant	
20	LXI	Sefui	Seveux	
21	LX	Cuscei	Cussey-sur-l'Ognon	
22	LIX	Bysiceon	Besançon	
23	LVIII	Nos	Nods	
24	LVII	Punterlin	Pontarlier	
25	LVI	Antifern	Yverdon-les-Bains	
26	LV	Urba	Orbe	

Stage no. from English Channel to Rome	Sigeric's stage no. from Rome to English Channel	Sigeric's place name	Modern place name	Guidebook stage no.
Via Francigena Part 2: Lausanne to Lucca			
27	LIV	Losanna	Lausanne	1
28	LIII	Vivaec	Vevey	1
29	LII	Burbulei	Aigle	2
30	LI	Sancte Maurici	Saint-Maurice	3
31	L	Ursiores	Orsières	5
32	XLIX	Petrecastel	Bourg-Saint-Pierre	6
33	XLVIII	Sancte Remei	Saint-Rhémy	8
34	XLVII	Agusta	Aosta	8
35	XLVI	Publei	Pont-Saint-Martin (Montjovet?)	11
36	XLV	Everi	Ivrea	12
37	XLIV	Sancte Agatha	Santhià	14
38	XLIII	Vercel	Vercelli	15
39	XLII	Tremel	Tromello	18
40	XLI	Pamphica	Pavia	19
41	XL	Sancte Cristine	Santa Cristina e Bissone	20
42	XXXIX	Sancte Andrea	Corte San Andrea	22
43	XXXVIII	Placentia	Piacenza	22
44	XXXVII	Floricum	Fiorenzuola d'Arda	23
45	XXXVI	Sanctae Domnine	Fidenza (Borgo San Donino until 1927)	24
46	XXXV	Metane	Costamezzana	25
47	XXXIV	Philemangenur	Fornovo di Taro	25
48	XXXIII	Sancte Moderanne	Berceto	26
49	XXXII	Sancte Benedicte	Montelungo	27
50	XXXI	Puntremel	Pontremoli	27
51	XXX	Aguilla	Aulla	28
52	XXIX	Sancte Stephane	Santo Stefano di Magra	29
53	XXVIII	Luna	Sarzana (Luni)	29
54	XXVII	Campmaior	Camaiore	31

Stage no. from English Channel to Rome	Sigeric's stage no. from Rome to English Channel	Sigeric's place name	Modern place name	Guidebook stage no.
Via Francigena Part 3: Lucca to Rome				
55	XXVI	Luca	Lucca	
56	XXV	Forcri	Porcari	
57	XXIV	Aqua Nigra	Ponte a Cappiano	
58	XXIII	Arne Blanca	Fucecchio	
59	XXII	Sce Dionisii	San Genesio near San Miniato	
60	XXI	Sce Peter Currant	Coiano (Castelfiorentino)	
61	XX	Sce Maria Glan	Santa Maria a Chianni (near Gambassi Terme)	
62	XIX	Sce Gemiane	San Gimignano	
63	XVIII	Sce Martin in Fosse	San Martino Fosci (Molino d'Aiano)	
64	XVII	Aelse	Gracciano (Pieve d'Elsa)	
65	XVI	Burgenove	Badia an Isola (Abbadia d'Isola)	
66	XV	Seocine	Siena	
67	XIV	Arbia	Ponte d'Arbia	
68	XIII	Turreiner	Torrenieri	
69	XII	Sce Quiric	San Quirico d'Orcia	
70	XI	Abricula	Briccole di Sotto	
71	X	Sce Petir in Pail	San Pietro in Paglia (Voltole)	
72	IX	Aquapendente	Acquapendente	
73	VIII	Sca Cristina	Bolsena	
74	VII	Sce Flaviane	Montefiascone	
75	VI	Sce Valentine	Viterbo (Bullicame)	
76	V	Furcari	Vetralla (Forcassi)	
77	IV	Suteria	Sutri	
78	III	Bacane	Baccano (Campagnano di Roma)	
79	II	Johannis VIIII	San Giovanni in Nono (La Storta)	
80	I	Urbs Roma	Roma	

A VIA FRANCIGENA GUIDE IN THREE PARTS

Certified by the Council of Europe as an official Cultural Route, the Via Francigena brings to the modern pilgrim the amazing cultural heritage of four nations – England, France, Switzerland and Italy – and highlights their immense natural beauty and deep, ancient heritage. This guidebook is one of a set of three volumes that covers the route.

Part 1 – From Canterbury to Lausanne
The Via Francigena officially begins at Canterbury Cathedral, crosses the English Channel, then makes its way along French canals, battlefields, farmlands and historic villages to arrive at Lake Geneva in Switzerland.

Part 2 – From Lausanne to Lucca
Beginning at easily accessible Lausanne, the Via Francigena climbs toward the headwaters of the mighty Rhône River before branching off to summit the historic Great Saint Bernard Pass. The route descends the Alps along the Aosta Valley, traveling through the Po River Valley and then crossing the scenic Passo della Cisa into Tuscany. After a few days near the coast, the trail swings inland to Lucca, one of Tuscany's medieval jewels.

Part 3 – From Lucca to Rome
From Lucca to Siena the Via Francigena is at its most evocative. As it passes through dazzling Tuscan towns like Lucca, San Gimignano and Siena, the route crosses the Orcia and Paglia Valleys into the volcanic tufa stone ridges and basins of Lazio where the centuries-long rule of the Popes is felt in every village. This amazing pilgrimage ends at one of the world's great treasures – the Eternal City of Rome.

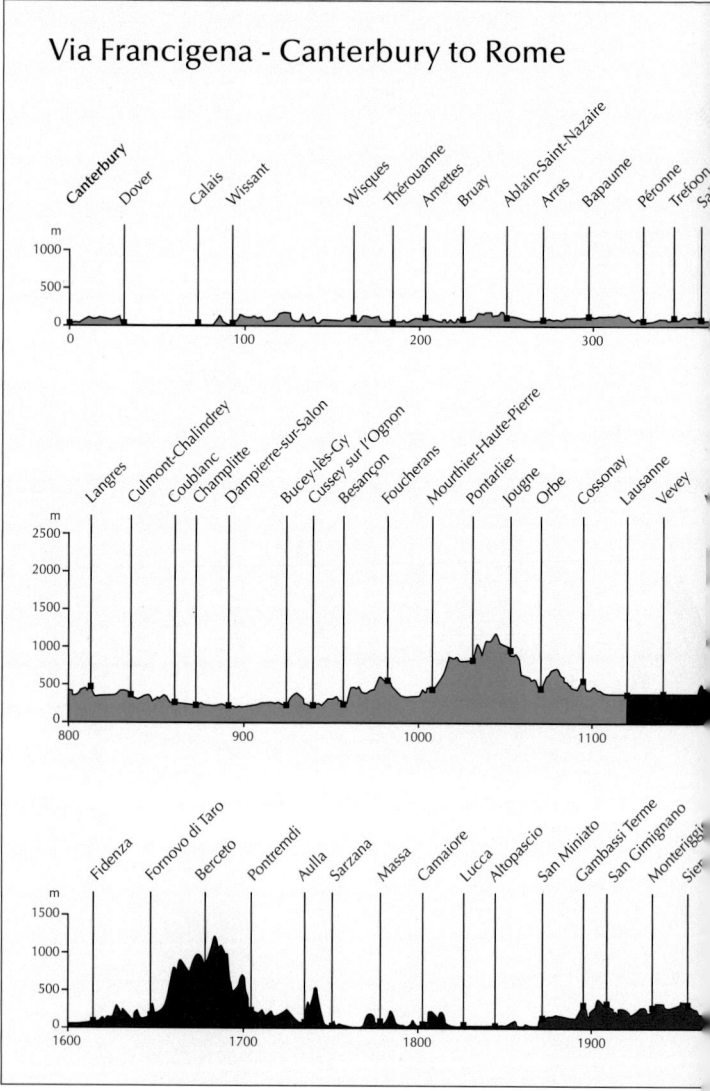

Via Francigena - Canterbury to Rome

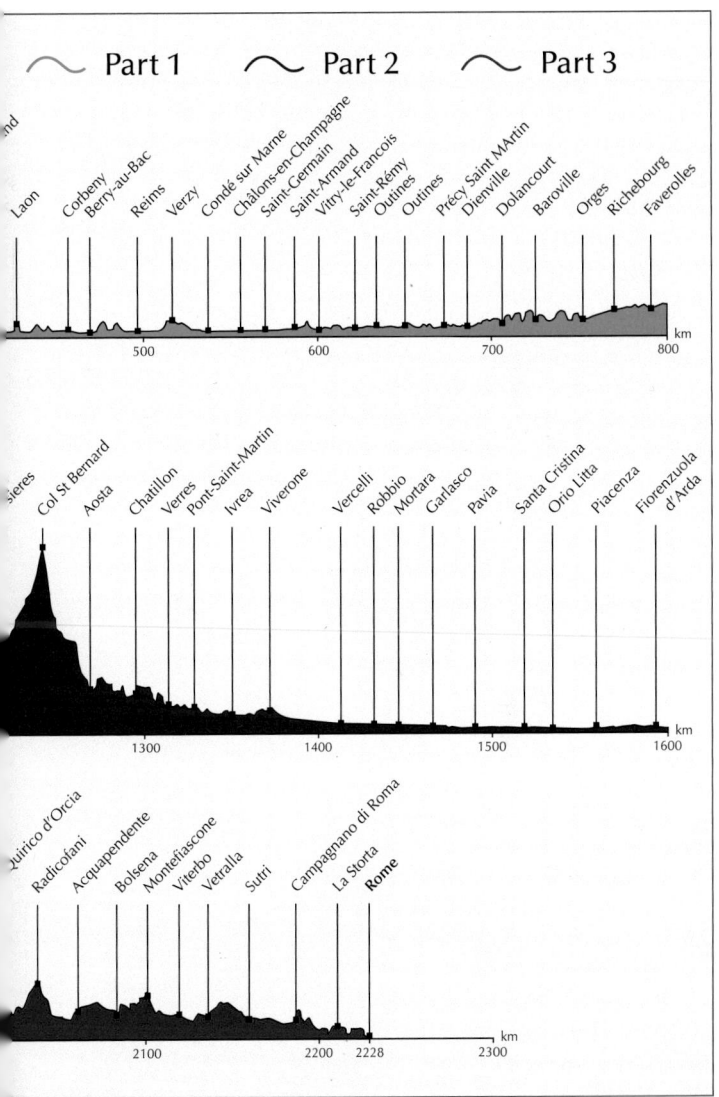

NOTES

NOTES

DOWNLOAD THE ROUTES
IN GPX FORMAT

All the routes in this guide are available for download from:

www.cicerone.co.uk/1086/GPX

as GPX files. You should be able to load them into most formats of mobile device, whether GPS or smartphone.

When you go to this link, you will be asked for your email address and where you purchased the guide, and have the option to subscribe to the Cicerone e-newsletter.

www.cicerone.co.uk

LISTING OF CICERONE GUIDES

For full information on all our
guides, books and eBooks,
visit our website:
www.cicerone.co.uk

CICERONE

Trust Cicerone to guide your next adventure,
wherever it may be around the world...

Discover guides for hiking, mountain walking, backpacking,
trekking, trail running, cycling and mountain biking, ski touring,
climbing and scrambling in Britain, Europe and worldwide.

Connect with Cicerone online and find inspiration.

- buy books and ebooks
- articles, advice and trip reports
- GPX files and updates
- regular newsletter

cicerone.co.uk